D0812576

31
by Lawrence Clayton

edited by
Lou Rodenberger

with a foreword by
David Coffey

McWhiney Foundation Press
McMurry University
Abilene, Texas

CONTENTS

PHOTOGRAPHS

Acknowledgments

This book would not have been possible without the tireless effort and dedication of several people. It is with tremendous gratitude that we acknowledge the following contributions: Laura Zullo typed the manuscript from the original stack of essays handed over by Lawrence Clayton. Barbara Darnall performed the difficult task of copyediting these essays, originally written over a span of twenty years, to make them all flow with a single voice. Sonja and Lea Clayton and DeLys Clayton Mitchell answered endless questions, and worked diligently to provide the photographs for the work. Daniel Price and Jay Hardaway created an excellent index, and Henry Rosenbohm, of Rosenbohm Graphic Design, designed the book, all under significant pressures of deadline. Finally, we are grateful for the partial underwriting of this project by a grant from the A.V. Jones Foundation of Throckmorton County, Texas, a donor-advised fund of the Community Foundation of Abilene.

FOREWORD

Late Texas folklorist and historian Lawrence Clayton found beauty where many might see only mesquite and limestone; he found humor in unlikely places, and he found nobility in the hard lives of cowboys and roughnecks. He was intrigued with the idea of *place*, the impact of *place* on the people who shared it, and, indeed, the literature of *place*, of which he was a master. To him, *place* usually meant the Clear Fork Country.

For years, Dr. Clayton chronicled the history of the Clear Fork Country—the stretch of land cut by the Clear Fork of the Brazos River—of Shackelford and Throckmorton counties. His thoughtful prose on the region's colorful past and its equally colorful characters has appeared in dozens of publications over the years. His efforts to record the stories of area ranches and the men who built them and worked them represent a major contribution to the state's recorded history. Indeed, few writers could capture in words the ranch life of West Texas the way Lawrence Clayton did—fewer still might bother to translate the nomenclature and nuances of a working ranch to underexposed readers of all backgrounds.

Unfortunately, much of Clayton's work resides in scholarly journals or magazines not easily accessible to a wider audience. But these stories and others long unpublished belong in books to be passed down through generations. Before his death, Dr. Clayton worked diligently to see that this history—these unique tales—remained available to all who are interested (and to some who don't yet know it). This volume goes a long way toward honoring his wishes, and we are all better off for it.

Even before I moved to Abilene in 1998 I had heard of Lawrence Clayton, and I had read some of his work. We even had mutual friends in Jo and Wallace Cox of Haskell. But I didn't know Lawrence Clayton until a fortuitous meeting at the famous Perini Ranch Steak House in Buffalo Gap, Texas. He was pretty much what I'd expected and a lot more. He looked the part, for sure, in his black cowboy hat, but it was his easily recognizable good humor and notoriously playful smile that struck most everyone who met him, and I was no exception. He had a way about him that made me feel (and I've heard many others say the same thing) like we were indeed old friends.

We no doubt would have become social friends—linked by common interests and associations in the Abilene area—but I got the chance to be his publisher, and I couldn't improve much on that. I worked as managing editor for Abilene's McWhiney Foundation Press when Lawrence and Cliff Teinert asked us to publish *Tracks Along the Clear Fork: Stories from Shackelford and Throckmorton Counties.* Lawrence and I labored together to bring the book to press, then I got the rare pleasure of watching Lawrence sign copy after copy as the book quickly sold out. Wherever we appeared to promote *Tracks*, we found enthusiastic buyers; it seemed that everyone knew Lawrence and that he knew them back. He was quick to credit those who contributed to the book (he insisted once that I autograph the index for one customer) and always modest about his own contribution, but there was no denying that folks who bought the book loved Lawrence Clayton.

Tracks was a truly satisfying project for Lawrence because it allowed him to bring the history he loved to a wider audience and, at the same time, feature the writings of the local historians he admired. But there was more to the story, and Lawrence still had dozens of underexposed or unpublished pieces that he wanted to share and preserve. He soon approached me about the possibility of publishing these neglected works in another anthology. Thrilled with the prospect of working with Lawrence again, I took the proposal the Don Frazier, Executive Director of the McWhiney Foundation, who readily endorsed the concept.

Lawrence and I met three or four times during the year 2000 to discuss the project, what works to include, what might be left out. The last couple of these meetings took place after he announced that he suffered form Amyotrophic Lateral Sclerosis (ALS), better known as Lou Gehrig's Disease. The project took on a new meaning, and we proceeded with a melancholy frankness, but Lawrence refused to surrender his sense of humor. I'm sure that Lawrence doubted that he'd see the book to publication, so there was no urgency to throw something together. He left it to me to shepherd his stories and to get them into a book. He also made sure I understood the subject matter by exposing me to many wonders of the Clear Fork Country; he even fixed it so that I got to judge the 2000 Fort Griffin Fandangle Parade. We didn't make much progress on the book, but I enjoyed those few precious times I got to spend with Lawrence.

When Lawrence died on December 31, 2000, he left a big hole in many a life. The book remained largely conceptual—it didn't even have a title. But a perfect title came to me as I sat with Don Frazier during Lawrence's memorial service. Lawrence had a thing for numbers, particularly 31 and 13. These tended to show up at significant times in his life. I knew we had about thirty stories accumulated, and we could add more if need be, so the title became clear—*31 by Lawrence Clayton.* Lawrence's wonderful wife Sonja liked the idea, as did his daughters DeLys and Lea.

But best laid plans and good intentions do not a book make. During the summer of 2001 I left Abilene for a teaching job in Tennessee, and I brought *31* with me. It would be more difficult for me to edit and introduce the stories Lawrence had selected, removed as I was to the old country east of the Mississippi—it was a *place* thing—but I still planned to honor my commitment. Fortunately, Don Frazier and Robert Pace at the McWhiney Foundation Press had a better idea. They proposed, with Sonja's blessing, to turn the project over to Lawrence's good friend and fellow West Texas folklorist Lou Rodenberger. While I hated to give it up, I knew that the book would be in capable hands. My friends at the press were kind enough to allow me these few words, for which I am ever grateful, and an opportunity to thank Sonja, DeLys, and Lea for their kindness and encouragement.

I miss Lawrence Clayton, but I'm better for having known him, and I have a much better understanding of *place.*

David Coffey
The University of Tennessee at Martin

A Scholar on Horseback: The Last Gathering

Introduction by Lou Rodenberger

This last gathering of essays by Dr. Lawrence Clayton, late Dean of Liberal Arts at Hardin-Simmons University, could include no less than thirty-one. The numbers three and one in combination carried considerable significance for this teacher, writer, cowboy, rancher, folklorist and historian. His first football jersey number in high school was 13. His last at Ranger Junior College was 31. His office at Hardin-Simmons University was No. 313 and his Abilene house number was 3126. The last two digits, he would point out, were a multiple of 13. His first book, *Clear Fork Cowboys*, was released on November 13th, and the cattleman Watt Matthews, the subject of Dr. Clayton's acclaimed biography, significantly to his biographer, died on April 13, 1997. Interrupted by two years at Texas Tech University for graduate work, Lawrence's years of service at HSU numbered 31. In the final months of his life, as he battled ALS (Lou Gehrig's Disease), Lawrence produced essays, finished works in process, and read proof for two new books in press. He worked steadily until December 13, 2000, when he could no longer concentrate on writing. After celebrating Christmas with his wife Sonja, his daughters DeLys and Lea, his son-in-law Matt Mitchell, and his granddaughters Amanda and Ashley, Lawrence Ray Clayton, who had reached the age of 62 (31 doubled) died in the early morning of New Year's Eve. He had predicted that his final day would be this one, December 31, 2000.

Lawrence Clayton, Number 31

It would please Lawrence that his friends see this unique connection with two numbers as the stuff of good storytelling. Lawrence, himself, was a talented raconteur. Like all good storytellers, Lawrence treasured the well-told oral tale. He cultivated friendships with family and community members who recognized the elements of a good story and knew how to share a good yarn. Scholar that he was, Lawrence soon came to believe that without storytellers, the history of a region, bereft of knowledge of its colorful personalities, unique landscapes, and sometimes scandalous human behavior, would likely become descriptions of battles between natives and frontiersmen, accrued statistics on population distribution, and examination of major events in the development of its towns. For Lawrence Clayton, who lived in several Texas regions during his childhood and acquired his personal sense of place late, history without knowledge of its makers would be dull indeed.

Lawrence Clayton as a young man

Lawrence Clayton and Sonja Irwin were married in 1958, and Lawrence soon connected with his wife's native region, the country around Fort Griffin in Throckmorton and Shackelford Counties. Originating in his close relationship with his wife Sonja's father, rancher J. C. Irwin, Jr., who was a masterful storyteller, Lawrence developed a kinship with the landscape and with other ranchers living along the Clear Fork of the Brazos. He and his family spent holidays at the Irwin ranch and as Lawrence listened to his father-in-law's stories of both family and community past, his life's work began to take shape. Soon after Lawrence became a member of the Irwin family, this young schoolteacher realized that listening to and recording the stories his father-in-law told and those preserved through oral tradition in this region around Albany, Fort Griffin, and Throckmorton both enlarged and enriched his own experience. By 1983, in the *West Texas Historical Year Book*, Lawrence, already an active collector of oral history, had also become convinced that "Much of the social history of this region . . . can be found in oral narratives that often recount or interpret local events and customs" (161).

After teaching high school English and completing work for a masters degree at North Texas State University (now University of North Texas) in 1968, Lawrence took a position as instructor of English at Hardin-Simmons University. With his family, he settled in the Abilene area, first at Clyde, later in the city, and then not many miles from Sonja's early home in ranch country on the Clear Fork just upriver from Fort Griffin. Lawrence once declared that it was Sonja who "provided inspiration as well as credibility" for him as he became acquainted with her native culture. Sonja's connections with those in the region who knew its history and folklore became his own connections after a time. Sonja, a gifted storyteller in her own right, had performed in the Fort Griffin Fandangle many times, and her knowledge of its production and history provided yet another source of the region's colorful history.

At HSU, Lawrence taught English, became chair of that department in 1974, and after a dozen years, Dean of the College of Arts and Sciences, a position renamed Dean of the College of Liberal Arts in 1999. On leave from the university in 1971-73, he finished his work for a doctorate at Texas Tech University, where his interest in folklore, cowboy songs, and literature of the American West found focus with the steady encouragement of his research director, Everett Gillis. There, too, his friendship with Dr. Kenneth Davis, Texas Tech University professor who taught courses in folklore and literature of the American West, led later to collaboration on two collections of cowboy humor. For his dissertation research,

Lawrence Clayton, High School Teacher, Late 1960s

Lawrence Clayton, Young Professor at Hardin-Simmons University, ca. 1970

Lawrence chose to examine the folklorist John Lomax's collections of cowboy songs. Soon, essays by the newly minted Dr. Clayton on regional oral narrative, cowboy life and ranch history began to appear in professional journals.

The gathering of Lawrence's essays in this volume, first initiated by the author himself in collaboration with Dr. David Coffey, then associated with McWhiney Foundation Press at McMurry University, illuminates, as the author intended, his personal examination of devotion to place. A knowledgeable literary critic and author of several biographies of Texas literary figures, Lawrence Clayton decided by 1984 to concentrate on the colorful history and lore of the region around Fort Griffin. His sources were many. J. C. Irwin, Jr., in front porch sessions and around the dinner table, told stories from both his early life and his family history. Lawrence became acquainted with such repositories of regional history as the ranchers Watt Matthews and Bob Green and Sonja's cousin Morris Ledbetter, whom Lawrence has said, "knew more of the history of the area than anyone else and lovingly shared it."

With the encouragement of the four Peacock brothers, whom Lawrence admired as traditional cowboys, the scholar became a cowhand himself and rode annually with the Nail Ranch wranglers. Both foreman George Peacock—his brothers Troy, Dean, and Benny—and cowboy friends, among them Sonny Edgar, Tunny Hollingsworth, Bobby Williams, Johnny Stewart, Terry Moberley, and John Caldwell, taught Lawrence techniques for rounding up, driving large herds, and working calves. Becoming fully aware through these experiences of the contribution of the ranching industry to Texas culture and economy, he began research into the history of ranches in the area. During his visits to the Fort Griffin area, he also interviewed community storytellers, including Raymond Little and Litt Perkins, and began his field work as a folklorist with interviews with oldtimers who told of the early life in the region and taught the folklorist techniques for leather working and other crafts.

By 1985, Lawrence's first book, *Clear Fork Cowboys*, a study of cowboy life in the region illustrated with photographs by Sonja Clayton, was issued. Self-published, the press run of 2000 copies soon sold out. Lawrence once observed that this in some ways was his most important work because it "set the tone and the direction" of his future books. *Ranch Rodeos in West Texas*, again featuring Sonja's photographs, was published in 1988. Soon, these successes encouraged Lawrence to begin research that would lead to one of his most successful and prestigious books, *Historic Ranches of Texas*, published by University of Texas Press in 1993. Shortly after Lawrence's untimely death, the University of Texas Press published his further study of Texas ranch life, *Contemporary Ranches of Texas,* and a co-authored history entitled *Vaqueros, Cowboys, and Buckaroos.* Passion for a place had inspired this college professor to preserve all he could learn of its history, leading to production of his first books and regional acclaim. Dedication to the subjects he found worthy of the time required for intensive research and writing—modern cowboy life and ranch history—brought finally the statewide recognition such devotion and talent deserved. In September, shortly before his death, Lawrence was awarded the American Cowboy Culture Award for lifetime excellence as a writer at the National Cowboy Symposium. In January 2001, state Rep. Bob Hunter sponsored House Resolution 148 and state Senator Troy Fraser spnsored Senate Resolution 130 in honor and memory of Lawrence Clayton, and they each read this tribute to the assembled legislators: "This estimable individual has bequeathed to the world a treasure of research and erudition, many generations of former students who were inspired under his tutelage and a host of family members and friends whose lives are richer because of this remarkable man."

Lawrence Clayton, Public Speaker, ca. 1970s

Lawrence Clayton at Work on the Ranch

Selected from more than one hundred essays Lawrence published in his lifetime, and many that were never published, included here are only those that expand his definition of the sense of place that Lawrence felt "a source of focus" in his writing and life. His discussion of how close connection with a place provides inspiration for his work introduces this collection. Logically following the author's discussion of his dedication to a region as inspiration for his writing is his personal definition of the family saga. The late Mody Boatright, professor and folklorist, perceived the stories told by family storytellers about past family events, if they were worthy of being told over and over, as a folklore genre. Boatright called this form "living folklore." Lawrence modifies Boatright's definition by pointing out that the Irwin family stories he heard were "more personal and less spectacular" perhaps than the examples Boatright provides. Most importantly, the stories for the author provided "a sense of community within the family." Following the author's discussion of family saga as he defines the genre are the stories J. C. Irwin, Jr. told that share both family and regional folk history.

Collected in the section "The Storyteller" are the stories Lawrence recorded as he visited with Litt Perkins, old cowboy, leather worker, and storehouse of cowboy songs and stories. In the company of his father-in-law and his younger daughter, Lea, Lawrence recorded not only the stories of this master raconteur but songs and carefully observed techniques Litt used in his craft. The author shares here not only the stories and the craft of Litt Perkins, but he also conveys the storyteller's personality and sense of humor.

Cowboys and cowboy life provided subjects for much of Lawrence's work, once he became convinced that this lifestyle deserved his writer's skills to share not only cowboys' lives but their values, their stories, and their roles in the community. Lawrence was convinced that "not everyone has what it takes to be cowboy." He also believed strongly that no school teaches how to be cowboy. Wannabe cowboys learn the hard way from veteran cowboys, who are not likely to do much instruction but provide example of how to do the job during their daily work.

That the author himself had learned the basics of his chosen avocation well is exemplified in his careful accumulation of cowboy terminology, which in this section he collects with full explanation in a glossary.

For his professional reputation, the essays in "Ranching Histories and Their Significance" led to the author's most successful books, the elegant ranch histories published by the University of Texas Press. In the introductory essay to this section, Lawrence discusses the importance of preserving the history of the large ranches in Texas, which in turn emphasizes the importance of the cattle culture to Texas history. He also makes clear that smaller ranches with interesting histories deserve attention. Following discussion of the importance of preserving ranch history, the author shares his knowledge, through both experience and interview, of three Fort Griffin area ranches and of the Long X in the Big Bend area, established by the Reynolds brothers, who grew up on the Clear Fork of the Brazos.

The final section of this gathering of Lawrence Clayton's major essays about his beloved region is a rich collection of stories gleaned from oral history and early accounts of both major historical events and of family history as part of regional history. Some stories, told often and by many storytellers, have assumed the status of myth in the region. Others only family members treasure, but the assemblage is a fitting conclusion to Lawrence's more than forty years kinship with this unique section of Texas that converted Lawrence into "an avowed regionalist."

In the author's last account of an interview with Litt Perkins, he makes a poignant and now particularly significant observation.

Lawrence Clayton Rests at Hardin-Simmons University Western Heritage Day

Lawrence and Sonja Clayton

Lawrence writes, "Litt was full of stories, and I intended, of course, to get more. It's odd how we too often assume that a good situation will last forever. We realize only when it's too late that it won't." Aware even then of the unstoppable impetus of time, Lawrence's own acknowledgment of his mortality, "My Last Christmas????," concludes this last gathering of his work. Appearing in *A Christmas Pudding 2000,* the annual collection of essays and poetry by members of the Abilene writers group which calls itself The Almost Every Wednesday Club, the author, with the courage and honesty he demonstrated throughout his career, discusses with candor his fast-approaching death. "Dying is a part of living," he says, and accepts his fate with the uncommon grace that his students, his colleagues and his friends knew well.

It is easy to discern clearly many of Lawrence's admirable attitudes and his philosophy of life from reading his work. It is not only Lawrence's strong sense of place but his intelligent defense of the contemporary working cowboy, his admiration of the subtle humor of cowboy and family storytellers and his own practice of the art, and his scholarly tenacity in uncovering the truth through research that impress his readers. He was a careful gatherer of facts and a gifted collector of oral history. He was a determined and talented teacher of southwestern life and literature. This gathering of the writing he most enjoyed doing about the region he most loved is presented here as lasting tribute to the memory of Lawrence Ray Clayton, mentor, colleague and friend.

ONE
Place as a Source of Focus: Confessions of a Regional Writer

A regionalist or regional writer is one who focuses attention on one area or place to the exclusion of others. I know this is true because I am an avowed regionalist and have been for most of my professional career. My lifelong interest began to have professional focus when I began teaching Life and Literature of the Southwest to students at Hardin-Simmons University in the late 1960s, a time when the focus of much intellectual life was directed in a very different direction in a tumultuous decade. Researching and writing my dissertation on a collection of Western folk songs by John A. Lomax solidified my interest and provided the research background for what has proved to be an enjoyable career as a regional writer.

The label *regionalist* is one shunned by most of my peers in the university professoriate. To them, the term connotes a narrow focus, a lack of perception of the big picture. I crossed that bridge long ago, and I am grateful that my supervisors and colleagues at HSU seemed not to worry that I was turning out a body of work unashamedly regionalistic.

Because of my training in literature, my papers, articles, and reviews first centered on literary figures and works—Elmer Kelton, Forrest Carter, Ben Capps, Leslie Silko, Frank Waters, and James Welch, all fine writers who set their works west of the Mississippi River and, therefore, are considered by the literary establishment to be Western writers. In 1984, I took a new focus. I decided to write a book tentatively entitled *Fort Griffin Sketches,* a play on the title of Don Biggers' important work *Shackelford County Sketches.* Without knowing, I set my direction and have never wavered from that focus.

My place or micro-region is southern Throckmorton and northern Shackelford counties of Northwest Texas. My point of inspiration is a stretch of rolling mesquite-dotted rangeland on the hills overlooking the Clear Fork of the Brazos River near Camp Cooper and Fort Griffin about twenty-five miles north of Albany. The small ranch is on the hills north of the river, but through the feathery leaves of mesquite I can see the course of the Clear Fork of the Brazos River and some of the smaller valleys and canyons feeding into it. One of these, Plum Branch, runs through the property. Here, one can almost hear the echoes of Col. Robert E. Lee's commands as he took charge of now long-abandoned Camp Cooper just up the river a few miles from the long-ago abandoned Fort Griffin, and the yells of Comanches and Kiowas and Tonkawas who inhabited the region. The site of the town of Fort Griffin, also known as Griffin Flat, now a prosaic stretch of gravel county road that reaches from the base of the hill on which the fort once stood across an aging suspension bridge across the reddish waters of the Clear Fork of the Brazos River, was once a thriving, albeit sinful, place where gamblers, prostitutes, ne'er-do-wells, gunfighters, rustlers, and other assorted thieves created legend without realizing it. It was home for a few years after the Civil War for units made up largely of black or "buffalo" soldiers, freed slaves in military service of the U.S. government. I drive periodically down Griffin Avenue, lined with pecan trees and a few grazing cattle, and imagine what once went on there. I am regularly reminded of that every time I drive from Abilene into

Albany when I see the old Fort Griffin store, a box and strip structure that continued to be operated after the town was abandoned by its more flamboyant characters and became instead the post office and general store for rural dwellers in this still isolated part of the state. Today it is a restaurant and watering hole, for years the only legal one, in Albany. The approximately 800 acres, that I have sweated and shivered over under summer sun and winter winds as I fought prickly pear, mesquite sprouts, aging and rotted fence posts, and other ingredients which that particular place puts in my way, have given me a focus. I am constantly reminded of how important that place is to me and to the heritage about which I have written for the past fifteen years. Carl Coke Rister in his *Fort Griffin on the Texas Frontier* describes the area as "one of the West's most nearly unique geographical and cultural entities" (p. ix). I came to realize that fact even before I found Rister's comment.

I was not alone in my quest. My wife Sonja was a ready partner and photographer. Her roots trace back to the earliest days of settlement here. Indeed, her great-grandparents, John G. and Emily Irwin, were among the three earliest white families to settle in the area. Her cousin Morris Ledbetter, with whom she shared a brother-like relationship, was also a ready guide and confidante.

I never finished the initial book. I began a chapter on cowboys and never left the subject. That interest led to a number of books and pamphlets on that and related subjects, such as ranch history, cowboy humor, biography, and vaqueros and buckaroos. My wife and I have resurrected the notion I hoped to address in the first book by issuing a pamphlet series using the title *Fort Griffin Sketches.*

The sense of place that permeates my thinking and working is as strong today as it ever was. It is a source of comfort and inspiration to me. I hope that the following information proves as interesting to you as it has been to me.

The Family Saga

The writer and teacher Leo F. Buscaglia once gave his students an unusual assignment. Write about your parents' lives, where they came from, how they met, the roles your grandparents played. Then he saw by the puzzled looks on their faces that they knew very little about their parents' history. From his own parents' stories, he had learned what he had hoped his students might learn from theirs: "that things didn't start with me. I was part of an ongoing history—full of pride, survival and love." Lawrence's own sense of becoming a part of an ongoing history through careful attention to family stories drawn from the store of past events remembered by his wife Sonja's family inspired this series of essays. Fortunate to be part of his audience when father-in-law J.C. Irwin, Jr., began a storytelling session, Lawrence was also savvy enough to realize what remarkable tales these were. His careful record not only of J.C.'s mannerisms and language but of his ability to make the family's past life vitally alive preserves history of value both to the family and to others who are interested in this region where the Irwin family has lived for well over a century. Note that Lawrence's account of Irwin's grasshopper and hailstorm stories appear in both the first and second essays of this section to illustrate different facets of family storytelling.

TWO
THE FAMILY SAGA

Although bonafide sagas stem from Medieval times in Scandinavian countries, the form has evolved into what C. Hugh Holman in *A Handbook to Literature* calls "a form lying between authentic history and intentional fiction." One modern type of saga consists of stories that develop in families and serve as the oral, traditional lore of that family. These narratives, which resemble the early sagas in scope, tend to be even more episodic, less chronologically arranged, and less "heroic" in content than examples of the early Scandinavian form. Folklorist Mody C. Boatright considers family saga the "lore that tends to cluster around families, or often the patriarchs or matriarchs of families, which is preserved and modified by oral transmission, and which is believed to be true. Lore that is handed down as folklore is excluded." Boatright continues by saying that family sagas are "not concerned with a type of tale, but with clusters of types, not with a motif, but with many motifs."

The stories of my concern differ somewhat from those Boatright discusses because they are more personal and less spectacular than his, and they provide more of a sense of community within the family. These family narratives are universal only in the sense that they represent a framework for particular events related to the life of a given family. Some of the stories involve members of other families in the action, either as antagonists, as co-protagonists, or as observers.

The cycle of family saga is a fragile organism developed in a sympathetic environment and is susceptible to upheaval and decline when the circumstance that created the saga changes, especially when the context around the pivotal figure alters in any way to break the dynamic chain of creativity and recreation through telling of the stories. For example, my initial awareness of these narratives developed years ago from the stories my grandfather told of his exploits as a young man in South and East Texas, which are now, unfortunately, so dimmed by time and by not being told that they are lost. He told and retold these stories as we worked together when he was teaching me of life and of farm and ranch work in East Texas in a tutor/tyro relationship. He was one of the most important heroes of my early years, and his philosophy and outlook as revealed in these stories have shaped my life. When my family moved back to town, the link between my grandfather and me altered, and the tales told freely in the work environment were stymied in the more polite circumstances in which we only occasionally found ourselves after that. When he died some years later, I realized how fatal to the cycle is the loss of the pivotal figure, for that absence destroys the environment necessary for the development and continuation of these stories. Usually the family gatherings so vital to the cycle either cease or alter in structure to avoid the tales and thereby to avert the poignancy of loss felt by other members of the family when the central figure is recalled through the stories.

My interest in this form of folklore was rekindled by the tales I heard my father-in-law tell and retell after 1958, when I married into the West Texas pioneer Irwin family and began to spend weekends and holiday periods at the Irwin Ranch near long-abandoned

Fort Griffin, a post-Civil War military post located on the Clear Fork of the Brazos River between Albany and Throckmorton in Northwest Texas. These stories dealing with the western frontier sparked my interest, as had those my grandfather told me. The setting for the Irwin stories is much like that found earlier in my grandfather's stories, a rural one, this time loaded with the romanticized elements of the West Texas ranch country. This region is still dimly peopled by figures from the past like then-Colonel Robert E. Lee, commander of the nearby pre-Civil War military outpost named Camp Cooper; early-day cattlemen like Hittsons, Gentrys, Reynoldses, and Matthewses; outlaws like John Wesley Hardin, John Selman, and John Larn; and even living legends like Watt Matthews, son of Sallie Reynolds Matthews, whose family saga is told in *Interwoven: A Pioneer Chronicle.*

The patriarch of this cycle of stories is J. C. Irwin, Jr., a mild-mannered, reserved, but vivacious modern-day frontiersman. Mr. Irwin was born in 1902 within a mile of where he lived during most of the years I knew him. A third-generation Texan, he grew up along the Clear Fork of the Brazos River on the Irwin Ranch where he helped farm and tend the cattle. He worked in the West Texas oil fields as a tool dresser, roustabout, and pumper until he retired in the early 1960s and moved a house onto his part of the family ranch. This modest structure provided a home for Mr. Irwin and his wife, Lee Ita. Although not large, the Irwin ranch, which has been in the family for over one hundred years, encompasses some four hundred acres of rolling, mesquite-dotted range land which has provided the opportunity for the extended Irwin family to work cattle, hunt, fish, and spend sizeable amounts of time together in a relaxed environment with little structure on the language or content of the fairly cohesive set of stories that became the Irwins' oral storehouse. The twenty miles of space between the ranch and Albany, the nearest town, provided a healthy degree of isolation from outside influences during our visits there.

I came to realize just how crucial a productive context—an outdoor work/recreational one—is to the development of this oral tradition as I have known it. Given this kind of context, it seems that the development of the cycle is a natural manifestation of a narrative tendency in people and will occur unless negative circumstances are present. For example, the tendency of some religious groups to treat jokes and stories with disdain is detrimental to the cycle's development. The reluctance seems related to the religious injunction against "idle tongues." Also the desire of that generation just out of the rural experience to sever ties with that part of their past and join in the urban existence seems another negative factor. There are likely others as well.

J.C., Dale, and Lee Ita Irwin

The cycle of relating the stories seems predictable. I found that as new members have joined the family, usually through the marriage of one of the family members, such as my own daughter and later a niece, the same spate of stories would be retold in no particular order over a period of several gatherings. Some of these were told by my father-in-law; others were related by those of us who had heard the tales and repeated them from memory. New stories have been added in the form of narratives of adventures involving me, my two brothers-in-law, and other members of the family. Upon occasion, when only those individuals familiar with the stories were present, an allusion by a phrase or two from one of the stories would elicit the desired effect associated with the complete tale. The purpose might be to evoke laughter, emphasize a point, or note a contrast in a situation or behavior. I found as well that many of the tales were told and retold either at the dining table as we sat after meals or on the front porch, a favorite spot for relaxing on a summer evening, usually with a chorus of coyotes in the background. Significantly, no radio or television set is found in either location to interfere with the flow of conversation. I began writing these stories down some years ago and have continued to add to the overall collection since that time.

The specific incidents in the cycle of stories in families vary, of course, from family to family, but the general makeup of the saga has similarity in the kinds of material included. The stories are typically of a few distinct kinds. One concerns coping with hard times growing up and is related to stories dealing with the Great Depression, a common motif for those who lived through that dismal period. Another category involves jokes and pranks, which may or may not be work related. A third kind recounts remarkable occurrences or tales of adventure. A fourth variety includes stories related to historical events or personages. Some examples will illustrate.

The story which actually got me started on this project involved Mr. Irwin's childhood and is a "hard times" tale. Although similar to depression stories, this one does not involve the Great Depression at all. It seems that during his childhood he faced a series of depressions. I will relate the story as nearly as possible in Mr. Irwin's words:

"Yes, I've had plenty of hard times in my day. I remember once when I was a kid, my brother Firl planted a crop of watermelons in that old sand field west of the Robinson place, and the folks planted some cotton too. This never was farming country anyway, but it rained some that spring for a change, and we were hopeful. Grasshoppers were real bad, too, though—those old big jumbos, some were three or four inches long, and they did like cotton stalks and leaves, nearly ate us out of house and home. Dad put me and my brothers in the field with wooden paddles, almost like flat baseball bats, walkin' the rows and killin' 'hoppers. It wasn't much sport after a time, I can tell you. Human insecticide I guess we were, but there wasn't much other kind. We also took a turnin' plow and cut a furrow all around the field with the straight side toward the crop. The 'hoppers would try to climb that—they can't fly, you know—and they would fall into that trench. We'd mixed wheat bran with strychnine and syrup and put that in the trench. They'd eat that poison and die by the thousands, but it didn't kill nearly all of 'em. But we just couldn't give up and let the hoppers have the cotton. We killed grasshoppers all through late June, but we looked forward to the Fourth of July. We usually had a get-together with the neighbor families at the Red Top School, which Dad built in 1907 for us kids to go to school in. I figured we could let them ole 'hoppers rest for one day. I hoped maybe the hot sand would kill 'em, but I noticed they seemed to thrive in it. It didn't appear to hurt their feet like it did my bare ones, 'cept I do recall [he chuckled] how we used to kid about some of those 'hoppers carrying other 'hoppers across that hot sand to save their feet. We knew about 'hopper reproduction, I guess; it was just a kind of a kid joke.

"About the first of July, Firl carried off and sold a wagon load of his big, sweet melons. Me and my brother Stanley sneaked one down to the draw and ate it that day; we didn't tell little Jimmy. He never could keep a secret. The Fourth dawned kinda mixed. By late morning, a cloud was coming up, and I knew there'd be no party at the schoolhouse that day. By noon the sky in the northwest was as green as winter wheat, and I felt a puff of cold wind when I was out at the barn puttin' stuff up from the wettin' we knew was comin'. Before two o'clock it hit, the wildest hailstorm you ever saw. Come right out of the northwest, broke out all of the windows on the north and west sides of the house. Covered the ground! Hailstones as big as golf balls piled up two or three feet on the sides of the house! Lasted about twenty minutes, I guess. When we went out, it was awful. Trees were stripped; everything was beaten down. It even killed some rabbits and bruised up the cattle some. My brother grabbed a saddle horse out of the barn and rushed over to check his melons. It was as useless as everything else we did to try to get ahead in those days. Those melons looked like somebody had shot all of 'em with a Winchester 30-30. Cotton stalks were stripped bare of leaves, just stalks standing there. I knew it was all lost. We all went over and ate all of the melon we could hold, knowin' that was all we'd get out of it. When we got back home we noticed those hailstones just melting there. Ice in July! Now, that was a treat too good to pass up! We gathered up some while Maw mixed some sugar and milk and eggs together. We put that in an old crank freezer, filled those hailstones in around it, put some stock salt on it, and kept crankin' 'til we had a freezer of cream. That was one of the few times I had ice cream in the summer 'til years later. Never have quite got all I wanted, even yet.

"Well, that wasn't the worst of it. You know, the rain and all that melted hail fed that cotton, and it come out green as could be, grew a second growth like crazy. We were foolish enough to get excited about pickin' cotton that fall. The strippin' had set it back considerable, and that fall, kinda late for cotton, it began to make squares. Just before those squares would have opened to make cotton, frost hit it. It wasn't particularly early; the cotton was just late because of the backset caused by the poundin' hail. All the cotton we picked that fall was just 'bout enough for Maw to make three quilts. It struck me then—we'd worked hard all summer; we killed grasshoppers and hoed that cotton and those melons. All we got to show for all that hard work was all the melon we could eat one day and a freezer of ice cream the same day. The two together gave me the worst bellyache I nearly ever had."

Life was undoubtedly hard, but those who survived responded with humor, often seen in the form of jokes and pranks. These are easily illustrated from the Irwins' storehouse of tales. The following prank served to straighten out a problem for the group and had a useful, not a destructive, purpose. It occurred when Mr. Irwin was still a child in school.

"Well, I learned to throw rocks chunkin' at the outhouse the girls had out behind the school. Us boys just went to the creek. I got where I could hit that pipe comin' up out of that outhouse every time I throwed. My throwin' nearly got me in trouble one time, though. Louis Overton—we called him Sandy—and I were older than most of the other kids by this time, and we felt an obligation to help out around the school. Robert Tuton, Grace's brother, had trouble gettin' along at Fort Griffin School and was moved up to Red Top with us—an exchange student, I guess you'd call him now. His mother, who had a nickname for everybody, called him Dobbin. 'Be beautiful, Dobbin,' she'd say to him. It didn't work much, though. He was bad to pick on the little kids, bullied them a lot. Well, one mornin' Sandy and I were out playing catch before school when Robert began to pick on some of the little kids. I knew he needed a fire built under him; Sandy and I got the idea at the same time. He moved over to put Robert in line between us and waved at me to throw the ball. I lined up on Robert and hit him right in the back of the head, just below the roundin' spot on his skull. Whump! He went down and was out like a light. The girls screamed and ran, and the teacher came chargin' out. Robert came around after a little and began to cry and say he was bad hurt. The teacher decided he wasn't, but she had us all in and asked around and decided it was all an accident. She told me and Sandy to go back to playin', but she made Robert stay in. He slowed down some after that, but not much."

In this case, the story has a moral—bullies deserve to get abused—and illustrates the ability to inflict punishment with impunity for a right or just cause.

Another incident related to the school experience involves getting the best of the teacher who, as misfortune decreed, lived in the Irwin house, near which the small school had been erected. She treated the situation with some disdain, which prompted Mr. Irwin to pull the prank on her that he did. He recalls the incident this way:

"Her name was Margaret Robinson, and she was from somewhere up in North Texas. Her sister taught up at Throckmorton at that time. She stayed in the east bedroom of the old ranch house on the river, the one that burned. There was a piano in her room, and she could play a little. We had a telephone by then—it was about 1912 or so—and she'd call up her sister in Throckmorton and talk to her. She didn't take to country livin' too much and didn't make any bones about it. It was Halloween. Donald McKechin was due to come visit, and she'd been sittin' around on the porch, waitin'. But she got bored and called up her sister in Throckmorton and said, it bein' Halloween night and all, she didn't know how to act out in the sticks. When she lived in town, they'd always go out and trick-or-treat on Halloween night.

"Well, I listened to her runnin' down where we lived and decided I'd scare her a little bit. I've always been a little devilish, I guess. Well, Dad had an old bearskin rug that was lined real nice. We used it for a lap robe or cover in a buggy. It was 'bout dark, so I got that old bear robe and a set of buffalo horns that'd been made into a hat rack. By this time she was off the phone and was back playin' the piano. I got to the door and propped it open just a little bit. Then I scratched on the screen. She quit playin' and listened. I was real still. Then I scratched on the screen a little bit more. She got up to see what was goin' on. Well, I had that robe all around me and those horns tied on my head, and I came growlin' and groanin', jumped in that door and hollered 'Whee Hoo!' When she saw me she lit a shuck screamin' that the ol' devil who was out there was out there with his horns on. She ran the length of the house, through that bedroom, the room next to it, just a flyin'. My brother Ennis was sittin' in the third room, which was the kitchen, in a chair by the cookstove. She was so scared she left a string of water all through those three rooms and still had enough left to wet Ennis down good when she jumped into his lap. Maw was there and laughed so hard she could hardly catch her breath, but it was tough at home and at school for me the next few days after that. I don't think that teacher ever forgave me. She finally married Joe Overton and lived around here 'til she died."

Mr. Irwin had many exciting adventures, but one which has come up regularly in the conversation involves an experience he had some years after I came into the family. The Irwins at that time had Lucky, a small, part-bulldog canine that served as a watchdog. He often treed varmints in the post oak trees that surround the Irwin house. Mr. Irwin loves to relate this story:

"One evening as I was fixin' to go to bed, I heard Lucky barkin' and recognized the bark that he had treed somethin'. I knew if we were to get any sleep that night, I'd just as well go out and take care of whatever Lucky had up that tree. Takin' my flashlight and my .22, I walked up nearly to the road where I could tell Lucky had something in one of the oak trees. When I got to him, I shined my light into the tree and saw a pair of eyes and fired. Something dropped from the tree, and Lucky grabbed it and ran into the broomweeds before I could tell what it was. When I walked under the tree to see if I could figure out what had fallen, I felt somethin' warm drippin' on my head. I raised one hand to my head and came away with blood on my head and shoulders. I backed up under the tree, shined the light into the branches again, and saw eyes gleam back. I shot again and a half-grown bobcat came crashin' down.

"As near as I can figure out, the bobcat must have grabbed a rabbit; lots of 'em live in the grass and weeds around the house; it's safer for 'em there. Lucky saw 'im get it and took after 'im. The bobcat, rabbit in its mouth, got up the tree to get away from the dog. My first shot wounded the bobcat and made him drop the rabbit, which Lucky grabbed and carried into the weeds. The second shot, of course, brought the bobcat down."

That story is guaranteed to send the grandchildren to bed early any time it is told. The effect can be elicited by referring to Mr. Irwin as a man who shoots rabbits out of the trees. The horror element—the narrow escape from being clawed by a dying bobcat—is strong in the tale.

The Irwin family had strong historical ties in the region. Mr. Irwin's grandfather came to the Clear Fork area from Fort Chadbourne to the southwest as the first sergeant of a dragoon company stationed at Camp Cooper and later, after he had left military service to begin ranching, provided beef to the soldiers at Camp Cooper under a contract signed by Robert E. Lee, by then the Commander of the Department of Texas. These events happened in the late 1850s. In addition, the family "forted up" at Fort Davis in Stephens County during the latter stages of the Civil War, a period documented ably by Sam Newcomb's diary appended to Sallie

Reynolds Matthews' *Interwoven*. Elmer Kelton used that material at the beginning of his novel *Stand Proud*. This body of lore, however, has been in oral tradition so long that it has lost much of the detail necessary to provide a narrative framework and any characterization at all. None of us alive, even Mr. Irwin, knew the grandfather, who was killed by a thief in Fort Sumner, New Mexico, in 1867 as he returned from a trail drive to Santa Fe. Therefore, the personality around which the tale would revolve is too dimmed by time to be an anchor point for the narrative. Tristram Coffin makes a point in regard to folk ballads that seems relevant here: the longer a ballad is in oral tradition, the less narrative and the more lyric it becomes. The same seems true of these tales which, lacking the mnemonic devices of rhythm and rhyme, have less support for recall than do the ballads and lose any narrative structure or cohesiveness. Massive distortion of facts is also likely in that part of the narrative that remains.

One history-related story still told about Mr. Irwin's father, whom he does remember well, involves an incident in which John Larn, notorious cattle rustler and former sheriff of the town of Fort Griffin located in the flat below the military post on the Clear Fork of the Brazos River, nearly killed Mr. Irwin's father, John Chadbourne Irwin. The younger Irwin usually tells the story this way:

"My dad knew John Larn was rustlin' cattle because Larn sold beef to the army nearly every day, but the size of his herd didn't drop off any. Dad lost three big ol' steers he used as oxen and went to the Larn place to check on 'em. Larn's slaughterhouse stood on a bluff on the river, and a deep hole of water was just below that bluff. Dad walked out to the edge of the bluff and looked into the river, and he could see lots of beef hides weighted down with rocks in that hole of water. He wondered how many brands were on those hides, but he never found out. Larn walked up about that time and said, 'Mr. Irwin, do you see anything?' Dad glanced over and saw that Larn was patting the pistol he always wore. Dad said, 'No, John, I don't see a thing,' and left. But later Dad was part of the posse that arrested Larn and carried him to Albany, where some masked men broke in and killed him." The historical authenticity of this story is borne out in Carl Coke Rister's *Fort Griffin on the Texas Frontier,* but the account is somewhat embellished by legend.

These stories stabilized or gave focus to countless family conversation sessions that otherwise included a plethora of current gossip, information about the affairs of past and present friends and acquaintances, and stories related to the families established by the Irwin children in their own communities. The gatherings were richly rewarding. As in all things temporal, however, these times could not last forever. Regrettably, I have rediscovered how fragile is the existence of the context producing these stories. After I had pretty well completed collecting the principal tales, the eighty-three-year-old Mr. Irwin had a stroke and lay three days and nights before he was found in the ranch house, where, after his wife's death in 1973, he had lived alone. He now lives in my home, paralyzed on his left side, his mind clear and his speech still audible. But the happy context for telling the stories is gone. The tension generated by disagreement concerning his care among the three sisters—one of them is my wife—has fragmented this family unit probably forever. The family circle is broken and with it the cycle of stories. It is fortunate that the research was completed before this development in the life of this family, for these stories would otherwise be headed toward extinction since the framework for rehearsing and renewing them is gone.

The value of these stories to the formal study of folklore is yet to be fully understood, but the tendency to tell tales is as old as mankind. In this age of fascination with prepared stories in books and films, this may be the most natural form of oral narrative still being practiced.

THREE
Hard Times At Griffin, As Recalled by J.C. Irwin, Jr.

J.C. lay back on the frayed webbing of an aluminum-frame lawn chair holding a homemade fly swat in his hand. The dry heat of the one hundred degree-plus mid afternoon was oppressive, but the old man seemed not to notice. Glancing up, he grunted and eased upright, his litheness belying his eighty years. Taking careful aim, he swung the swat in a horizontal path with the porch ceiling and hit the horsefly, bouncing it off a rough beam. He stepped on it and left a small blood stain on the cement. Twice more he swung with the same result. "Those flies come in here by the hundreds in weather like this, and they'll bite the blood out if you're not careful. One of those already had." He grew tired of the sport and turned his attention instead to a devil's horse inching its way up the wall of the house toward the grayish horseflies that buzzed and darted incessantly near the ceiling. He smiled and sat down, speaking after a pause to me as I sat, pretending to doze, in the straight-back wooden chair at the front edge of the porch in a futile effort to catch a little breeze. There was none. I knew if I gave him time he would talk and that was what I wanted.

"See that old devil's horse over there? He'll climb up to the ceiling and catch one of those flies. It'll be a waitin' game, but he'll eat before we get around to supper."

I injected, "Couldn't you spray and cut down on the numbers?"

He continued, "Not really, and no fly powder will touch 'em. Those horseflies drive cattle and horses crazy. They're tougher than houseflies. When I was a kid, though, the houseflies were so bad somebody had to fan the table while the food was put on until everybody got there to fan for theirselves. We didn't have screens on windows or doors. That reminds me of an ol' preacher that I heard about—baldheaded as a slick rock—who put a handkerchief over his head at meal times. Tied the ends of the handkerchief into little knots to hold it down on his head. Seems those little legs crawlin' on the bare skin were awful distractin' to him and kept him from enjoyin' his food. And he did like to eat, like most of the preachers I've known."

J.C. Irwin, Jr.

"I can't tell that's changed much," I said.

"This has always been a hard land, almost like it didn't want us here. We've fought drought and flood, often the same year. They say this was a 'prairie sea' in the early days, grass was stirrup high on the horses. Now we have overgrazed it, and mesquite and prickly pear have taken it."

"I've heard the longhorns brought those trees up here from South Texas," I said.

"Some say that the trail herds of ole steers brought 'em up here in their stomachs after eating the beans. Seeds sprout real good in manure, you know. Every year they brought 'em a little bit further north. Those trail herds used to come by here in the late '60s, but that didn't last long. Buffalo used to come through here by the millions before that, taint the waterholes, fight and breed and raise cain and drift on, till the hunters took them all away. Those buffalo hides made good leather after, I believe, some German figured out how to process it. A man could make a mint of money in those days killin' buffalo and sellin' the hides."

"How much was a hide worth, anyway?" I queried.

"A good robe sold for a dollar up to three dollars and more each, dependin' on the market; a man could kill a hundred a day in good years. Lots of money made then."

"Have you heard the story of old Crego, who supposedly left Jacksboro in 1873 to hunt buffalo up in the Pease River country west of Wichita Falls?"

"No, I don't reckon I have."

"It's in a folk song. It says his crew killed him up there when he tried to cheat them out of their season earnings."

"I haven't heard it, but I don't doubt it. People don't take to cheaters much out here. But there were so many buffalo, they tell me, some folks back East covered their walls with buffalo skins. I've even heard the ol' Ledbetter picket house had a coverin' of skin at one time. Very few buffaloes left now. Watt Matthews has got some on his ranch, but he guards 'em pretty careful. When he's gone, who knows what'll happen to them old buffaloes and to us other old-timers.

"But I wandered off from the hard times and the bad times, didn't I? And I've seen plenty of both in my day. I remember once when I was a kid, my brother Firl planted a crop of watermelons in that old sand field west of the Robinson place. This never was farming country anyway, but the folks planted some cotton too. It rained some that spring for a change, and we were real hopeful. Grasshoppers were real bad, too, though—those old big jumbos, some three or four inches long, and they did like cotton stalks and leaves. Nearly ate us out of house and home. Dad put me and my three brothers in the field with wooden paddles, almost like flat baseball bats, walking the rows and killin' 'hoppers. It wasn't much sport after a time, I can tell you. Human insecticide I guess we were, but there wasn't no other kind. We took a turnin' plow and cut a side on a furrow all around the field with the straight side toward the crop. The 'hoppers would try to climb that—can't fly, you know—and they would fall into that trench. We'd mixed wheat bran with strychnine and syrup in that trench. They'd eat that and die by the thousands, but it didn't kill nearly all of 'em. And we just couldn't give up and let the 'hoppers have the cotton. We killed grasshoppers all through late June, but we looked forward to the Fourth of July. We usually had a get together with the neighbor families at the Red Top School they built in 1907 for the kids in these parts to go to school. I figured we could let them ole 'hoppers rest for one day. I hoped maybe the hot sand would kill 'em, but I noticed they seemed to thrive in it. It didn't appear to hurt their feet like it did my bare ones, 'cept I do recall [he chuckled] how we used to kid about some of those 'hoppers carrying others across that hot sand to save their feet. We knew about 'hopper reproduction, I guess; it was just a kind of a kid joke.

"About the first of July, Firl carried off and sold a wagon load of his big, sweet melons. Me and my brother Stanley sneaked one down to the draw and ate it that day; we didn't tell little Jimmy. He never could keep a secret. The Fourth dawned kinda mixed. The sky was real red, so we knew a storm was brewing. You know the old saying: 'Red in the morning, a sailor's warning; red at night, sailor's delight.' Heard that all my life, and it worked that day. By late morning, a cloud was coming up, and I knew there'd be no party at the schoolhouse that day. By noon the sky in the northwest was as green as winter wheat, and I felt a puff of cold wind when I was out at the barn puttin' stuff up from the wettin' we knew was comin'. Before two o'clock it hit, the wildest hailstorm you ever saw. Come right out of the northwest, broke out all of the windows on the north and west sides of the house. Covered the ground! Hailstones as big as golf balls piled up two or three feet on the sides of the house! Lasted about twenty minutes, I guess. When we went out, it was awful. Trees were stripped; everything was beaten down. It even killed some rabbits and bruised up the cattle some. My brother grabbed a saddle horse out of the barn and rushed over to check his melons. It was as useless as everything else we did to try to get ahead in those days. Those melons looked like somebody had shot all of 'em with a Winchester 30-30. Cotton stalks were stripped bare of leaves, just stalks standing there. I knew it was all lost. We all went over and ate all of the melon we could hold, knowin' that was all we'd get out of it. When we got back home we noticed those hailstones just melting there. Ice in July! Now, that was a treat too good to pass up! We gathered up some while Maw mixed some sugar and milk and eggs together. We put that in an old crank freezer, filled those hailstones in around it and put some stock salt on it, and kept crankin' 'til we had a freezer of cream. That was one of the few times I had ice cream in the summer 'til years later. Never have quite got all I wanted, even yet. Sweet stuff was scarce in those days. All the sweets we had was fruit pies in season. Maw made a few pies out of those cactus red berries—not prickly pear fruit—but those red berries in those cactus that grow close to the ground. Other than that, vinegar pie was about it. I wouldn't trade cookin' today to go back to that, no way!"

"You didn't get anything much out of the crop, then, did you?" I responded.

"Well, that's not the worst of it. You know, the rain and all that melted hail fed that cotton, and it come out green as could be, grew a second growth like crazy. We was foolish enough to get excited about pickin' cotton that fall. The strippin' had set it back considerable, and that fall, kinda late for cotton, it began to make squares. Just before those squares would have opened to make cotton, frost hit it. It wasn't particularly early; the cotton was just late because of the backset caused by the poundin' of the hail. All the cotton we picked that fall was just 'bout enough for Maw to make three quilts. It struck me then—we 'd worked hard all summer; we killed grasshoppers and hoed that cotton and those melons. All we got to show for all that hard work was all the melon we could eat one day and a freezer of ice cream the same day. The two together gave me the worst bellyache I nearly ever had."

"Why did people stay in those days, J.C.? There were other parts of the country less hostile, I'd think."

"I thought about leavin' here, but this country will put its mark on you, brand you, I guess, is a way of puttin' it. Then you can't leave. I never could. Them that did regretted it and tried to come back. Some made it; others died before they could.

"The Ledbetter boys left and came back. I can remember them—George, Seaborn, and Joe. They're all dead now. They went to Dakotas in the early days and homesteaded up there. Lived in a dugout. They raised cattle and trapped mustangs. Got wiped out once in a blizzard. They stayed out on horseback in that snow and wind, stirrin' them cows until about four in the mornin' and finally froze out and went on in. By the time they got back after daylight, most of those cows were dead. They built back, but then got smart and sold out. Brought their money back in a towsack on the train. None of 'em ever worked another day as long as I knew 'em. But I can't face winters like that. They went to Dakotas, but they came back to Griffin. I guess things are pretty hard wherever you go. It used to get colder here than it does now. When I was a boy, around 1916, the winters were colder than they are now. Each family had at least one pair of ice skates, and in the winter the Clear Fork and the tanks would freeze over. I've skated on that river many a time, sometimes with the skates and sometimes just in my shoes. The houses leaked air. Boy, it was tough, especially with outside toilets in those days. But I can't take the cold like I once did. I've come to enjoy this heat. I can sweat and feel real good about it.

"See that old devil's horse up there? That's his trancin' dance he's goin' into now. He'll nail him one of those flies in a minute." I looked up and watched the mantis in its hypnotic movement, but this fly was too smart and flew away. The mantis seemed undaunted and started moving in on another fly.

"You know, this heat reminds me of how cold I got last winter when it got down to five and ten degrees and stayed. I had to chop ice for the cows down at the tank. When it gets cold like that and stays, those tanks will freeze six or eight inches deep, and deeper, I guess, and an old cow, starved for water, will walk out on the ice and maybe find a soft spot around the middle somewhere and fall through. She can't get out and will drown. Well, you know, you all couldn't come over during Christmas, and Tom stopped by to stay with me so he could hunt. I thought he was a cowboy, since he worked on the Nail Ranch as a kid, 'til I took him down to chop that ice on the tank that first mornin'. It was plain to me that he was a summertime cowboy and had no experience a'tall choppin' ice on a tank." J.C. grinned as he brought up the point.

I felt inclined to follow up on that and asked the leading question, "What difference does it make how you chop it as long as you get it chopped?" That gave J.C. the opening he was looking for.

"Anybody who's chopped much ice knows that you got to hold that ax so that the sharp part of the blade strikes that ice flat. If you just chop down at it, nothin' but the point of your ax is hittin' that ice, and those chips will fly ever'where. And as you begin to hit through the ice and get to the water, then water will splash all over you and you'll get wet. Of course, when it's that cold, the water freezes and creates other problems. Ol' Tom, he'd just stand there, as tall as he is, and short as that ax handle was, and chop down into that ice, and chips and water were just flyin' ever'where. So I said, 'Tom, let me show you how to do that.' He didn't much want me to have that ax because he prob'ly knew I was right. Even though I showed him my way was better, you know him, he never did admit I was doin' it any better than he was. As a matter of fact, I believe I remember, he tried to tell me he was doin' it better than I did anyway."

I stretched in the heat, "Yeah, I remember last winter, J.C. I promised myself then that when it got hot I wouldn't complain. I guess it's as hot today as it's been, but I'm sure going to follow through on my promise. I don't want any more ice day after day. I'm not geared to take much to that."

"Yeah, heat is tough. I remember when I was just a young man, I got a job on a thrashing crew up on the Matthews' Ranch, not far down the river from Reynolds' Bend where they do those

"Fandangle Samplers." Well, it was hot that time, too, and we were harvestin' oats. I remember that well enough. A fellow was cookin' lunch for us there and had barbecued a goat. I never have cared for goat meat since then, but boy, I was hungry that day, and I ate a big bait of that stuff. Well, by two o'clock, I was sick as I could be. I laid in the loft of that ol' rock barn there right by that field for three days not knowin' whether I was goin' to live or not. Wasn't anybody there that could take care of me. Wasn't nothin' anybody could do. They just had to wait and see if I was goin' to make it. Well, I made it, but I tell you, that was the end of the barbecued goat for me. That convinced me, too, that farmin' was somethin' I didn't want any more to do with than that. That's when I decided the oil patch is where this ol' boy needed to be."

I got interested at that point, too. "J.C. , how'd that ol' boy cook everything? Did he use Dutch ovens?"

"Yeah," J.C. responded. "He even cooked bread in a Dutch oven."

I said, "How did he cook it without burning it?"

J.C. grinned and said, "I didn't know you could cook it without burnin' it. All I ever ate was burned."

I said, "Well, I've learned over time if you keep the amount of coals small, it won't burn. But it is hard to do if the wind is blowing."

"Another time I was cuttin' posts 'way up the river for the Matthews. It came a weekend, and I decided I'd go home for a visit. It'd been rainin' quite a bit, and the Clear Fork was at flood stage. I came on down to Fort Griffin thinkin' I'd cross the bridge, but the water was too high to do that. It got over the approaches to the bridge there quite a ways, and I decided I'd just swim it. The current was pretty swift, but I didn't try to fight the current—I just let it carry me along and finally made it over the river by holdin' on a log. That ol' river must have been a mile wide at that point. Scared me after I thought about it later, but there wasn't any other way to get across it, so I took the chance and it came out all right that time.

"I have had some interesting experiences on the Matthews Ranch. One time in 1924, Charlie Overton and I stopped there at the cook shack. It was just about dark. The ol' judge and Watt were there in the cook shack, and we went in and talked to 'em a minute. The judge said, 'Watt, go get these men one of those hogs apiece.' Well, Watt went back there and gave us a dressed hog apiece. Those things weighed about a hundred and twenty-five pounds apiece, I guess. They were wild hogs that they'd just captured. Well, I took mine home. We were stayin' up at the Stockton's, Ita's folks, then; and Mrs. Stockton, she was real conservative, wanted to know where I'd got that hog. I said, 'Well, I was just drivin' around and decided I wanted a hog and saw that one and killed it.' Well, she got awful nervous about that and said, 'Oh, good night, boys, we'd better get rid of that hog. J.C.'ll get in trouble over that.' Ita already knew that wasn't the truth, that I wouldn't just kill a hog, but Mrs. Stockton sure did get nervous over that before I finally convinced her it was all right, and we ate that hog. The Stockton place was not far, you know, from where I was born."

I nodded assent.

"The old chimney is still standin' where I was born. That dirt road was the old Albany/Throckmorton highway then. This highway here in front of the house wasn't there then. We used to walk all over these oaks huntin' when I got bigger, but in 1906 we moved to the river and lived in the Lowe house. It was one large room, about sixteen by twenty. We lived there while we built the ranch house over on the river. That's the one that burned in 1953. I can remember movin' over there on a wagon, sat on a spring seat, and we went right by the Stockton place. Didn't know the woman I was goin' to marry was there then. The Stocktons were camped along Plum Branch. They'd sold four hundred acres of land around Weinert and bought two sections of the land down here. That's the difference then in land prices here and there—that's good farmin' country; this isn't. The Stocktons owned land that the Kunkles and the Sheltons own now. Their land went nearly to the Wilhelm place. The Stocktons sold it off a little at a time as they needed money. I remember Mr. Kunkle bought three hundred and twenty acres at one time. They finally got down to just that hundred and sixty acres

I bought—that's my Plum Branch place."

J.C. continued, "You know land was cheap down here, but everythin' was cheap then. I noticed one time in lookin' at my abstract that once this land around here was leased for coal. That was in 1912. The company was goin' to pay eight cents a ton for the coal if they mined any."

I said, "J.C., they were just stealing that coal."

"Well, they may have been, but that's all they were goin' to pay. I'm glad they didn't tear up the land for that. Things were hard back then.

"I remember Dad sayin' one time he rode over to the McKeichan place to see Mr. McKeichan. He got there 'bout the middle of the morning. When he rode up to the front of the house, Mrs. McKeichan came out on the porch to meet him. She said her husband had been gone since early that mornin', and she didn't expect 'im back 'til that evenin' sometime. Dad said he was sorry he'd missed 'im, and then Mrs. McKeichan asked if he'd like to come in and see the new baby. Being a congenial man, Dad got down from his horse and walked into the house and looked at the child lyin' in the crib. 'How old is the baby, Mrs. McKeichan ?' he asked. 'Oh, about two hours,' she said. Obviously, she had given birth to the child with her husband gone and had cleaned the infant up and had it in the crib and met Dad on the front porch when he arrived. People were tough in those days, or they just died. I had my share of trials, too, growin' up.

"When I was a kid, they'd give us those ol' cathartic pills in the spring. Maw would look at us and say, 'You boys are lookin' bad.' She'd give all of us a round of those pills. Your ole belly would just cramp for a couple of days because of it. I'd finally decided I'd had all of those pills I needed, so I'd play like I swallowed that pill. In another day or two, Maw would say, 'You boys sure are lookin' better. You needed that pill, I guess.' We'd smile and agree, but I knew I hadn't taken any pill and wasn't goin' to.

"Another thing about those pills was that all the time I was at home, we never even had an outhouse. The girls went to the creek, and so did the boys. Why, Litt Perkins built the first outhouse for Maw and Dad after us kids were gone from home."

"Well, J.C.," I spoke up, "Wasn't that awful hard, especially on the girls?"

He said, "We didn't know any difference. We thought we were gettin' along fine. We were doin' at least as well as ever'body else. It was just tough to get along.

"Even schoolin' was hard to get. That's why I got so little. Our teachers in those days were contracted to teach through the sixth grade, but they would usually agree, to get the job, to carry the older kids on as far as they could take 'em. By the time I was in the eighth grade, I was beginnin' to lose interest because the teacher's main concern was for the little kids. She might get to the lesson I had every three or four days, and that got pretty borin'. Really, the teacher usually bogged down by that time anyway because teachers just weren't trained to go on up through the kind of math that we had at that level even then. We just got what we could and had to get the rest by experience. I guess I had some bad experience. I remember once, toward the end of the eighth grade, Sandy Overton and I were taking a test. The teacher put me on the front seat and him on the back. Sandy needed a little information, so as he came to the front of the room pretending to talk to the teacher, he dropped a note in the floor for me. I caught her lookin' off and reached for it, but she looked back at the wrong minute and caught me dead to rights. She was about to get us both, and I knew it, but at that time my brother, who was older than me and out of school, showed up to get me to go help pull some cows out of a bog hole over at the east side of the pasture, up in the oaks, not far from here. I sure was relieved."

"The weather was pretty droughty at that time, and I had to stay out of school to drive those ol' cows back to water every day. So I missed several weeks that way. The teacher had told me when I left that she'd settle up with me when I got back, and I sure did dread that. On a Monday, I was supposed to go back and was runnin' late, on purpose, I imagine. Maw just said, 'Oh, just wait and go tomorrow.' That was a relief, but I knew it was just one day. Well, my sister had come in from New Mexico not long before, and she broke out with the measles that day. Mother decided I'd have them anyway, so she just kept me out of school to drive the cattle and help burn pear for the cows to eat. I never did go back that term, and that ended my formal education."

"What ever happened to that old school, J.C.?"

"The old school was closed sometime before 1940, I remember. It was moved to Throckmorton where it was the Baptist church for awhile. I do remember that Pauline Pickard was the last teacher. That was in '36 or '37. In the late 1950s, the buildin' was moved to the Kelly ranch and the neighbors all fixed it up for a community center."

"Okay, that's where we went for that barbecue when I was out here in '61, wasn't it?"

"Yes," J.C. responded. "Before Charlie and Ella Kelly died, the ranch sold, about '63, and again after that. The owner didn't want the buildin' there, so my brother Stanley moved it to his place in '81 or '2 without saying boo to anybody. It's still there and in pretty good shape, considerin' it was built in 1907. Dad bought the lumber, and they built it on the Peeler place. I remember goin' to Albany with Dad in a wagon and bringin' the lumber back. That was in August, and school opened in September in that buildin'."

"You grew up pretty tough, then, didn't you?" I observed.

"Yes, in a way, but we didn't know any better. Livin' like that will teach you patience, though, 'cause you couldn't do anything else. In the early days we just got along as best we could. We had cattle and pretty well depended on them for a livin'. I remember one hard job when I was a kid foolin' with cattle. Dad decided we needed a dippin' vat. Government regulations at that time required all cattle to be dipped, anyway, to kill out the Texas fever ticks. We dipped them ol' cows every twenty-one days as long as the inspector could find even a few ticks per hundred head of cattle. The old vat is still there right along side the old road 'bout a mile west of here. That little tank just above it we built special with a mule team and a slip in order to catch the water to fill that vat. The job my brothers and I had was to get that water in buckets out of that tank, walk up that tank dam, and then go pour it in that vat. It took many a bucketful to fill up that ol' vat. Once we got it full, we'd add chemicals—I forget what kind—and dip cattle. We'd jump every old cow off into that vat out of a little crowdin' pen at one end. The entry was slanted and had a slick board on it. When that board got wet, the ol' cows couldn't get their footin' and went on in. On the other side we had two by twelve planks bolted to the floor for cleats to help them climb out. My dad stood about halfway across with a pole and punched the heads under so that the water with the chemicals in it would get down in their ears and kill the ticks that hid there as well. He had a stick with a hook on one end for the little calves that jumped in and sank to the bottom. He'd fetch 'em up and help 'em out on the other side. On the other end was a drain pen with a floor of flat stones fitted together with cement. It was higher on the edges and sloped off into the vat and would hold about ten or twelve head. We'd let 'em stand there while the water drained off and went back into the vat. Neighbors drove their stock over, too, and we dipped them, chargin' them a dime or so a head, I believe. But there I was totin' those buckets of water up that dam; pourin' them into that old vat, the government inspector standin' there, grinnin' as he watched me sweatin' in the sun. We'd have to dip it down with a bucket on a rope once in awhile to allow for new chemicals to recharge the water. 'Bout once a year, we'd have to dip the old vat dry, shovel out all the mud accumulated in the bottom. We had to be sure the old cow couldn't walk across because if she didn't get her head under, the inspector made us run her through again. Sure was hard to get that ol' cow off in that vat the second time. I heard a story once 'bout dippin' longhorn cattle. It seems the horns were so wide they wouldn't fit down into the vat. One ol' steer leaped off into the vat and hung there on the rim, swingin' on his horns. One old cowboy took a fence post and knocked off one of his horns so he'd fall down into the water."

"Wasn't there an easier way to get that water in that vat?"

"I've been asked that a lot of times, why with the lay of the land the way it was we just didn't get a rubber hose and siphon that water out of that tank into the vat? I'm quick to admit that sure would've been easier, but I was grown before I ever saw a piece of rubber hose. We finally did build a wooden sluice box—a v-shaped trough made of two one by sixes jointed and dabbed with tar. It had a box at the head; we poured water into it and watched it run down into the drain pen. Then we could pour the water from the top of the dam and not have to walk all the way down to that vat. We thought that was a heap better. Now with the kind of pump units we've got, that wouldn't be any problem a' tall. But let me tell you, in those days it was tough."

"What did you all do when people got sick?"

"It was sure tough on 'em. I remember once when I was workin' on a threshin' crew up in Reynolds Bend. I ate a bunch of barbecued goat. Never have cared for it since. I got so sick I thought I was goin' to die, and laid in the loft of that ol' stone barn along the river for three days. Wasn't anythin' anybody could do, but just hope I'd pull out of it. I finally did. That stomachache reminds me, though, of the first operation I witnessed. I was just a kid, 'bout five or six. There was a house up near the entry to the Brown Ranch about three miles north of here. The house was on the south side of the road right there where you turn into the ranch. It was a young woman who, as I recall, married an older man, but her appendix went bad on her. Well, folks sent word out all over the country for ever'body to bring their kerosene lamps. They knew it would be night by the time the doc got there. Sure enough, it was and ever'body gathered around and stayed. They laid her out on the dinin' room table, as well as I can remember. They put all the kids in the kitchen, but I figured out if I went outside I could watch through the window. All the neighbors gathered, just like a big party, except for the family that was involved, of course. I'm sure they didn't enjoy it much, but I can remember seeing her a layin' on that table bein' mostly covered with a sheet. I believe ol' Doc King from Throckmorton is the one who did the surgery. But they got it done, and the woman got all right. I don't know what finally become of her, but she lived through that.

"When I was eighteen, I got a piece of steel in my right eye while workin' on a car. It was a fairly small piece, but it lodged in the linin' of the back of the eye and wouldn't come out. They tried magnets and ever'thin' else to get it. The eye began to swell then. The doctor told me I'd have to have it out. The folks were too busy to take me, so I caught a ride with my brother Firl to Fort Worth. He was haulin' a load of cattle to the stockyard in his truck. I checked myself into the hospital in Fort Worth and had the eye out. They deadened it, but I was awake through the whole thing. They fitted an artificial eye in the next day, and the day after that, I caught the bus back.

"I've had it so long, it looks pretty natural, I guess. When I went to Dr. Tucker in Abilene to get my glasses checked back in '69, the girl put dilation drops in that glass eye before I told her it was artificial. It sure did embarrass her. Luckily, I'm left handed, but a blind right side has been a handicap to me. The kids all enjoyed the eye—showed it at slumber parties, and the grandkids are awful spooked by that eye when I put it on the chest at night to go to bed. I lost one once in the river when I was divin'. I ordered a whole box of 'em from a supply house and selected the best match for me.

"Look at that old devil's horse. He's got him another one lined up." I watched as the mantis eased closer and closer to a fly obviously entranced by the hypnotic movement of the mantis. Suddenly the fly realized its plight and flew, but too late. The fly and mantis met in mid air and hit the hard concrete porch two feet from my chair. We watched as the mantis drilled into the fly in the crease between the small head and body. Before long, the fly quit struggling. The mantis set about immediately devouring its prey. "There's a lesson in that—patience and hard work, that's the only thing that can let you survive in this country. If you don't get it the first time, wait and get it the next time."

"It has taken that kind of tough people to hold on out here, as long as we've been here. Folks had to keep tryin', battlin' drought, flood, hail, and wind, and even an occasional grass fire. My family's had this land in continuous ranchin' use for over a hundred years now. I'm sure goin' on that trip to Austin in November and get my Family Heritage Award from the Department of Agriculture. Sonja's going to get all of that paperwork fixed up for me. My dad got most of this land by paying back taxes on it. The oldest part is from the Hudler Survey. Governor Sam Houston gave a patent to Hudler in the 1850s, but then Hudler couldn't do anything with it, I guess. He apparently just let it go, or he died, maybe. Anyway, in 1880 Dad got 320 acres for about $12.00. Then in 1881 he got 990 more acres for about $20.00. All that land was split up among nine of us kids, and I got my 240 acres. You remember when I fenced it how Jimmy and Jack put up their double fence on each side? I never could understand why they did that. They just cheated themselves out of the use of about ten feet of their ground for a mile on each side."

"Sonja and I got married about that time, J.C., I remember when it happened."

"Now Stanley and I are the only ones who still own our land, except for Berthol's kids. They've lived in California for so many years they really don't count anymore. The whole time Maw was sick, we kept cattle on the place, and I had power of attorney. That means having control of the property, even though it was in the estate at that time."

"Lea, Sonja, and I intend to go to Austin with you, J.C., to get the award. We'll party all the way down there and back in the travel trailer."

The old man rose to his feet, knocked two more flies dead, and moved toward the door. "Seein' that mantis eat reminds me that it's been awhile since I had anythin'. These dern teeth make eatin' rough as a cob. A man has got to eat and exercise to stay healthy. That's the only reason I made it this far, though I guess there is an element of luck in it, after all. You know, some days I feel like one of those ol' buffalo, passed by time, but I'll be darned if I'll give up. I don't want my hide nailed up on some Easterner's wall. Let 'em put paper on it. Trees grow back; tough ol' men and buffalo are scarce these days." He rose from the chair, opened the screen door, held it open for me, and we eased into the dim light of the interior room heading for the kitchen and a drink of ice water. I followed him, trying not to smile at the apparently easy way of life existing in such a setting as I found myself in.

Some time later, J.C. said, "When I was at home and a big kid, my little brother, Jimmy, was big enough to be a problem for us. He was a real whine bag. Whatever he did, though, because he was the little one, he could get away with. Folks always assumed it was the fault of us big kids when Jimmy got in trouble. Well, we didn't like that much, but there wasn't a lot we could do about it. I remember one time, we were all dressed up to go somewhere and Jimmy was bein' his usual obnoxious self. He'd run by and throw a little sand in my face, and I didn't like it much but did put up with it for a little while. Finally, though, I saw out of the corner of my eye that he picked up another handful of sand and was about to make another run at me. Well, when he came by, I just put my foot out to trip him and gave him a little shove. Well, he fell down and this time he hit wrong and broke his arm. He cried like it had broken his neck.

Dad had already cautioned us about roughhousin', and he just assumed this was my fault, that I was pickin' on little Jimmy. Well, Dad went down to the peach orchard and got him a handful of switches about three feet long, and he came back up there and began to work me over with those things. He worked each one over until there wasn't anythin' left but a stub, and then he would start over on a fresh one. Well, he just about striped me all I could stand. When he ran out of switches, I went in the house to clean up, 'cause I was bloody in a few places by then. Mother said, 'I was about to stop him,' and I thought, 'Goodnight , if you were going to stop him, you should have stopped long before he ran out of switches.' I worried over that for a long time and would have left home if I had had any other place to go. I really felt that was about as unfair as I had been treated."

J.C. smiled and said, "After I was married and gone from home, I would go back and visit pretty often. One of my younger brothers, Jack, was an awfull' strong young man by that time. Jack was so strong that one time later he picked up one of those six inch drill bits and walked off with it just to show the men he could do it. He liked to wrestle. He was good at it. So he was followin' me around the kitchen talkin' about how he could throw our younger brother, Jimmy, who was married at that time and livin' at home there with the folks. He finally looked at me and said, 'J.C., I think I can throw you, too.'" J.C. said, "I knew better than to let him get the upper hand, so I just slipped around him and updid him right quick, and got him pinned to the floor. Well, he was so strong that he was just about to throw me off, but I finally got my feet caught under that old pie safe that Aunt Sis used to have. Then I had the leverage on him, and he couldn't throw me off. Our mother didn't like us wrestlin' there in the kitchen, and she kept tellin' us to quit. But my brother wouldn't give up. Finally, mother got all she wanted of it, though, and she took a piece of stove wood and broke it up, and that put an end to the wrestlin' in that house for a while."

J.C. leaned back and half closed his eyes. Then he said, "I can remember when I was young, and 'specially when I was livin' at home, things sure weren't very convenient like they are now. We would come in from work and try to clean up—it was a mess to have to draw the water, put it in a pot, and build up a wood fire to get the water hot; put that water in a tub in the kitchen floor; your feet would hang out. If you were greasy, you'd have to try to get all that grease off. I tell you, that was the biggest mess! It doesn't compare none a'tall with the way things are now."

FOUR

A Gunslinger Confesses: And Finally Reveals the Fate of John G. Irwin After More Than 100 Years

Fort Chadbourne—the short-lived military post east of Fort Concho (in present-day San Angelo, Texas)—was in its heyday when John G. Irwin, First Sergeant of Company C, 2nd U.S. Dragoons, was transferred from the post to Camp Cooper, a military post north of the present town of Albany, Texas. Robert E. Lee had earlier commanded the Clear Fork post and later called it his "Texas home."

Along with Irwin went his wife and four-year old John Chadbourne, his first child (and reportedly the first white child born at Fort Chadbourne during those days of Comanche hostility). The record of Irwin's life is scanty, but the experiences of this frontiersman and the long-concealed circumstances of his death constitute one of the fascinating stories of the settling of West Texas.

When Irwin was transferred to Camp Cooper in September 1859, at age forty-seven, he began looking for a way to make money. Soon after his arrival he began to accumulate a herd of cattle. The

Comanche Indian reservation near the post had recently been abandoned, following the confrontation between the Comanches, under Chief Katumse, and enraged settlers led by John R. Baylor, a former Indian agent. As the land became available for settlement by whites, Irwin homesteaded 160 acres of old reservation land near the Clear Fork of the Brazos River and built his herd.

John G. Irwin, Jr.

In 1860 his prosperity was assured when he received a contract, signed by Col. Robert E. Lee, then Commander of the Department of Texas headquartered at San Antonio, to furnish fresh beef for the soldiers at Camp Cooper at the rate of 6 24/100 cents per pound. He was to be sure the meat was of good quality and was to deliver it in quarters.

Ex-Sgt. Irwin was not drawn into the Civil War when it broke out, but continued his ranching enterprise in West Texas. He also took steps to increase his holdings and livestock, despite the fact that citizens of the region had moved to the relatively secure refuge of Fort Davis, a family fort in Stephens County, because of a lack of military protection from the Indians at home.

After the Civil War, trail herds began serving the beef trade in distant markets. The renewed presence of soldiers, this time at Fort Griffin, established nearby in 1867, promised some security for the region. So that same year Irwin left his family to take a herd of cattle up the trail for sale, reportedly in Santa Fe, New Mexico. Among the herd was stock from other ranches in the Fort Griffin area. The drive was successful, a suitable sale was arranged, and Irwin received the money from the transaction. Then the men began the trek homeward, passing through the eastern part of New Mexico on their return trip.

This much was known for years by the family and friends. What happened next, however, was the subject of much speculation over a long period of time because the only other certainty was that John G. Irwin never reached Texas with the money.

When the trail hands returned home they reported that Irwin had decided to spend a few days with friends in New Mexico. That story caused no serious concern because Irwin was always an independent sort. When the next few days did not bring his return, however, suspicions of foul play began to form. Had the "friends" killed him? Had the hands killed him? Had he been the victim of some other devious plot? Or, of more interest to some, had he decided to begin a new life elsewhere? After all, he was an immigrant from Scotland and had started anew at least once before. So had he decided to begin again, perhaps back in Scotland, where the money would set him up in grand fashion? Many explanations were offered, but nothing was known for certain—not until years later.

The town near which Irwin's New Mexico friends lived was Fort Sumner, a spot that was later to see its share of outlaws. Even though Billy the Kid is the best known, others had their share of cause for suspicion. Along with them were a host of individuals involved in the Lincoln County War some years after John Irwin disappeared.

Among these outlaws was an old gunslinger whose name has passed into anonymity. Apparently with several dead men to his credit, this gunfighter was fated to live a long life and die of natural causes.

On his deathbed, this aging gunslinger began to talk of his exploits. More than one man has had second thoughts at this time about the kind of things he has done and has given some thought to reconciling himself with the Master.

The information relative to the missing Texas rancher was revealed to the family years later when another frontiersman was growing older and decided it was time to share knowledge he had held for years—knowledge known to few others. In 1981, the details of the death of John G. Irwin were finally revealed. John G. did stop in Fort Sumner to spend a few days with friends. Word of his recently acquired wealth became known, and the gunslinger decided he had a better claim to it than Irwin did.

This is the story the gunslinger told years later as he was dying. He said, "I only regret killin' two men. One was old Uncle Johnny Irwin."

"Why'd you kill him?" asked one of the bedside watchers.

J"For his money," was the reply.

"What did you do with the body?"

"I buried it," replied the killer, and gave directions to the grave. A search followed, and at the indicated spot was uncovered a human skeleton. In the grave were buttons and shreds of a linen coat of the kind known to have been worn by Irwin. The grave was covered over and, if marked, was later lost. The family has no knowledge of the site.

But why was the knowledge so late in getting to others, in particular J.C. Irwin, Jr., who still resides on land homesteaded by his grandfather? The killer obviously died years ago. The truth is that after the news became known, word came to Irwin's son, John Chadbourne Irwin, who confided it to Litt Perkins, a resident of the Fort Griffin area for many years and a ranch hand for the Irwin family. But this information was withheld from neighbors and even the children because of the trauma a murdered father may have caused them. As Litt grew older, and only six months before the knowledge died with him at age eighty-four, he told J.C. Irwin, Jr., the fate of his grandfather, and ended the family's speculation about the guilt of the trail crew, the New Mexico friends, and the "new life somewhere else."

The Old West continues to reveal its secrets, almost by coincidence, of a day when violent death was common in remote, unsettled areas of mountain and prairie. The fate of a former soldier who sold beef to Robert E. Lee, homesteaded ranchland among the Comanches, bossed a herd up the trail, and died in an ambush finally comes to light after more than a hundred years of obscurity.

The Storyteller

Much has been made in recent years of the value of examining our personal stories as a way of discovering our true selves, but the breed of storyteller that the author shares in this series of essays would have laughed at such a concept. Litt Perkins told stories because he liked to weave tales as he worked at his leather craft, and because he had many colorful tales that demanded telling. Good storytellers have at least three traits in common. They know just which details to include, they understand timing perhaps even better than a comedian, and they all possess a subtle sense of humor. Here, Lawrence provides, through careful observation and his knowledge of recording oral history, a profile of the master raconteur, Litt Perkins, who possessed in full all of the characteristics of the good storyteller.

For the benefit of those unfamiliar with ranch terms, Lawrence provided the following glossary, which will explain many of the terms used in the next two sections.

Glossary

Bedroll—the cowboy's bed, composed of a tarp used as an outer cover for sleeping and for enclosing blankets, clothing, and personal effects.

Bit—a metal device for controlling a horse by putting pressure on its mouth. The side bars are attached to a bar that goes through the horse's mouth. A "low" or "shallow" port has a gentle or small curve in the center; a "high port" has a sharp, high curve. There are numerous variations of the basic bit.
Blackleg—a deadly disease affecting cattle.
Bosal—a band made of plaited leather, horse hair, or fiber, often reinforced with wire, that fits over the horse's nose about eight inches from the animal's muzzle. A rope or reins are attached to it to control the horse if the bosal is used as a part of a hackamore. Often referred to as a nose band.
Breast collar or harness—a strap of leather, or, less often, of mohair, attached to the front cinch rings of the saddle and encircling the chest of the horse. The breast collar is most useful to keep the saddle from slipping to the rear when the roper is pulling an animal by a lariat attached to or dallied around the saddle horn.
Bridle—The device composed of a headstall, bits, and reins that gives the rider control of the horse's head.
Browband—that part of the headstall that fits around the top part of the horse's face.
Buckaroo—a cowboy from the Northwest United States.
Bunkhouse—a sparsely furnished building where bachelor cowboys live when not working off the wagon.
Calf cradle—a term sometimes used to identify a working table.
Camp—usually a barn, corrals, horse pasture, facility for storing feed, and a house where a cowboy and his family live. The man is usually responsible for the pastures that surround the residence.
Cantle—the rear part of the seat of the saddle. It may be short and the leather "rolled" back for a rolled cantle, or rise up several inches to form a straight cantle.
Cattle van—large trailer trucks designed to haul livestock.
Chaps—coverings for a herder's legs. Made of a soft but durable leather, the chaps resemble pants with the seat cut out. Also called leggings.

Chuck wagon—a wagon outfitted with a box, the back of which folds down to make a working surface for the range cook. It also has drawers and bins for storing foods and utensils. This rolling kitchen, first built by Charles Goodnight, is the range cowboy's home away from home.

Chute—1. An area two to three feet wide between two strong fences. This area may be several yards long. The chute is used to force cattle to form a single line in order to be worked or sorted. The various working tables can be attached at one end of the chute, and the cattle driven into the chute from the other end. 2. The narrow confine from which bucking stock is released for that eight-second ride in a rodeo arena.

Cinch—(n) the braided band of mohair or horsehair, or in buckaroo culture even of burlap, that passes beneath the horse's stomach to hold the saddle in place. See also girth. (v) to pull the latigo tighter to hold the saddle on the horse more securely. This is called "tightening the girth" or "cinching up."

Cookhouse—a building where a cook prepares meals for cowboys.

Corral—(n) one of the names for a set of pens, or just a pen for holding or working stock. (v) to drive cattle into a set of pens.

Cow—(v) the instinctive and trained response of horses to the movements of cattle while working in a pasture or pen.

Cow horse—a horse trained to work cattle. It will have cow sense.

Cow sense—innate tendencies, found especially in Quarter Horses, to do cattle work with little or no training. A good cowman has this sense as well.

Crease—the pattern impressed into the crown or top of a hat.

Crew—the assembly of men and women for a given period whose job it is to work livestock. It may include temporary hands (day workers) and others from nearby ranches who are neighboring.

Cutting alley—a long chute designed to facilitate the separating of animals.

Dally—from the Spanish *de la vuelta*, meaning to wrap the lariat around the saddle horn when roping stock. The alternative is to tie the rope to the horn. See Hard-and-fast.

Day work—doing ranch work by the day rather than being hired by the ranch on a full-time basis.
Double-rigged saddle—a "Texas style" saddle with two girths—one attached to the saddle below the fork or swell and the other below the cantle. This style is still preferred by Texas cowboys. Also called "Rimfire" saddle.
Flank girth or cinch—a heavy leather strap attached to the rear cinch rings on a double-rigged saddle. It passes beneath the horse's stomach and keeps the rear of the saddle from being pulled up by a taut lariat holding an animal located in front of the horse.
Flanking calves—the technique a cowboy uses to throw calves to the ground in order to work them. The man grasps the rope around the calf's neck with the left hand and the loose skin in front of the right hind leg with his right hand, and lifts the calf off the ground in order to throw the animal to the ground.
Foreman—the man in charge of the cowboys on a ranch. He gets his orders from the owner or manager.
Fork—that part of the saddle that forms the front. These can be slick (with no swell) or swelled (with a noticeable swell.)
Gelding—a male horse that has been castrated.
Girth—the braided band of mohair that holds the saddle in place. The front girth is so called to denote its location; the flank girth is attached to the rear cinch rings. The term is usually pronounced "girt" in some sections. See also cinch.
Gooseneck trailer—a trailer pulled by a truck and characterized by a hitch which attaches to the bed of the truck over the rear axle and arches over the tailgate. This arching tongue resembles the neck of a goose—hence the name of this style of trailer.
Green-broke—said of a horse willing to accept the saddle but otherwise untrained.
Green horse—See Green-broke.
Hackamore—headgear used for training young horses, made of a bosal and a leather strap for a headstall.
Hard-and-fast—the cowboy style of attaching the lariat to the saddle horn by tying the rope, half-hitching it, using a slip-knot made

especially for the purpose, or employing a *honda*. The alternative style is the dally method. See Dally.
Head and heel—the method of roping an animal first by the head by one roper and then by the hind leg or legs (called the heels) by a second roper. Larger animals may be roped by the head and heel method, and, thereby, thrown to the ground.
Headquarters—the residence of the boss or the foreman as well as the central offices, main horse herd, the bunkhouse, and other centrally significant operations. "Branch offices" for the ranch are usually called "camps."
Headstall—the part of the bridle that attaches to the bit and goes over the horse's head. It may have a browband, noseband, and throat latch.
High-port bit—a bit on which the cross bar has high curve or port.
Honda—a metal ring used to form a slip knot to fasten the lariat to the saddle horn; the small loop of rope, metal, or rawhide on the end of a lariat rope through which the rest of the rope is passed in order to make a loop for catching livestock.
Lariat (rope)—often called by one or the other term (sometimes both), the lariat is one of the basic tools of the cowboys' trade. The variety used by cowboys is usually thirty or so feet in length and made of 3/8 inch nylon.
Latigo—the leather (less often nylon) strap used to tighten the girth of the saddle to hold it securely to the horse's back.
Neighboring—a time-honored practice of the cowboys on one ranch helping a neighbor work cattle on the neighbor's ranch.
Padded seat—a saddle which has some padding added to the seat.
Palpate—a procedure for determining if a cow is bred.
Poverties—extremely poor cows.
Prowling—the practice of mounted cowboys riding slowly through a pasture looking for signs of danger, illness, strays, or other problems in the pasture.
Punchy—a slang term to describe a person or event epitomizing cowboy life. From Cowpuncher.
Quarter Horse—the preferred breed of horse for cattle work. These horses are characterized by stocky conformation and well-devel-

oped hindquarters and are known for quickness, agility, speed over short distances, and innate cow sense.
Quirt—a short whip, often of braided rawhide, attached to a handle, used by horsemen.
Railroad corral—the set of pens from which cattle were loaded into cars of the train.
Ranch rodeo—contested rodeo events between teams of ranch cowboys as opposed to the traditional rodeo where professional rodeo cowboys compete as individuals.
Rein—(v) to give directions to a horse through pressure applied by the reins. (n) the strips of leather, rope, rawhide, or horsehair attached to the bits to guide the horse.
Remuda—the herd of horses, usually geldings, kept on the ranch for the cowboys to ride.
Rigging—a general term to indicate the girth, latigo, and other parts of the saddle used to hold the saddle in place.
Rim-fire saddle—one with girths at the front and rear.
Rodeo—(n) a competition between professional rodeo cowboys in such events as calf roping, bareback and saddle bronc riding, bull riding, and the like. See ranch rodeo. (v) to compete in rodeos.
Rodeo cowboy—a man who makes his living competing in one or more of the events in the rodeo. He will likely belong to the Professional Rodeo Cowboy Association.
Rolled cantle—low cantle on the rear of the saddle.
Rope and drag—the method of roping calves by the neck or heels and dragging to a crew waiting to work the calf.
Rowel—the round spike-like piece of metal attached to the shank of the spur. It is the part that touches the horse when the cowboy spurs the animal.
Saddle house—a small building where saddles and related gear are kept. "Tack house" or "tack room" is an equivalent term.
Saddle tree—the wooden base to which the saddle leather is attached. The best are still made of wood (hence, tree) and covered with rawhide for strength.
Screwworm—the larvae of the screwworm fly, which can cause serious injury or death to livestock.

Screwworm fly—a bluegreen fly that breeds in the living tissue of mammals, having penetrated through open wounds.

Shallow port bit—the bit preferred by cowboys. The raised part of the bar that passes through the horse's mouth rises only an inch or less.

Shipping pasture—a pasture used only to hold the collected herd ready for shipping to market.

Shotgun chaps—leather leg coverings with long, cylindrically shaped leg pieces resembling the barrel of a shotgun; hence the name. Long zippers are used to open and close the pieces for each leg.

Snaffle bit—a type of bit characterized by a large ring on each side of the horse's mouth and a hinged bar across the animal's mouth. When the rider pulls on the reins, the snaffle applies pressure on the sides of the horse's mouth.

Snuffy—a term to describe an agitated bovine looking for some human being to charge and hurt. The term may derive from the expulsion of air from the animal's nose when about ready to charge. Also "on the prod" or "sully."

Spook—to startle livestock.

Spur—a steel device attached to the cowboy's boot heel by a leather strap. The spur consists of a band of steel fitted around the heel of the boot, a shank attached to the rear of the band, and a rotating rowel attached to the end of the shank.

Split reins—two usually leather reins, six feet or longer in length, typical of the cowboy. Each rein is tied to one side of the bits to control the horse.

Spur leathers or straps—usually two leather straps attached to the heel bands on each side and fastened by a buckle positioned on the outside of the wearer's foot.

Stove pipe boots—cowboy boots, the tops of which are straight without the traditional scallops in front and back.

Straight cantle—the raised rear part of the seat of the saddle. It rises some four to six inches or more rather than being laid over in the style called rolled cantle.

String (of horses)—the horses assigned to a cowboy to ride in regular rotation. The string may include from three to as many as twelve horses, depending upon the amount of riding done, the amount of feed given the horses, and the roughness of the terrain.
Swell—the term to describe the part of the saddle on the front, to which the saddle horn is attached.
Tack—horse-related gear to include saddles, parts of the bridle, blankets, pads, stirrups, girths, latigos, and the like.
Tack room—room in a barn where saddles, bridles, and other riding gear are kept. Also Saddle house.
Tapaderos—leather coverings over the front of a stirrup, sometimes in buckaroo culture, with flaps extending twenty-eight or more inches below the stirrup. Also called "taps" and "toe fenders."
Texas saddle—see Double-rigged saddle.
Throat latch—that part of the headstall that goes over the top of the horse's head behind the ears and fastens, usually with buckle, under the throat. Its purpose is to hold the bridle securely on the horse's head.
Tie-down—a leather strap attached to the bosal around the horse's nose, run through a ring on the front of the breast collar, and then attached to a ring on the front side of the front girth. This girth is attached by a short leather strap to the flank girth.
Vaquero—a Mexican cowboy.
Wagon boss—on large ranches the man in charge of the cattle working crew. He gets his orders from the foreman or manager, who does not accompany the crew when doing the actual work. The term derives from the practice of managing the men who work "on the wagon" on a large ranch.
Work cattle—(v) a general term to describe any of the several routine practices necessary to move through the annual cycle. This includes vaccinations, ear tagging, castration, branding, palpating, sorting, and the like.
"Work on the wagon"—an expression designating the routine of a group of men who live for varying periods around a chuck wagon.

They sleep, eat, and spend their free time far from the headquarters. The chuck wagon is their home away from home.

Working table—a device constructed of metal sheeting and pipe to trap, hold, and lay the animal on its side for ease in working it by the cowboys. See also Calf cradle.

Wrangle the horses—to round up and bring in the remuda to the corral or other location so that mounts can be selected for the work day. Sometimes called "jingle the horses."

Wrangler—the person whose job it is to bring in the remuda, separate the horses needed for the day's work, and feed the horses early enough so they have finished eating before the men arrive before break of day to saddle up.

Wreck—a term describing any of the numerous accidental falls, kicks, and other injuries common to working cowboys, spilling cattle, or generally descriptive of anything going wrong.

FIVE
THE TALES

My interest in formal narrative art from Homer to Chaucer to modern time has been with me a long time. I came later upon oral narrative or storytelling as it springs up in spontaneous presentation. Those are the types of stories which follow. The sessions in which the tales are related usually lack a cumulative climax and often take unpredicted directions as one anecdote leads to another on a related subject or theme. Many of the anecdotes were taken from tape recordings made at informal gatherings. In transcribing and preparing them for reading, I found some editing necessary. Oral presentation, for instance, relies more on intonation and stress than upon clear pronoun-antecedent agreement and concise syntax. This form is often characterized by redundancy, false starts, interjections, and digressions, with a return to the main chord or thread of the narrative from time to time. In retelling something heard earlier, the speaker often relies on the word "said" rather than quotation marks. When J.C. Irwin, Jr., for instance, relates his experiences, this is not always true. Mr. Irwin is more to the point and relates more of his own experiences. In the case of Litt Perkins, however, he related many experiences of others as well as his own. I also discovered the unique nature of Mr. Perkins' language flow. Often he seemed to "prime the pump" by continuing to speak, more to keep himself going. This would occasionally lead him on a tangent. At other times an idea stated by himself or others would start a new tale or elicit a detail that he felt needed to be entered. Any remark could bring a new direction into the conversation at any time, but this new direction did not preclude returning to the original narrative thread later. The same is true of the other speakers.

I have tried to relate as nearly as possible the styles of the various tellers, though certainly there is much similarity in the styles of most people as they relate stories. The conversation seems to lapse into a style or level of usage that is a common denominator for all speakers present. Individual eccentricity, in some cases, becomes less apparent than if the person were in a different setting. This practice stems from a desire, perhaps unconscious, to make the entire range of speakers feel a comfortable part of the group.

These tales represent a kind of oral tradition which is perhaps universal among people. The subjects tie the stories closely to individuals themselves as well as to the culture peculiar to a given region. There are no stories about knights in shining armor or damsels in distress in this section. These tales concern the events and the lives of the people who live in the region and whose interests have caused them to tell and retell these stories many times. This is the lifeblood of the tale's existence. Many times the stories deal with difficulties overcome, battles won, or reputations saved, though few are cataclysmic. Often the stories concern lapses of memory or concentration, or lack of skill. By telling these stories, the speakers reinforce their enthusiasm for life, and improve their self image in the struggle for survival in an otherwise harsh environment. It is a form of bragging about prowess that seems reduced from the "tall tale," with its outrageous events or exaggerated actions, such as the Pecos Bill type of tale. The events here are often understated or at least simply stated or told, without fanfare, for the entertainment of the audience and to reinforce their recall of events. I hope that these tales show you some Fort Griffin folk at their relaxed best.

The Dramatis Personae:

The people involved in telling these stories deserve to be introduced:

J.C. Irwin, Jr., grew up along the Clear Fork of the Brazos River and as a lad hunted over the land where he lived for many years. Indeed, he was born about a mile from his current ranch. He worked in the oil fields in the Abilene area much of his life. In 1962 he retired and moved onto his portion of the Irwin estate, where he lived, still pumping two oil wells on his own property, raising cattle, and since 1973, looking after himself. He often rode his three-wheeled Honda All-Terrain Cycle as he made his rounds. He is the father of five children—three girls and two boys. I married his middle daughter, Sonja, in 1958 and came to appreciate the uniqueness of this man. Quiet and straightforward, J.C. was often the calm in the center of a storm. Not prone to dote on the past, he could nonetheless tell stories of the "good old days." He died in 1993.

Morris Ledbetter, my collaborator in the history section of this work, is an inveterate collector of everything valuable as well as useless. A World War II veteran of the African Campaign, he uses his medic background to doctor his cattle and himself. A cowboy in his early days when he rodeoed some, he is a descendent of the famous Ledbetter family. He would likely have a degree in archeology had he known in time that schools gave a piece of paper for what he has been doing most of his life, digging for artifacts and verifying historical facts of his region gleaned from his extensive reading.

Litt Perkins, frontiersman, folk artist and singer, informant *extraordinaire,* figures prominantly in these tales. You will know him well by his works and his words before you finish reading.

Lea Clayton, my late-life daughter, is the apple of my eye. She has heard more folklore and history papers than many beginning scholars, and has accompanied me on more collecting interview trips than she cares to remember. I secretly hope she eventually becomes the scholar I have long wanted to be, if I do not burn her out.

And now for the tales...

SIX
How Litt Perkins Treats Hides and Makes Leather Goods

In an article published in 1958, E. J. Rissman made a commendable effort to record the rapidly disappearing techniques of the wheelwright. In 1969, before a meeting of the Texas Folklore Society, Mody Boatright made a similar effort to give posterity information on the tools and methods used by his brother Will, a do-it-yourself blacksmith, to make bridle bits and spurs. I would like to make a similar effort with the leather worker, whose skills have largely gone the way of numerous other disappearing folk crafts. I had the opportunity to visit a leather craftsman in his home workshop, where from time to time he plies his trade, and to discover how he learned his craft and what articles such a craftsman sometimes makes.

The man is Litt Perkins, former cowboy and farm hand. He was born in Palo Pinto County, Texas, about five miles southwest of Mineral Wells, in 1896. When he was eleven years of age, the family moved to nearby Graford, where he lived for some time. He has lived for many years in the area of old Fort Griffin between Albany and Throckmorton, just inside the northern edge of Shackelford County.

Litt Perkins

When I first approached Mr. Perkins to see what techniques he utilized in practicing his craft, I found an open, affable man. Although aging, he is erect in stature and serious in demeanor, with a twinkle in his eye suggesting the sense of humor which becomes obvious when he begins to talk. He answered my request by explaining that he would demonstrate his craft to anyone interested in it. As I watched him work, I could tell he obviously found the work a fulfilling and productive outlet for a creative spirit evident in his whole person. I have since heard him sing numerous songs, some legitimate folk pieces, which he learned from oral tradition and later wrote down by hand in a spiral notebook. In addition, he plays many of the tunes by ear on a harmonica. With unfeigned vigor, he relates local legends and tales involving persons whose names constitute a "who's who" of the settlers in this still sparsely-settled section of ranch and oil country. Embodied in Mr. Perkins is the spirit of this frontier region—a region rich in cattle, Comanche Indian, and cavalry lore from the days when Robert E. Lee was on assignment at Camp Cooper near Perkins's home. John Wesley Hardin lived for a while in the nearby town of Fort Griffin, one of the chief outfitting points of buffalo hunters for a brief time after 1874. Mr. Perkins unashamedly admires the old ways and desires that young people not let those ways die.

The principal concern in this regard is his craft. The revenue from the sale of his goods is modest, especially in these days of inflation, and is usually expended in buying more material for use in making additional goods. He expresses his personality in the items that he makes, and while they are all on the same design, each is unique in some way—colors chosen, pattern of colors, or length.

He is not a mere copyist, but a folk artist at work expressing, much like a musician, variations upon a theme as he creates what is, in the eyes of some, at least, a work of art keeping alive one of the traditions of western life.

His specialty is not in tooling leather; it is instead in treating hides and then cutting those hides into strings to fashion such items as quirts and nose pieces for hackamores. Although he buys some leather in small bundles from commercial suppliers such as the Tandy Company, Mr. Perkins prepares most of his own hides, especially the rawhide and the buckskin, which he prefers to use.

He explained the processing of the hides in the following way. He first soaks the hide in a solution of three or four cups of regular hydrated builders lime and enough water to cover the hide well until the hair begins to "slip" or turn loose. This will be about three days in warm weather, longer in cold. Then he removes the hide and scrapes off the hair with a tool fashioned from the cutting part of an old carpenter's wood plane. He has ground the cutting edge at a ninety degree angle to provide an edge unlikely to cut into the hide but sharp enough to catch the hair and pull it out, not cut it off. He has another scraper for use on the flesh side of the hide, which is the next concern in the process. Since the small patches of flesh left on the hide in the skinning process are soft from the soaking, they are easily removed with the tool. This scraper is made from the head of an old garden hoe with the neck straightened and fitted with a wooden handle. The edge of this tool is ground thin in the same fashion as a knife blade and kept very sharp.

When both sides of the hide are clean, he immerses the hide in a solution of baking soda (sometimes with some Epsom salts added) and water (about one pound of baking soda to the desired amount of water), which he feels counteracts the action of the lime. This soaking lasts about twenty-four hours. The hide is spread to dry and, when dry, is ready for use.

If "buckskin" is desired, the hide should be treated with the lime and soda solutions and the hair and flesh scraped off. But when the hide is taken out of the soda solution, it must be soaked for four or five days in a solution of two pounds of pulverized alum with enough water to cover the hide, which is then wrung out and pulled and worked with the hands until it is dry. It is best to do this in a strong breeze to aid in the drying process. Mr. Perkins says that this pulling and working by hand is difficult for him to do at his age because of the fatigue in his arms and shoulders brought on by exertion.

He related to me another process for treating a small hide, such as that of a squirrel. When the animal is killed, it should be skinned immediately. The animal's brains are removed and mashed into a paste, which is spread onto the flesh side of the hide, which is then exposed to the heat of a small fire. If one continues to rub in the brain paste and hold the hide before the fire to keep it warm, the hair will begin to loosen and can be plucked off, a process best accomplished outdoors, since a large quantity of hair floats into the air. When free of hair, the hide must then be pulled and stretched as it dries. This is all of the treatment that the hide requires. Mr. Perkins feels that the best use of this kind of leather is for shoe and boot laces. The same technique can be used on a larger hide, but the amount of rubbing, plucking, and pulling is a handicap to this method.

Before hydrated lime was available, one way to treat a hide was to put it in a bank of ashes, which most homesteads would have had available, and then pour water on the ashes. The hair on the hide would begin to slip in a few days and could be scraped off by the method explained above. Mr. Perkins said, "If you are allergic to loud smells, don't go into this. An old deer hide can stink, my . . . can it stink! It will durn nigh rot in those ashes. . . . The lime, however, has a tendency to sweeten the hides."

Some of his tools Mr. Perkins has fashioned from what is available. In addition to the scrapers mentioned earlier, he often trims the leather with a tool made from the blade of a straight razor. The handle has been made from a piece of deer antler soaked in water for several days, forced onto the tang of the razor, and then allowed to harden. By this process the material is firmly attached to the metal. He has strengthened the handle by wrapping a piece of braided cotton cord around the leading edge of the antler so that the cord also serves as a guard to keep the fingers from slipping forward onto the sharpened steel. Other punches and heavy needles he has fashioned from old screwdrivers and ice picks. Some of these have antler handles attached in the same fashion as the razor tool. He also uses a standard leather knife. All of his tools he keeps extremely sharp by using a medium grit stone lubricated with light oil and, for finishing the edge, a small razor hone of very fine grit. Occasionally he uses a strop.

Mr. Perkins learned his techniques from several persons, but the art of cutting strings—his most unique skill—he learned from Bob Donnell, who lived in Throckmorton some years before his death in the 1950s. Mr. Donnell had learned the technique from some Mexican hands on a horse ranch in Southwest Arizona "around the turn of the century," as Mr. Perkins puts it. The technique is simple and involves the use of a notched block of wood and a sharp pocket knife, two tools that would be available to most people even in primitive areas. The block of wood has a notch about one inch wide and half an inch deep cut into the right hand end of the block. The horizontal section of the notch is slightly slanted toward the portion of the notch facing the worker. The block itself can be made from any kind of wood. I have one made from a block of oak, the remnant of an old chair leg; and another from a block of pine wood. Mr. Perkins has one made from a mesquite limb. In the case of the round pieces of wood, it is desirable to square up the edge facing away from the person doing the cutting so that the protruding surface will not interfere with the positioning of the knife blade.

This technique is used mainly to cut strings of uniform width or thickness from irregularly cut leather. Making one long string out of a single hide by cutting in a gradually descending circle is not served by this technique, even though once the string is cut, it can be "trued up" with the block and knife technique.

To cut the string, one must secure the piece of leather to something able to withstand a fairly heavy pull. I have seen Mr. Perkins secure the leather to a vise mounted on a workbench, and another time I saw him tie on to the bumper of his pickup. Facing the secured end of the piece of leather, he aligns the left edge of the leather with the left hand side of the cut in the block of wood. He holds the block near the left end with his left hand. Holding tension on the leather with his right thumb, he cuts through the piece of leather from beneath at a point that will give him the desired width. Then holding the left end of the block with his left hand while at the same time keeping tension with his thumb and holding the knife blade firmly against the piece of wood, he draws the block of wood and knife toward him, thus making a uniformly proportioned leather thong as long as the piece of leather will allow.

If the string is to be used for a quirt, he adds two steps which allow him to cut or bevel the edges so that the piece will fit neatly into the plaits. He does this by holding the knife blade at an angle so that the sharp edge of the blade bites slightly into the wood at both the bottom and top. As he again draws the block of wood and the knife toward him, a thin string is cut from the larger piece, thus providing a cleanly cut bevel on the right edge. He repeats the step after changing the location and angle of the knife blade so that the left edge is beveled. If the piece of leather is too thick for use, as the case might be with a piece of cowhide, he holds the string and block in the same manner, cuts down into the string from above to the desired thickness while holding the knife parallel to the flat side of the string, and then pulls the block and knife toward him, thus "splitting" the hide and leaving it the desired thickness throughout its length. The quality and uniformity of the thongs are generally excellent. Using this technique allows one to cut a round string, that is, one with all four sides beveled much as a leather shoelace or a piece of leather string used for sewing would need to be.

One of the principal uses of these leather strings by the Mexican ranch hands in Arizona was the making of rawhide lariat ropes. Mr. Perkins recounts that it was customary for hands to spend some of their leisure time during the winter months carefully cutting and shaping the strings and rolling them into bundles, much like modern binder twine or balls of string. One reason for this bundling is that the process of plaiting necessitates crossing the strings over each other repeatedly. Having them in neat bundles makes it easier to keep the strings from becoming tangled. Only when all was in readiness would the men begin plaiting the ropes. The lariats were usually four plaits and were often thirty-five to forty feet long and approximately three-eights inch in width. When the ropes were made for someone else, the cost was usually $1.00 per foot. In 1900, that was a significant investment.

A rope that was important to the work and expensive besides was well cared for. It was never oiled by the horse wranglers. The only treatment was application of raw liver when a beef was killed. The application was made by rubbing onto the rope a piece of fresh liver about the size of a man's fist or smaller. Mr. Perkins recounts that it was common for the men to sleep with the ropes inside their blankets, or at least on top of their ground sheets, when they slept outdoors. If, during the day, a cloud came up and threatened rain, the men would raise their shirts, coil the rope around their bodies, and replace the clothing. In this way, the rope was kept protected from the elements. To keep the rope from being damaged when in use, the men never tied it to the saddle horn. Instead, they dallied it around the saddle horn so that slack could be given. If it were tied to the horn, the shock of the animal's hitting the end of the rope would usually break one strand of the rope.

Much care was given to the selection of the leather to go into ropes. The men preferred the hide of a solid red cow in poor condition. Evidently, a fat animal was thought to have a hide less tough than a poor one. They would not under any circumstances use the hide of a spotted animal, apparently believing that the blotched hide would have weak spots in it. This idea could grow out of the uneven coloration of the finished product. When cutting the string out of the hide, the men carefully cut out the neck and flank portions, since the thick neck and thin flank sections were deemed unsuitable.

Even though he learned the skills from men most interested in making ropes, Mr. Perkins' main work with the leather is in the making of quirts and hackamores, there being little demand for leather ropes these days when nylon, polypropylene, silk manila, sisal, and hemp are used. Mr. Perkins also does not have access to sufficient quantities of hides for making these ropes. Most of the hides available to him are deer skins given him by friends and neighbors who are interested in his craft. He occasionally buys a beef hide from a butcher shop or is given a hide from a stillborn calf. The quirt that I bought from this craftsman is made up of twelve strips in a neat round shape over a wooden dowel at the top joined to a piece of rope near the bottom to allow for flexibility of the lower portion. Overall it is thirty-five inches long. The main body measures seventeen inches. The remainder of the length is made up of a narrow retaining strap that goes over the wrist (seven inches in length, the entire piece being more than twice that long, to allow for the single knot securing the two ends). This string is inserted through a hole about one quarter of an inch or so from the top of this main body. The popper, about thirteen inches long, is attached to the bottom of the quirt in a unique way. A one inch split is cut in a piece of leather approximately twenty-seven inches long. The piece is wet, and the strings of the quirt are pulled through and plaited below to secure the popper.

There appears to be nothing significant about the measurements, but the quirt is a handy size for a man about six feet tall. Not all of the quirts that Mr. Perkins makes are exactly this length; I have seen several quirts smaller and shorter than this one. Some are plaited over a flexible wire core. My quirt ranges in thickness from slightly over three-fourths of an inch at the top to one-half inch at the bottom. It is crowned about three inches from the top by a Turk's-Head knot, an interwoven binding of two leather strings side by side and interwoven under each other. This slightly bulging knot affords a kind of grip that will aid in holding the small whip when it is being used. The quirt is made from tanned leather mixed with rawhide made from a deerskin, thus giving a contrasting white and brown effect. About six inches from the bottom of the main body, the brown is left out, and rawhide is used to make up the lower portion. Some of the quirts are similarly made with black rather than brown leather, and others are of only one kind of leather.

The nose piece for a hackamore is made in a four plait over a flexible aluminum wire core. This core is an example of adaptation of the technique as more satisfactory materials have become available. Formerly the core was made of rope, but this material has a tendency to lose its tension and droop when exposed to the elements over a long period of time. The section that touches the front of the horse's face is double the size of the rest of the elliptical shape. There are two Turk's-Head knots on each side; their function is to hold the piece that goes over the horse's head and behind the ears and keep the headpiece from slipping out of position on the nosepiece. The wire is joined at the rear of the piece and bound with a Turk's-Head knot. The bridle reins would be attached to the piece at this rear position.

Mr. Perkins also makes other articles. He fashions chair bottoms out of leather by lapping the edge of the piece of leather under the edge of the seat and lacing it in position with a leather string. He has also made protective cases for rifles. These he makes to fit the individual article. When making deerskin gloves, he uses a pattern from which he cuts the leather. He stitches the pieces together with a glover's needle, one with a sharp point but with flattened sides so that the point has a cutting edge on two sides. For sewing heavier leather, he uses a pegging awl to cut holes and then sews with a blunt harness needle. He customarily uses two needles when sewing, one on each end of a long string with a knot located in the middle. In this way, he can push the needles through both sides and speed up his progress. He has fashioned a thimble by sewing to fit his thumb two layers of buckskin from the neck portion of the hide, which, because it is thicker, gives needed protection but, because it is pliable, allows him to control the direction of the needle as it is forced through the material being sewn. For this last reason, it is far superior for this use to a metal thimble.

Mr. Perkins does custom hide preparation and sells some of his items to area residents. He also repairs whips and other such items.

In short, he is a folk craftsman of the finest order who is keeping alive skills that he has learned from others who possessed the skills. And in his richly hospitable way he was willing to show me on several occasions how he practiced his folk art.

SEVEN

Litt Perkins: Leather Worker, Storyteller, and Singer of Songs

I first met Litt Perkins on Easter Sunday, 1979, the day after the close of the annual meeting of the Texas Folklore Society in Waco. I was looking for a folk craftsman to interview with an eye toward next year's program for the Society. I had heard of Litt for some years, actually before I came to appreciate just what Griffin folks and life were really like. The first thing I had heard was that he made things out of leather—quirts, nose bands for hackamores, or bosals, whips, and gloves—and that he had a special technique for cutting leather strings to make them smooth and straight. Also, I heard he liked to talk. I found both of these true, and more. He was a marvelous storyteller, and he could sing folk songs and play the heck out of a harmonica.

That Sunday afternoon was cold and windy, even for early spring in West Texas, but J.C. Irwin, Jr., and I drove the seven miles of red gravel road from J.C.'s place to Litt's house, one he and his wife, Jewel, had moved in off the railroad property and fixed up in a grove of live oaks up on a high hill overlooking the Clear Fork of the

Brazos River bottom. It wasn't fancy. Covered with asbestos shingles, it looked like a number of other such houses from the 1930s and '40s that I had seen moved in and set up elsewhere. A couple of old tractors and some plow tools were scattered around, and an old Mercury Cougar, obviously past service, was rusting on the hillside. As we drove up to the back, Litt came out from behind the house. He had seen us coming up the hill and recognized J.C.'s pickup. I saw a small man, a little stooped by age and hard work but proud, with large, strong hands and twinkling eyes. His hair was gray, what of it showed beneath his hat—a felt one because of the chilly wind.

After the introductions, J.C. told him that I was interested in seeing how he cut leather strings. That's all it took to open up one of the warmest friendships I have ever known. Whenever I returned, as I did on several occasions, I was welcomed and encouraged to come again. I sensed a certain loneliness because of the isolation—the nearest neighbors were nearly two miles away and gone most of the time. Mrs. Perkins was not well at the time, so they stayed mostly at home. For a frontiersman who had "bached" for years on ranches around West Texas before he married and then raised a son, Litt liked company but didn't totally rely on it. He was a private kind of person, reluctant to mingle with a crowd; but one-on-one or with two or three, he was excellent company. I asked him if he would demonstrate his art at the International Cowboy Campfire Cookoff festival in Abilene that summer. He said, "No, I won't. But I'll show you anything about leather that you want to see." He did that.

That day in March, we walked out to the garage that doubled as a shop, and he got out his tools. "I learned this from Bob Donnell in the '50s. He'd learned it from some Mexican vaqueros workin' out on a horse ranch in Southwest Arizona around the turn of the century. These vaqueros would sit around a lot in the winter and to pass away the time they made rawhide lariat ropes. They got hides and cut them into strips and then 'trued' the strings using a knife and a notched block of wood, two tools they always had with them." He was obviously proud of his skill and eager to show me how to cut the thongs.

"Where do you get your leather?" I inquired.

"Oh, I buy some of it in those bundles from the Tandy Company and leather shops, and occasionally I buy a raw beef hide at the locker plant in Throckmorton. But a good bit of what I do is made out of deer hides that I get from people I know." We walked out into the yard where a discarded bath tub sat. In the bottom was about six inches of murky water covering three deer hides. He said, "I've had these hides dried and am ready to use them now. That's lime water, about a gallon of lime in that much water. The hair ought to be 'bout ready to slip in a few more days. I put 'em in yesterday." We wandered back toward the garage. "Now," he said, "winter deer hides are all right, but you don't want to use winter cow hides. Those old hides over there are winter hides," he said, pointing to two skins lying in the corner, obviously discarded. "Those old worms work their way up into the backs and leave holes in the hides if you skin 'em in the winter. A cow hide is just too thick, anyway. You see," picking one up, "you can't plait leather or do any good with it that thick. And those is bug holes. That was a beef hide that Cliff Garrett brought out here. He give me a couple of beef hides and wanted me to make him a whip. And I tried to make a whip, but I couldn't get the leather soft. I didn't have time, for one thing. They're just winter-time hides anyway, and you can't get much for 'em on the market because of the holes. I tell you, I've peeled a lot of ol' hides off old poverties when they died in the winter, and you could get hardly half for one of 'em as good as spring or summer hides, after them, them ol' bugs work 'em over.

"I'll tell you what them bugs make. They make them big ol' horse flies, them ol' big fellers as big as the end of your finger. 'Cause I've been skinnin' and I've cut them ol' cocoons under there that were shaped, and I've actually cut 'em out that had wings on 'em that was 'bout ready to hatch out, come out, and I know that's what them grubs are, those in the old cow's back, you know.

"There's an old man in Archer City that was raised in Mississippi, and somebody said that heel flies go from the cow's heel up inside and works up to their backs. This old man Ray said, 'Bull shit.' Said, 'In Mississippi, we don't have no heel flies.' Said, 'Them old black flies is bad down there.' Said, 'They're a lot worse than they are here.' Said, 'I've killed a many a one of them old black flies; they'd land on my pony's back and hips. I'd just holler "whoa" and go around there and smack 'em.' He said that's where they come from, hatch out of that old cow's back. Said, 'Mississippi has "grubs" down there. Mississippi cattle has got "grubs" in their backs. Mississippi is as bad, if not worse, than Texas. And,' and said, 'they have got no heel flies; there's no heel flies in Mississippi.' And so I told him, 'You're right, I've skinned a bunch of them old poverty hides, and I've seen 'em.'"

"I've heard that heel fly business all my life," I said.

"That's a fake. That feller is a little black fly, and I don't know where he hatches out, but he looks kinda like a big bee and he pesters the horse."

"Under the neck?"

"Yeah, and the reason it comes up there and hits him under there, this old horse will stop and pull his head up; and if it can get him standing still, then it'll put a bunch of them little ol' eggs on his leg on the hair."

"I've seen those," I said. "They are those little yellow…."

"Yeah, sticking to the end of the hair; well, that's what that heel fly, that's what he's a doin'. There's an old veterinarian in Wichita Falls; he said he'd give a thousand dollars to anybody who'd show him a heel fly. And we nearly done it. I was helpin' with some cattle we had in the lot in late February one time. The weather had been nice, and there was two men horseback, Pete and George Parrish, they were both horseback, and a man called Tom Allcorn, who was workin' for George Parrish. We's down between 'em puttin' the cows in another lot, and a little old black fly landed down on George Parrish's saddle horse, on its heel. And Allcorn was pretty close there, you know, when that fly lit. Old Tom said, 'Damn.' He just reached there and put his hand on his ol' horse's hips and said, 'Whoa, boy!' and reached down with his hat, a little ol' Stetson hat, he reached down and whopped that fly and picked 'im up and looked at him, said, 'Well, b-b-by G__, I-I-I got a th-th-thousand dollar fly here.' He was kind of a stutterin' kind of feller. He said, 'I-I-I'm goin' t-t-to sh-show that to ole d-doc. Wh-what in t-t-the world am I-I-I goin' t-t-to put 'im in?' He said, 'Say!' and he reached in and pulled out a Prince Albert can, had a little tobac' in it. He just dumped that in his Levi pocket, and put that little ole fly in that Prince Albert can. I don't remember how long it was, but I thought about it one day, and I said, 'Tom, did you ever get to show old doc that fly?' He said, 'N-N-No, a-a-a little later I w-w-was l-l-looking' it over, and said it s-s-swiveled up so, it was just a l-l-little ol' black speck, and I c-c-couldn't have convinced d-d-doc he was a fly, anyway.' Said, 'If I-I-I coulda showed 'im to d-d-doc that evenin', might h-h-have been a-a-all right, but' said, 'w-w-when I did g-g-get a chance, there w-w-wasn't nothin' there to show.'"

Litt chuckled and shook his head. "Those old flies have given us a lot of trouble, but I heard of one time they did an ole cowman a favor. You ever hear that ole story about a Kansas man comin' to Texas to buy some cattle? They'd had a pretty hard winter down here, and the ole cows was poor. The buyer came in the spring when the heel flies were bad. He looked at the cows in the pasture. The old buyer says, 'Seem like they're awful' poor.' The old man said, 'Yes, they liked to starve to death on me.' About that time the heel hit 'em, and, boy, they went down across that pasture, them tails up. This Kansas feller said, 'By George, they're sure thin, but they've got a lot of pep; I'll just buy 'em.'" We all laughed.

J.C. reached down to tie a loose shoestring. Litt said, "By Jucks, I can tell you how to make you some shoestrings out of a squirrel hide if you don't mind a hairy job. You just skin that squirrel and build you a little fire, take his brains out, rub the brains on the flesh side and hold that hide up to the fire, and keep rubbin' those brains in. Directly, that hair will start slippin'." He said, "Just slip or pull that hair off, but be sure you do it in the yard. Don't try that plan in the house. You'll get the house full of squirrel hair, and there's many a hair on a squirrel, and that hair is sure fine." He said, "Whenever you get that hair pulled off the hide, just keep a warmin' the hide and pullin' it and stretchin' it.

"And, you know, I've dressed out a good many squirrel skins, and the strings won't be very big, but brother, are they tough. You can lace your shoes up with 'em, by George. I lived with Uncle Jim and Aunt Kate, down there in that Possum Kingdom country, close to Graham. Me and Jim's boy, we'd hunt them squirrels; we'd eat 'em, by gosh, but we'd always save the head, wouldn't let Aunt Kate cook the head. We'd use the brains on the hides to make us some shoestrings."

"But you'd put the brains on the flesh side?" I said, "but it would cause the hair to slip off on the other side?"

"Yes, it did. An old man named Arch Hemphill, who taught me this, said the same thing would happen on a deer hide. I 'xpect it would, but good Lord, couldn't nobody rub it in, and pluckin' hair off deer hide would be somethin.'"

"Yeah, that would be a pretty tough job," J.C. noted.

Litt turned to a small hide with definite Hereford markings on it. "I'm doing this hide over here for Morris Ledbetter," he explained. "That calf was stillborn, and Morris wants me to tan it for him. That's goin' to cost him five dollars, too." Litt was tanning the hide with the hair on it—white and deep red were still brilliant. Litt was sanding the hard membrane from the underside of the hide with a large rounded stick covered with coarse sandpaper.

Litt's songs were yet another matter I discovered quite by accident. My brother-in-law, Gene Irwin, visited Litt in 1979 to see about buying the old sewing machine that belonged to Litt's mother-in-law, Mrs. Shelton. Gene bought it, and wisely so, for it was in mint condition—a Singer with a wooden cover and all of the tools that came with it intact. It was over a hundred years old. In the course of this conversation, Litt mentioned his songs, and produced a spiral notebook into which he had hand copied twenty-nine songs he had learned as a youth. I know he could still sing them because he sang some of them for me; and as well, he played some old tunes on his harmonica. Fortunately, I had that marvelous invention, a cassette tape recorder, with me and preserved some of it.

Like many folk singers, his voice was gravelly and unpolished, but he sang with a gusto and verve refreshing in this day of amplified and arranged discord. He began singing to me:

There's an old spinning wheel in the parlor
Spinning dreams of the long, long ago,
Spinning dreams of an old fashioned garden
With a maid and her old fashioned beau.

It seems like I see her in the twilight
As the organ softly plays 'Ole Black Joe.'
There's an old spinning wheel in the parlor
Spinning dreams of the long, long ago.

After Litt had sung and then played awhile, he stopped to rest and said, "I just give out of wind. I'm too dern fat, I guess."

The collection contains some songs Litt learned in 1912-15 and others, of course, later. The fact that he bothered to write them down marks him as one who realized what he possessed, and he did so in the generation that had little appreciation at the time for the songs. My personal interest is in the songs of the cowboy, so I was attracted to "When the Work's All Done This Fall," "California Joe," "Sanantonio," "No Use for a Woman," "Out West," and "Streets of Laredo." Since I was familiar with Lomax's songs, I discovered only incidental variations from Lomax's definitive texts. Here is Perkin's version of "Streets of Laredo," which Lomax calls "The Cowboy's Lament":

-1-

As I walked out in the streets of Laredo,
As I walked out in Laredo one day,
I spied a poor cowboy wrapped up in white linen,
Wrapped up in white linen as cold as the grave.

-2-

"I see by your outfit that you are a cowboy;"
These words he did say as I boldly passed by.
"Come sit down beside and hear my sad story,
I'm shot in the breast and I'm going to die."

-3-

"Once in saddle I used to go to go dashing,
Once in saddle I used to ride gay.
First to dram house, then to the card house;
Got shot in the breast and I'm dying today.

-4-

"Go write me a letter to my gray haired mother;
Go write me a letter to my sister so dear;
But never a word of this note shall you mention
When the cowboys gather round you my story to hear.

-5-

"Get six bold gamblers to handle my coffin;
Get sixteen bold cowboys to sing me a song.
Oh, play the fife slowly and beat the drum lowly,
And play the dead march as you bear me along.
Take me to the green valley and throw the sod o'er me,
For I'm a young cowboy and I know I've done wrong."

The stanza that shocked me is the fourth, which Lomax does not have but which fits the mode for songs of this type in which the dying frontiersman recalls home and family.

The collection also includes a number of Anglo-Irish songs—"Where the River Shannon Flows," "On Erin's Green Shore," and "Bonnie Black Bess," this latter one also found in Lomax. He also sang "On Erin's Green Shore" for me:

-1-

One evening so late as I rambled
By the bank of a clear running stream,
I sat down by a bank of primroses,
So quickly I fell into a dream.
I dreamed that I saw a fair maiden,
Her equal I'd ne'er saw before,
And she trimmed her hair with primrose
As she strolled along Erin's green shore.

-2-

She was dressed in the richest apparel,
An green was the mantle she wore,
She sighed for the wrongs of her country
As she strolled along Erin's green shore.
Her cheeks were like two blooming roses,
Her teeth of ivory so white,
Her eyes were like two sparkling diamonds,
Or the starts of a cold winter night.

-3-

So quickly so kindly I addressed her,
    "My jewel - pray tell me your name,
Knowing that in this country you're a stranger,
Or I would not have ask you the same."
"I've come to awaken my brethren
Who slumber on Erin's green shore."
In transport of joy I awakened
And found that alas this was a dream.
My beautiful damsel has fled me,
And I long to slumber again.

Some are typical American songs—"Too Late," "The Boys in Blue," "The Girl I Loved in Tennessee," "Darling Baby Ben," "Withered Pansies," "The Baggage Coach Ahead," and others. Perkins really liked "The Baggage Coach Ahead," which he sang mournfully with great feeling:

-1-

On a dark stormy night as the train rattled on
All the passengers had gone to bed,
Except a young man with a babe in his arms
Who sat with a bowed down head.

-2-

The innocent one began crying just then
As though its poor heart would break;
One angry man said, "Make that child stop its noise,
For it is keeping us all awake."

-3-

"Put it out," said another, "don't keep it here;
We've paid for our berths and want rest."
But never a word said the man with the babe
As he fondled it close to his breast.

-4-

"Where is its mother; go take it to her,"
A lady then softly said.
"I wish that I could," was the man's sad reply,
"But she is dead in the coach ahead."

Chorus

As the train rolled onward a husband sat in tears
Thinking of the happiness of just a few short years.
Baby's face brings pictures of cherished hopes that are dead;
Baby's cries can't awake her in the baggage coach ahead.

-5-

Every woman arose to assist with the child;
There were mothers and wives on the train.
And soon the little one was sleeping in peace
With no thought of sorrow or pain.

-6-

Every eye filled with tears when his story was told
Of a wife who was faithful and true;
He told how he'd saved all his earnings for years
Just to build up a home for two.

-7-

How when heaven had sent them this sweet little babe
Their young happy lives were blessed.
His heart seemed to break when he mentioned her
name
And in tears tried to tell them the rest.

-8-

Next morning at the station he bade them goodbye;
"God bless," he softly said,
And each had a story to tell in their homes
Of the baggage coach ahead.

Chorus

As the train rolled onward a husband sat in tears
Thinking of the happiness of just a few short years.
Baby's face brings pictures of cherished hopes that are
dead.
Baby's cries can't awake her in the baggage coach ahead.

He balanced that with a rendition of "The Preacher and the Bear":

-1-

Well a Negro preacher went out hunting,
'Twas on Sunday morn; 'twas against his religion
But he carried his gun along.
Well, he killed himself some very fine quail
And one little measly hare,
And on his road returning him that day
He met a great big grizzly bear.

-2-

Mister bear marched out in the middle of the road
Before this Negro you see;
This Negro got so excited that he climbed a persimmon
tree.

Chorus

Well he cast his eyes to the God in the skies
And these words said to him,
"Oh, Lord, didn't you deliver Daniel from the lion's den;
Also Jonah from the bosom of the whale; then
Three Hebrew children from the fiery furnace,
The good book do declare.
Now, Lord, if you can't help me
Oh, Lord, don't help this bear."

-3-

Well the preacher stayed up that tree, I think it was all
night.
And he says, "Now, Lord, if you don't help me
You gonna see one awful fight."
Well along 'bout day the limb gave way;
Poor Negro came tumbling down.
You ought to saw him get his razor out
Before he hit the ground.
Well, he began to slash at that bear,
First left and then to the right,
Mister bear marched up and took a hold of him
And he squeezed him a little too tight.

Chorus

Well he cast his eyes to the God in the skies
And these words said to him,
"Oh, Lord, didn't you deliver Daniel from the lion's den;
Also Jonah from the bosom of the whale; then
Three Hebrew children from the fiery furnace,
The good book do declare.
Now, Lord, if you can't help me
Oh, Lord, don't help this bear."

I could easily see that Litt whiled away long, lonesome hours entertaining himself with his songs.

We all have regrets, I guess, and one of my big ones is that I did not tape more of Litt's stories. He and Mark Twain would have gotten along just fine, though I feel that Litt stayed closer to fact than Twain did. The subjects of Litt's tales were so tall, the tales just tried to keep up.

One of his stories concerned Doc Hemphill, the younger brother of Arch Hemphill, who was going over from Peaster to Jacksboro, and to Fort Richardson. He said, "They was goin' up a little ol' place called Slip-down Mountain, where a little branch poured off into a deep gully. The father told the son, 'There is where Doc was in the Indian fight. They had a bunch of Indians hemmed up in that little pour-off hollow there and couldn't get them out. Every time they got up close, they got shot at by the Indians. The area was covered with tall dead grass but it was drizzling' rain! They couldn't get the grass afire. But there was an old dead blackjack oak nearby, and they set it on fire. Then they threw chunks of fire in the hidin' place. Some of the Indians tried to escape. One of them crawled up by Henry Gillam, who shot the Indian in the top of the head with his six shooter. Gillam was hid behind a tree nearby.' Arch said that the body was still lying there, pretty well dried out, a long time later. Arch got off and twisted the skull from the rest of the skeleton and took it to Jacksboro. It created quite a stir when it was carried into Jacksboro, but it has long since been lost, I guess. I thought of that thing a lot of times after I was grown and wondered whatever happened to it."

Another story involved John and Bill Hitson, well-known cattlemen in the Fort Griffin area. "They'd lost a small bunch of ponies to Indians, probably out of Oklahoma, and two years later, this little ole pony showed up one mornin' when the wrangler brought the saddle horses in. The old man did not know if the pony came all the way from the Nation by himself or if the Indians was a raidin' and the horse wandered off when he knowed it was near home. They said the ole pony was pretty well ridden out and stove up, but the Hitsons kept the ole feller as long as he needed a home. They knew the Indians would not likely take him again 'cause they'd know he couldn't run all night. Doc Hemphill told me that a white man could ride a pony 'til he was apparently dead on his feet, but an Indian could ride him fifty miles further. When an Indian gets off a horse, he don't go much further. And when an Indian abandons a horse, he's a give-out horse.

"Why, Frank Collinson, an ole Fort Griffin buffalo hunter, was tellin' about those shields those Indians carried. He said the lead slug of a .44-40 couldn't penetrate one. The old-timers would shoot low to hit the Indian in the lower body or legs in order to knock him off the horse. Doc Hemphill, an old Texas Ranger, told me that the Indian was sure hard to knock off a horse. Doc also told me one time that they were in camp one mornin' and had just finished breakfast. At a crossin' about two hundred yards from the camp, the men saw 'a little string of ponies' in single file a crossin' a little ole creek. Five or six of the ponies, there were, I guess, one after another. The old captain yanked out his field glasses, focused it on the ponies, and said, 'I see a moccasin stickin' up on each one of those ponies' backs.' The old bucks had got over on the side of those ponies and was clampin' him, by George, from the side. Course he was holdin' onto his mane with one hand . . . . His head wasn't stickin' above but he had to get that moccasin over that backbone. Old Doc said he doubted that an Indian could have ridden a fat pony that way. Most of the ponies they rode would be poor, rode down, you know. They never would get back to Oklahoma. They'd steal more horses to get back on. Those Indians didn't pick a fight, and the incident amounted to nothing, ole Doc said. He said he sure was glad. Those Indians would usually sneak down here and get a bunch of horses together. Most often the ponies they was runnin' out on would not be any good for riding back. They'd ride back on the ponies they caught down here, you know."

I asked Litt if he ever made leather straps for spurs. He responded with a twinkle in his eye that, yes, he had, and he'd go one better than that. He went to an old army wooden footlocker where he kept his good stuff safe from the mice and pulled out a pair of spurs he had made.

"I made these from the barrel of an old .22 rifle that was plum' worn out," he said. Seeing my disbelief, he continued, "You can see the riflings in the bore if you look through the back of the spur." I looked, and there they were. He went on to explain how to do it.

"You start with a section of steel rod (this ole barrel was just about right) about nine inches or so long, dependin' on how big the spurs need to be, and that depends on the foot a little bit, how big it is and all. You use a hacksaw to split the rod down about six inches. The you put two blades in the saw and cut out a notch about an inch long or so on the other end and lined up with the first split. This short part is where you mount the rowell. Then you heat the barrel and start bendin' the front parts out to fit the shape of a boot heel. You have to have an anvil to pound it on. It takes quite a lot of heatin' and careful hammerin' to get that done. After you get it shaped, you have to punch a hole in each side to mount a dog knot of some kind to hold the leather strap in place. Then you punch a hole in each side of the rear of the spur so that the rowel can be braded in. I didn't put any chain under the boot heel. My son Dale wore these for years, but when he went to work for the Texas Company, a drivin' a transport truck, he gave them back to me to keep for 'im."

"That boy of mine is something. I always remember one thing about him as a kid. The wife and I rented a place near Graford on the halves," he said, "back in the early forties. We had twenty acres of corn, and it was supposedly a good place to raise turkeys. We also had ten acres of cotton and two old horses to plow it with. Me and the wife was out there pickin' that dern little ole cotton out one day. We made maybe two bales off the ten acres. We had two little dogs, little wooly devils. Dale, the boy, was about nine or ten and was a playin' with the dogs. Jewel, my wife, she looked around and said, 'Litt, I wish you would get a cotton stalk and get after that young'un and put him to work. He ain't a doin' a darn thing back there but playin' with them dogs.' I looked around and, by George, there that kid was, a sittin' on his cotton sack, looking' at me and grinning'. I said, 'Jewel, they whipped my butt and made me pick this damn stuff when I was a growin' up, and I'll just be damned if I'm gonna be guilty of doin' my young'un that way. If that kid wants to help pick this out, that's all right; if he don't, that's all right too. He don't have to raise cotton; he can learn to do somethin' else.' And we just went on a-pickin'. Jewel said, 'Well, that's all right, but it's a devil of a way to look at it.' Directly, that kid was a pickin' right up with us and beat us to the end of the row. It done a sight more good than if I'd whipped him; that would've made him mad. But he's like me—a cotton patch is what that boy don't want. He'll sit in a truck cab a many hour, but he don't want no part of a cotton patch."

J.C. and I rose to leave. "Do you want a glass of tea?" Litt asked, "Or a cookie or a cracker?"

"No," I responded, "we need to get on back. My wife and I need to get on into Abilene before dark. But we'll come again if that's all right."

"Do that," he said. "I'll show you how to make one of these bosals," showing me a handsomely done object that I recognized as the nose piece for a hackamore. He knew me too well already. He knew I'd be back.

EIGHT

Litt Perkins Talks About Snakes, Skunks, Cats, and Sheepherders; Or How To Spend a Pleasant Afternoon Learning to Make a Bosal

One afternoon in mid-June, J.C. Irwin, Jr., and I took my daughter Lea—she was about five at the time—and drove the seven miles of red clay and gravel road to the Perkins's place situated on a hill overlooking the Clear Fork of the Brazos River about three miles upriver from Fort Griffin. Litt Perkins had promised to show me how to plait a bosal, and I knew he would tell us more than one yarn in the process. As I drove up the gravel road snaking its way up the steep incline toward the house, I had to honk two young black calves out of the road. They pretended to butt at the pickup but then bawled and turned tail to run, kicking up their heels as they went. Two does grazing at the edge of a live oak clump did not like the noise and raised their white flags as they trotted off, prancing in the warm southerly breeze.

"Get out and come in," Litt called as we pulled to a stop at the back door. "Come on in. I've been a-lookin' for you two for a couple a weeks now."

Since he had some up on the driver's side, he reached me first. "Litt, I got tied up and couldn't get back. Having to work sure gets in the way of my doing what I like to do. We've come to J.C.'s to go to the Fandangle tonight."

J.C. responded, "We left his wife and my other two daughters and their kids at the house to come over. They told us not to spend the whole day, but we wanted to see you plait that nose piece. We brought this little girl; she was afraid she'd miss somethin'."

"Well, I'm ready to do it. As a matter of fact, I've already got it started. Hello, there, young lady," he said to Lea as we walked to the garage, Lea tagging shyly behind me, eyeing the cows and chickens she saw roaming freely through the yard and on back of the barn and the corral.

Litt limped some, because of age and working hard around livestock, I figured. The hard licks and falls taken in that kind of work make men fortunate enough to grow old get around pretty slowly. Lea beckoned me down to ask a question. Litt asked, "What's the little girl want?"

"Oh, she just wanted to know if you had any horses around, Litt. She's awful big on horses right now."

"I don't keep horses around. I don't ride anymore; my grandsons would ride 'em to death if I had 'em. I'm just too damn old and stove up to ride anymore. Why, if I fell off ridin' one now, it would kill me. I rode a bunch of 'em in my day, though, by George. I know lots of the boys around here who still ride 'em, though. Most of 'em use bits in their bridles, but some like my nose bands better for their cow ponies. I worked around horses all my life and made a lot of gear for the cowboys and really like ponies. I hear a lot of people are eatin' the meat now. J.C., did you ever eat any horse meat?"

"No, not knowin' it," J.C. responded.

I laughed and sided with J.C. Lea's eyes were wide open by this time. We drew up seats around Litt's workbench. J.C. elected to stand. I sat on an old five-gallon can, and Lea wedged herself in between my legs, carefully watching an old hen pecking away at gravel near the door. Litt got out some coils of leather strings and a piece of heavy aluminum wire around which he had begun to neatly plait strings. The ends of the wire were tied together to form a long oval. He set about carefully plaiting the strings over the wire, being sure that the leather completely covered the metal. As his hands worked, he began to talk. "Now ole Joe Matthews—he's kin to Watt and them other Matthews—up in Colorado, no, that was Montana; yeah, he used to have a horse ranch in Montana and Boo Donnel, Bob's younger brother, worked up there for him. They were both cowhands for awhile. They went to work on that horse ranch. They liked workin' there pretty good because they only had to round those colts up once a year. They'd just turn a bunch of mares loose with a stud in a little valley and let him take care of 'em. And then once a year, they'd round 'em up and brand 'em. When they did ride, he said it was a lot harder ridin' than on a cow ranch, but they laid 'round the headquarters a heap. He said they didn't have any cattle on that ranch so they ate them young horses, the colts. It would be them that had a crooked knee or got an eye knocked out, anyhow, them that was blemished colts, they butchered, and ole Boo said, 'By George, I got to where I liked it.' Said 'It sure was sweet and tender.' I 'magine they cooked them crippled up horses, by George, with plenty of red pepper on 'em."

Litt Perkins Making a Bosal

"I imagine if you put enough red pepper on it, though, you wouldn't know the difference," I spoke up.

"Yeah, people are funny in different places. My daddy worked out in the Pecos Basin in the ol' days. He said there was an old Mexican seein' after sheep that belonged to the same outfit he was working for. Dad was pumpin' some, seeing after some little ole water wells for some cows. They had them little Fuller-Johnson engines on those wells. Now that's the ones they pumped water with when I was a kid. He said he went by one day to deliver some groceries from headquarters to that ole Mex. Said he took the little box by and when he got there, why it was about noon. He said the old Mex was shadin' a little for the noon hour and had his little black pot with him. He said, 'Well, you're just in time, just in time, Judge; let's eat these frijoles.' Papa said he looked in that pot, and them little ole red peppers was stuck down there plum thick. 'But,' he said, 'I was hungry as a bear,' said, 'Lord, Lord, I was hungry,' and said, 'I sailed into 'em, by George. I didn't have any of them peppers, but I did eat the beans. And,' he said, 'they's darn sure good.' And he said he went by one night, for some reason, he went by the old feller's camp, and he had a pot of beans on. Said there was that little pot of beans just bubblin' a little bit, and he asked him, 'Ain't you been to supper?' He said, 'Oh yeah, but,' he said, 'them's for tomorrow.'"

"I guess he'd have to cook 'em the biggest part of the night," I said.

" 'And then,' the sheepherder says, 'in the morning me and the dogs, we leave here just as soon as it gets good and light so's we can see.' Said 'The old sheep scatter out and do better when it's cool.' Daddy said, 'He cooked this pot of beans, you know, to have 'em. He put some coals around the pot. I guess the old cuss would wake up through the night to see about his beans. Anyhow, he'd have a pot of beans ready to go the next mornin'. He'd take 'em with him and eat 'em wherever he was at noon.' My daddy said the old feller trapped one of them old cougars out there, and made a rug out of his hide. Said, 'It was the nicest rug he ever saw.' Sit down, J.C., you'll get tired. I've got a stool here."

J.C. responded, "That's fine, you sit on the stool."

Litt said, "I need to stand up so I can work on this nose band." While Litt had been talking, the bosal was taking shape. The faster he talked, the faster he worked. With deft movements, he plaited the carefully prepared leather strings, about a quarter of an inch wide and beveled on both bottom edges to lay together like they belonged there. "This wire core won't lose its stiffness like rope does. I used to use a rope core, but out in the weather and when a horse sweats, that rope droops, and begins to look funny. This wire is a lot better. I get it out of pieces of this ole highline wire. It's sure good for nose bands."

Lawrence Clayton with one of Litt Perkins's Bosals

"I've seen one of those rugs made from a cougar skin," I said, "a nice one. A friend of ours out in the Devil's River country, out from Del Rio, killed it. It about put him out of the sheep business before he did, though. He had that rug on the living room floor of the ranch house. It sure did impress me as a kid."

J.C. responded, "Yeah, but you can't run cougars and sheep in the same pasture. I know several people who found out you can't run coyotes and sheep in the same pasture, either."

"That's sure right, J.C. Well, this here ole Mexican was a good hand to dress out buckskin. My daddy bought a little ole buck hide out there and brought it back with him when he grew up and come back in. He had TB when he went out there. He got where he could do pretty good, but he got over-heated pullin' a windmill and went to coughin' up blood again. He just give up and come on back home. But that buckskin was nice enough that Papa John Perkins, that's just younger than Daddy, his wife took a little piece of it and made her a powder rag and put it in her powder box. That piece of buckskin was just as soft as a chamois.

"He said he never could get a shot at one of them ole cougars. 'They'd come up there,' he said. 'I've heard the old devils growl at the skunks.' Said, 'the skunks would come up and pick up the scraps. They came to the tent,' and he said, 'I'd set up nights with my rifle barrel poked through the tent on moonlight nights to get me a cougar hide.' And he said, 'I'd just sit there 'til I'd just go to sleep, by gosh.' And he said, 'If I didn't have that gun barrel out, then I'd hear them growling out there in the dark. Just plop the tent back, though, and I'd just see just a streak a-goin' up through there. Boy, they're quick on the draw.' Said, 'Just lift up the tent flap just a little bit, and that cougar is gone.' He said, 'They've got a getaway, they can move, now, for a little ways. The boys would see a streak out through the bushes, and there'd be an ole skunk with his tail up, all flustered, you know.' He said those skunks kept his outfit smelling like a trapper's den most of the time."

That prompted me. "Now I've had some skunk experience," I said. "We had one come to the house one time just as a big snow was melting. He just crawled out in the sun, trying to warm up, it looked like. I couldn't shoot him because he was right in front of the garage and the shotgun pellets would hit the car. Well, after he'd had a nap, he headed for the tool shed and crawled up just in front of where I had my hoes and rakes and stuff like that standing up. My grubbing hoe was there, too. I slipped out the front door with a pump shotgun and lined up on him at pretty close range, about twenty yards, I guess. I knew I had to kill him dead before he sprayed, or I was in big trouble. I sighted down on him and shot three times as fast as I could pump the old shells out and the new ones in. He didn't spray, but those pellets spread and ruined the wooden handle in every tool I had. It just splintered several of them, really made a mess." Litt and J.C. laughed. Lea didn't quite understand, but she grinned anyway.

Litt started out again. "Dad said he killed more skunks than a little. And he said, 'That dry country, the drought and all, don't slow them skunks up to amount to anything.' Said, 'They can take that dry country. Yeah, them little ole speckled devils. By George,' he said, 'you could see the little devils in the daytime, catching 'hoppers.'"

"I killed a many a grasshopper in a cotton field as a kid," J.C. spoke up. "But they're good fish bait."

"I guess there's always plenty of grasshoppers. Everywhere I've ever been, there was plenty of 'em. I heard one time that grasshoppers are one of the two biggest problems in the world. The other one is lawyers, or so that woman told me. I've had hoppers eat corn stalks in my garden 'til they just fell over. They'll do it. You know, once I was working on a ranch a long way from town. Well, I was a sittin' one evenin' propped up against the house I was livin' in, bachin'. It didn't have no porch. But the way it was a sittin', why, out on the south side in the breeze, the sun would get down a little, there was a shade out there. And one Sunday evenin', I was propped up against the wall in the chair and kinda dozin', and so I roused up when I heard somethin' make a little racket and opened my eyes and looked. It was an ole skunk that had come out from under the house, and he jumped on a grasshopper; just slappin' with his front feet is what I heard, you know. I sat there, and he ate that one and went on, by George, directly there was another one come out. They was both catchin' them 'hoppers. This old house wasn't too tight, but it did have screens. I didn't have no mice in the house, you know. There was this ole brindle puss cat that lived there under the house, and she come around after I moved in and made herself known, yowled around a little bit. I was feedin' that ole sister, and I'd let her in the house when she wanted in. She'd prowl around through the rooms, you know, and I wasn't bothered with any mice, and I thought at first she was doin' it. The old man I was workin' for, I told him a couple of skunks were a-livin' under the house. Said, 'I didn't know what kind of arrangement they'd made with ole Puss, but,' I said, 'I find her at the back door a whole lot, there at the steps, and them skunks, by the way,' I said, 'I think they're under my bedroom. That's where they come out from at night.' 'Well,' he said, 'you won't have no mice.'"

"That's what I've heard—they'll sure catch mice," I responded.

"Then one day some dogs got in 'em, and those skunks left. Never did see 'em after that. But, of course, they left fumes. Dad gum, they left a record."

"They'll do that," J.C. spoke up.

"Man, I wish them dogs had let 'em alone. They was those striped-back skunks, not those little speckled cats, those little ole hydrophobic cats. Had they been, why I'd have just got my gun and shot them right then, but them plain ole skunks, those striped-back ones, they don't go mad like them little hydrophobies, you know. I wouldn't have killed them striped-back ones at all, and I was sorry the dogs run 'em off."

That triggered a memory I had tried to forget. "I've got a neighbor down the road who says he likes to keep a skunk under his house, especially in the winter. They catch mice, and he never has had any mice as long as he had a family of skunks under there. But we had one of those get carried away under our house, and boy, when we came in, we could tell something had irritated him BAD."

"That old house over there of John Dillers, rattlesnakes and skunks are still there. Don't know what's goin' on over there, but I know them skunks, ever' once in a while, sure would stink up the place. There was a feller told me there was a skunk under the house, and he wondered how to get it out. I said, 'By golly, just get ya a handful of mothballs and throw under there.' Said, 'he ain't going to stay around them mothballs; he'll leave there.'"

"Well," I said, "we tried that and never had any more trouble, but I don't know if that's what did it, or whether the skunk just left of his own accord."

The sun was beginning to slant toward the mid point in the afternoon sky, and Litt had worked his way all around the wire core. He began to tie the two ends together at the back of the circle with rawhide in a Turk's-Head knot. He used a sharpened steel rod with a deer antler handle on it to open the crack for the end of his string as he pushed it through. He said, "I made this tool out of an old screwdriver. I sharpened the blade end and then soaked a piece of deer horn in water 'til the center softened and then I forced the other end up in it. It's a good tight fit."

"I did a knife that way once," I said. "That makes a good handle. I've used it a few times to skin a snake."

"A friend of mine down in Coleman, he moved into an old house on a ranch he bought down there. Then he discovered there was rattlesnakes under it. He could hear 'em whizzin', and movin' around. One time he took a trailer of that fertilizer down there, some of that anhydrous ammonia. He had a place up there at Akin, and he used that fertilizer a whole lot on it. He took some of it down to fertilize a little ole patch there close to the house where he wanted to raise some horse feed. Said he stomped on the porch there and that old rattlesnake got stirred up and went to whizzin'. He went and cranked up that tractor and drug that trailer with the 'hydros ammonia down there in the yard and got the hose and went back and took a brace and bit and bored a hole in this porch and reached in there with a little stick, and oh boy, said, that ole rattler *sure* went to whizzin'. He knowed he was pretty close to him. He poked that fertilizer nozzle down in there, said that snake just shut 'er off kinda gradual. Said he got dimmer and dimmer and directly plum quiet. He said next day or two, flies was swarmin' around there, and he had to dig out the underpinning. [Litt got to laughing hard and had to quit his plaiting.] He said he got a big ole rusty feller out. Said, of course, he was swelled up so you couldn't tell nothin' about the feller. Said, I'm tellin' you right now, that anhydrous'll get 'em. I told him, I said, Boy, I know it.'" Litt began the first of the small Turk's-Head knots that he tied on the bosal to hold the head stall in place. While he was doing that, he started another story.

"A trapper down there in Palo Pinto County—I spent a lot of time there—was out one night back in '36, and his dog treed. He was a skunk huntin', you know, had one of those carbide lights on his cap. His dog treed and when he got there, the ole dog had a cougar up on a limb about eight or ten feet off the ground. So he just proceeded to shoot that ole cougar, by George, with a .22 automatic. There was a woman who lived there in Palo Pinto, a taxidermist. She mounted that ole cougar, and it sat in Ray Abernathy's drugstore for twenty years. When we were down there in '46 and '7, the old cat looked pretty well motheaten, you know. You could tell it was beginnin' to deteriorate. Some of 'em was askin' this man if he wasn't afraid to shoot that cougar with a .22. Said, 'Lord, no; that automatic .22 used long rifles.' Said, 'Good Lord, I can kill a bull with it, and ain't no cougar skull thicker than a bull.' Said, 'All I had to do with his ole eyes shinin' like a couple of headlights was shoot 'im between the eyes.'"

J.C. reacted to that. "I never faced a cougar, but I shot a bobcat real peculiar one night. That little ole part bulldog we had—Lucky, we called him—treed one night just as I was getting into bed. I knew that if I wanted to get any sleep, I'd just as well go on and shoot whatever he had up that tree. I figured it was probably a coon, so I got my little .22 rifle—it won't shoot anything but shorts—and my flashlight and went on out. There was Lucky, dancin' around and barkin' under a small post oak tree out by the road. I walked on out, shined the light up into the tree and saw two eyes a blazin' back. I held the light alongside the rifle and shot right between the two eyes and a little low. Something came tumblin' out of that tree, and ole Lucky grabbed it and run off. I walked on under the tree to see if I could tell what it was, but Lucky was out in the weeds, shakin' whatever had tumbled out.

"Then I felt somethin' warm drippin' on my head. The night bein' clear, I knew it wasn't rain and besides that, it was warm. When I rubbed my hand over my old bald spot, it came away bloody. I backed up and shined the light up there again, and there was eyes again. So I just popped it again with the .22 and out came about a half-grown bobcat. Lucky came at the shot and shook the ole cat some, but it didn't struggle much."

Lea's eyes were big. "But Grandpa, what fell out the first time?" she asked.

"Near as I could tell, it musta been a rabbit. I'd been seeing one playin' around the gate out there. Near as I could figure, the dog was watchin' the rabbit and saw the ole cat grab it. When the dog took in after the cat, it ran up the tree and the dog began to bark. I must have seen the same cat's eyes both times, but when I shot the first time, the cat dropped the rabbit. Lucky ran off with that. On the second shot, I got the cat."

"Well, I'll be damned, J.C.," said Litt. "I never heard such a tale."

"It sounds like I've been oil field pumpin' so long I've started lyin', I know, Litt, but it happened just that way." J.C. was pretty well wound up by this time and continued, "Now you were talkin' about rats under the house awhile ago; if you want to keep the rats out from under the house, keep some rattlesnakes under there."

Litt's eyes gleamed, "Now, J.C.," he said, "I'm tough, but not tough enough to live with any rattlesnakes under my house."

Lea was getting nervous just from the discussion, and she climbed onto my knee as J.C. continued his story.

"Right there on the east side of my back porch is a hole goin' under the house. I've plugged it up a bunch of times, but somethin' always digs it out. I keep a small steel trap set in there all the time and often catch a great big ol' wharf rat in it. Well, a den of rattlers moved in last winter, probably because of the rats, but maybe because my wood stove is over the floor right there by the porch. Whatever the reason, they were there. I first knew about 'em in the late summer. Late in August, the kids had all come and after they left, I climbed into my lounger on the front porch to take a little nap, rest up a little from the grandkids. I slept awhile, and when I woke up I looked down through the webbing and saw a little snake asleep under my chair. The little bastard was about twelve or fourteen inches long. I killed it with my fly swat and wondered if there were any more around. Well, I began to check under that piece of tin I put over that hole under the house. I'd get me a pitchfork and raise up that piece of tin to check my trap. One day I raised it up and there was a rattler warmin' under that piece of tin. He made a run for that hole, but I speared him with my pitchfork—it was too close to the house to shoot. Well, I dragged it out in the yard and killed it. In all, I got fourteen out from under the house, but the one I really remember was a great big rascal. One day when I raised the tin I saw two snakes there. I got one with the fork right quick, but saw the other one crawlin' into that hole. I speared him just before he got all the way in. I had not seen his head, but I kept workin' with him to get him out of that hole. In a minute he decided he couldn't get in so he just come out. And he did, and he just kept a comin'. When he got about four feet long outside that hole, I gave him the pitchfork and got a long handled shovel. When he was all out, I cut his head off. That thing was five feet or so long. Since I had him pinned at the tail, there was a whole lot more snake than I had pitchfork handle."

Litt laughed and slapped his leg, almost dropping the long needle-like tool he was using to finish up the Turk's-Head knots.

"I killed the last one," I said, "on Thanksgiving and skinned it out. Sure did make my brother-in-law nervous, the way that snake kept writhing after its head was off; it even coiled around my arm when I tried to pull the skin off. We went ahead and just pulled it off from the head down over the tail and then turned it right side out and tied up the tail with a string and filled the skin with dry sand and tied the other end off. After it dried good, I put it in some antifreeze to tan it, but it never did get very soft."

Litt answered, "I've heard of people using it, but I've never tried it. You know, I've heard of snakes attackin' people, but I never saw it."

"I did," J.C. spoke up. "I saw it too close, 'cause one attacked me. When I had the brush and prickly pear 'dozed off my Plum Branch place—that hundred and sixty acres that the Stocktons ended up with and I bought off of them—you know it, Litt?"

"Yeah," Litt responded. "I used to travel that old Albany-Throckmorton road when it ran through there. I know it well. Will Stockton lived in a dugout there on the south side of that hill, didn't he?"

"Yes," J.C. answered. "That's the place. Well, I was over there pilin' up pear with a pitchfork so the pads which were scattered wouldn't sprout and spread the stuff so fast. I heard this hissin' sound—figured it was a gas well blowin' out over at the Shelton place. But I looked up and caught a movement out of my good eye. It was a rattler raised up this high. [He held his hand about three feet off the ground.] It was comin' at me and hissin'. Boy, was he mad! I ran to the pickup and grabbed a few rocks on the way. I rocked him to death, but man, I was scared."

"Why was he doing that, J.C.?" I asked. Lea was holding both arms around my neck by this time.

"All I can figure," J.C. said, "was that he had gotten rolled up in some of that brush by the 'dozer and was plenty mad about it. He intended to make someone pay, and I was all he could find. I was by myself over there. I just loaded up and came home after that."

"Boy! I don't want any of that," I managed to say. I could tell by looking at Lea she didn't even want to hear about any more of it.

Litt started again. "Were those snakes you killed under your floor fat, J.C.?"

"I don't know. I just put 'em in the trash barrel and burned 'em."

"I remember one time I killed some big fat snakes in the fall of the year and skinned 'em. I saw all of that good fat and thought it a shame to waste it. I found an old iron skillet and rendered that fat out. It fried up just like hog lard, even smelled a little like it, but it stayed liquid, just as bright and clear as you ever saw. That fat is white when it comes out, you know. That grease is supposed to be good for arthritis. I got a quart and half out of those snakes. I wish I had some more of it now, but I'm too old to fool with it. My aunt, we called her Aunt Ella, had arthritis and wanted some so I saved her a quart of it. She was in the hospital when I got it ready. I waited for her to get home. By George, before I could get it to her, she died. That left me with a lot of snake oil I didn't need. I used some of it on my guns. I kept it for a year, and it got to stinkin' a little bit. I used it up as best I could.

"Frank Andrews killed a big ole snake over at his place a good long while ago when he was a kid. It was fat and they proceeded to cut him up. Frank said they fried over a pint of good clear grease out of him. Frank used it to oil his guns with, too. Frank said it was as pretty a grease as he ever saw, and it was greasy too—don't think it ain't. Just as slick and greasy as can be.

"I had a little old short-legged dog that was quite a snake dog. He would trail 'em. He'd find one and bay it and bark 'til I came to kill it. He wouldn't try to kill one. Whenever I shot it, he was through. Some dogs want to shake the snake when it's dead, but not this one. All he wanted was for me to rub it out. When I was through, he was through. He'd never put his mouth on one.

"Once on some snakes I killed, I rendered that lard out on a chip fire by the woodpile over at John Dillers in an old camp fry pan with a long handle. That ole dog sat there, and he could smell that stuff. I'd put the fat in and render it out and feed him what was left. Boy, he liked them cracklin's. I thought I'd just try that ole dog. I cut the snake up in short chunks and fried it good and brown, let it cool, and tried that on him. He acted like, 'Man, oh man, yes, bring on some more!' People eat it, especially at Sweetwater, I've heard."

"I've never eaten any, but I've talked to a lot of people who have," I said. I could tell by looking at J.C. he wasn't interested in trying any, and Lea didn't want to talk about it at all.

Litt continued, "Bill Perkins had a grandson. That little devil would kill a snake, skin it, and cook it and eat it. He was a snake-eatin' little rascal. He did like rattlesnake."

By this time, Litt had plaited another layer of string over the front third of the bosal, and it was done—a work of art I keep on the wall along with other memories of the life I love. "How much for the bosal?" I asked Litt.

"I get $6.50 for 'em," he replied, almost apologetically. I paid him before he changed his mind. I had more than a hundred dollars' worth of stories and a $25 or $30 bosal to boot, and all for $6.50. I was lucky and knew it.

"You could probably get more for these in Abilene," I said.

"I don't have nothin' for Abilene," he replied. "I haven't lost anything there at all."

J.C., Lea, and I rose to go. "I could fix some tea," Litt said, "and put a little ice in it. I've got ice. I've got only a little bread, but I've got a bunch of crackers—I'm long on crackers—if you'll stay."

"No, Litt," I responded. "This little girl is about ready to see her mother. We'd better be going so we can get to the Fandangle."

"Well, I wish you'd stay," he replied.

"We'll see you again," I said.

He beamed. "Do that. I know the story of Johnny Ledbetter, boy, do I know that one." He knew that I was hooked, deep, and that I would be back. And he was right.

Litt was full of stories, and I intended, of course, to get more. It's odd how we too often assume that a good situation will last forever. We realize only when it's too late that it won't. I visited with Litt in the late summer and then went back to get school started. That routine kept me busy, but I intended to see Litt that fall. I went to J.C.'s in November of 1980 for the traditional family gathering at the opening of deer season. We hunted on Saturday, and I killed a small buck in the afternoon. The weather on Sunday morning was cold and rainy, and it was after lunch before we got the deer dressed and ready for the freezer. I'd planned to go see Litt to tell him that my article on his leather work had been accepted for publication by *Western Folklore*, but we needed to get on home. I thought I'd go on Thanksgiving; at least I promised myself that I would. But that was too late. I was at school on Tuesday before the holiday when my wife called. A regular reader of the obituaries in the local paper, she had seen notice that Litt's funeral was in Albany that afternoon. Needless to say, I went. I had lost a friend.

The cause of Litt's death was never really determined. When old people die, most people simply accept that. I learned that the son and his family had visited Litt that weekend, a custom since Litt's wife had died. They left him some supper on the stove when they left in the late afternoon. When somebody stopped to check on Litt Monday afternoon, the supper was mostly untouched, and Litt was dead on the floor, flashlight in hand. Apparently, he had eaten a little supper before he went to bed and had gotten up during the night, probably to go to the bathroom, and died. He had been sad since his wife died. I remember his saying, "All those years I bached, and now I'm alone again. Damn it, I don't like it." Now he's not alone any more, and he left a rich legacy that makes him one of the richest memories I have of a Fort Griffinite.

Cowboys and Cowboy Life

Lawrence Clayton often discussed in his scholarly papers the reality of being a contemporary cowboy versus the beloved romantic myth so many like to believe. For this cowboy-professor, the romantic myth ignored the true and special nature of cowboy life. He was honest when he pointed out that "trotting on horseback can be painful to the inexperienced or clumsy, and working around the branding fire is difficult and dangerous work requiring skill, patience and often daring." In addition, he adds, "Few sing well enough to garner accolades for their voices, even if they had time and fortitude to sit around a campfire harassed by buzzing insects and campfire smoke and enduring the extremes of the weather." He would add later in an essay on the life of the modern cowboy that he believed, nevertheless, that cowboys "are a special type, a breed apart from the rest of us, and they are fiercely proud of the life they lead." Collected here are the author's stories of cowboys he admired and worked with as well as informed discussions of cowboy techniques and parlance. Lawrence wrote most of these accounts in the 1980s, so many of the people mentioned are no longer living, or, at least, are no longer located where Lawrence leaves them. Nevertheless, within these pages, the true life of the cowboy emerges with skill and grace.

NINE
George Peacock, A Cowboy in the Folk Tradition

Despite the ludicrous assertion by Jane Kramer and others[1] that cowboys no longer exist, men and women still carry on this way of life as they ride the ranges of the West. Their lives have changed from the days of the open range, but what way of life has not as conditions affecting the culture have changed? Cowboys are no longer drovers moving trail herds nor do they focus their daily existence on a chuck wagon. Nonetheless, these men and women continue in the work and spirit of their forebears and cope with the changes that have come to the way of life they love.

Despite the changes, cowboy life is one of the few lines of work still learned by informal apprenticeship in the folk tradition. That is, the only way to learn to "cowboy" is to work under the direction of one or more skilled in the trade. It is, in that sense, still a folk occupation. There are schools for rodeo performers and schools for range management, all skills needed by a cowboy, but the diverse, demanding, and dangerous work of the cowboy far exceeds what one can learn at all of these schools. And not everyone has what it takes to be a cowboy. A cowboy has to have cow sense, and horse sense, and a hard-headed stubbornness that keeps him from giving up in the face of overwhelming challenge. He has to know not only how to ride a horse but also how to break and train his horse, how to use the lariat, and how to keep out of the way of the danger that surrounds him and still do the job. He has to know what a cow is thinking about doing, and react before she can break from the herd or charge with the intent of injuring the man and beast she blames for bedeviling her. Working with large, strong animals is always a challenge. Not knowing what to do and when to do it can be dangerous or fatal.

One of the most obvious folk traditions of this way of life is found in the dialect in which the men communicate. Many of the words and phrases in the following discussion will be strange to readers unfamiliar with this kind of work. Terms such as lariat, saddle, spurs, boots, and hats are familiar enough. But what of remuda, foreman, wrangler, green horse, shallow port bit, snaffle bit, split leather reins, headstall, tie down, double rigged saddle, tapaderos, honda, working table, palpate, dally, tie hard and fast, rope and drag, and others? The Glossary, beginning on page 52, explains the specialized uses of such words used in this discussion.

The demands of this work vary somewhat from region to region depending upon the terrain, the vegetation, and the climate. The work, in another way, is the same regardless of the region. Regional variation is apparent even to the casual observer traveling from the Nevada, the home of the buckaroo; to Mexico, the home of the vaquero; to Texas, the home of the cowboy. The type and style of hat, the length of the lariat, the presence or absence of tapaderos on the stirrups, the kind of swell in the saddle, and other parts of the mounted herder's appearance and work habits vary but still have the same purpose—to manage a herd of cattle through the annual cycle of work necessary to send the animals to market at the right time in the best possible condition.

A cowboy that fits well into this mold is George Peacock,[2] currently manager of the ninety-nine section Nail Ranch north of Albany in Shackelford County, Texas. George went to the Nail nearly thirty years ago as horse wrangler and cowboy and has been there ever since. His duties include working alongside the three cowboys on the ranch and making the on-site decisions for doing the work day by day. This latter part of George's work is coordinated with Dub Sims, a member of the Trust Department for a bank in Fort Worth, which manages the Nail Estate. This business arrangement is one way to operate a ranch instead of splitting it up among the heirs. In fact, Mr. Sims oversees a number of ranches in this fashion.

George Peacock

George Peacock is qualified to run the ranch by birth and experience. He was born on a ranch north of Breckenridge, Texas, and lived there for several years. His father was a second-generation cowboy. The family lived a long way from town, to which they went infrequently. The children played with the tools of the cowboy's trade—ropes, saddles, horses, and cattle. Not until George was nearly ten years old did the family move to a ranch near a road on which automobiles traveled.

George's formative years were spent with brothers Troy, Dean, and Benny under the careful direction of their father, who worked on a number of ranches in Texas. All of the brothers became cowboys and eventually ranch foremen. This childhood was the beginning of George's apprenticeship. He learned to work cattle and to handle horses by doing the work. He also learned roping from horseback and training horses for ranch work, as well as how to ride calves kept in the pens to call their milk cow mothers in each evening.

George graduated from Breckenridge High School in 1952 and took a job with a crew of bachelor cowboys on a Ross Sloan ranch near Crystal Falls, Texas. The men lived in a bunkhouse on the ranch, as had become the custom in this life. The cracks in the walls of the bunkhouse required that in cold weather the men cover their bunks with a piece of canvas tarp to keep the rain and snow off their beds. They cooked for themselves over a wood-burning stove and warmed the cookhouse with a fireplace in winter. There was no heat in the bunkhouse, but having that shelter was better than sleeping in a bedroll out in the open, as men had done not many years previous to this time, and still did when working on large ranches where a chuck wagon was home away from home. The men cooked breakfast. For lunch they took small cans of fruit, Vienna sausages, and the like with them and ate whenever the sun reached high noon. Each man carried the cans in an old boot top cut off and laced up across the bottom. These carriers the men secured to their saddles. The first man back to the headquarters in the evening started supper. This was the routine seven days a week year 'round. This regular checking of cattle was essential in the days when screwworms were a menace.

Later, when George married Sue Fonville, the daughter of a cowboy, he rented a house in town. Mr. Sloan allowed him the use of a horse to ride back and forth. Once, the experienced horse he rode each day to and from work injured a foot. Mr. Sloan helped George catch a young green-broke horse and sent George on his way home, after dark, of course. This was one way of putting miles on a young horse. A rancher is always interested in practicing good economic policies.

Several operations on this ranch show how methods in a folk occupation change to meet new demands. Trail driving cattle to market took on a new twist. In those days, some ranches had started hauling their cattle in small trucks to the railroad corral, but not on the Sloan Ranch. The crew moved the cows along with the calves to be sold by driving the herd down the county road to the shipping point. Since some of the fences along the road were poor, one man rode on the other side of the fence to turn back any animals that tried to escape into the pastures alongside the road. One of the obstacles on this drive was the swinging bridge across the Clear Fork of the Brazos River, a barrier that cattle naturally feared to cross. When the herd got to the bridge, two men at the head of the herd roped a calf each and tied their ropes hard and fast to the saddle horn. Then the men spurred their often frightened horses across the bridge and dragged the calves behind them. The concerned mothers anxiously followed, and the rest of the herd trailed along as the other cowboys pushed the herd from the rear. Now, of course, cattle vans come to each ranch to load the cattle. Trail driving to market or even to the railroad corrals is a thing of the past.

George Peacock on Horseback

It is a widely accepted fact among cowboys that they do not compete well with rodeo cowboys in the events of riding rough stock or even calf roping. Some of them may have tried rodeoing when young. A cowboy has so many skills to master that he does not have the luxury of concentrating on just one or two skills needed by the rodeo cowboy.

One such skill is the use of the horse in working cattle. While many people can ride a horse with some proficiency, a cowboy must ride well enough to stay in the saddle while the horse is on a dead run and twirl and throw a lariat at a bovine or horse running at full speed as well and hope to catch the quarry. The work can be demanding, as the following examples illustrate.

I once observed George and two of his hands attempt to pen a cow that had decided not to go into the pen. She had become agitated in the drive and lost any rational thought, something cows are short on anyway. Once a cow decides not to cooperate, it is impossible to head her or drive her in any direction. The phalanx of three men rode their cow horses in a tight single file to force the cow to turn in the desired direction. If the cow went too far in the other direction, then the men had to shift their phalanx to the other side without allowing the cow to escape. No verbal communication went on among the men; each knew what to do and did it. It was one of the most dramatic examples of horseback work I had ever seen, and nobody learns that from a manual.

Another time, when a cow refused to go into the pen, one of the cowboys roped her around the neck. To keep from choking her, two men rode up behind her. The two riders then dallied their lariats to saddle horns and formed a kind of net with the rope passing around the back of the cow between her second leg joint and her tail. In this way, the three riders, with the cooperation of their well-trained horses, maneuvered the cow into the pen without hurting her. When a cow "sulls," as this one did, this maneuver is about the only way to get her into the pen except as noted with the phalanx maneuver described above. Allowing a cow to escape from the roundup one time convinces her that she might be able to do it next time, and she always tries. This is not the kind of roping and horseback skills one learns at a rodeo school. A cowboy learns this by doing it, not just by observing it.

A strong element of folk humor is found in the cowboy's workplace. Peacock himself says that a cowboy has to pull a trick or tell a joke or story to keep from being bored in what is often a lonely life. Curt Brummett, a cowboy and humorist, believes that boredom and revenge prompt this humor. Someone does something to someone else to break the boredom and that person responds in turn.[3] This returning of the prank can get serious and unless something happens to break the cycle, the pranks may end up being dangerous. Naturally there are personality conflicts and disagreements that prompt some of this.

One cycle of pranks involves Peacock. As the wrangler in his younger days, he got out of bed each morning long before the other men did because his job was to bring in the remuda of horses, feed them, and have them ready for saddling when the men finished eating breakfast at the cookhouse. With all of this extra time, Peacock started looking for a way to break his boredom. He did not have to look far. He chose one of the men who had an additional chore of milking a cow for the cook before breakfast. Peacock started toying with his mind. Knowing that one man in particular was not especially comfortable in the dark, Peacock stacked some feed buckets against the door of the feed room so that when the man opened the door to get feed for the cow, the buckets would fall out on him. It worked! The men soon figured out the prankster and determined to get revenge. The next day the man and some of his friends got to the pens early and waited for Peacock to arrive. They did not know that he was already there, further out in the brush than they were. Peacock had been telling the men that an old black tomcat was particularly vicious in his attacks on people early in the mornings and, as the men were waiting, Peacock sailed his black hat at one of them and screamed like an enraged cat. This worked as well. The cycle was beginning, and the men plotted revenge. They went after George where he worked.

Lawrence Clayton and George Peacock

One way that Peacock tried to make his work easier was by turning the horses into a patch of feed near the headquarters and closing the gate so the horses would be close to the pen the next morning. After Peacock went to bed early, these men went down and opened the gate so the horses would go to the back of the large horse pasture. This caused Peacock extra work. Then the men waited until he rode off to get the horses and wired the corral gate shut. They made sure the wire was wrapped tight and cut close so it would be difficult to open. When Peacock brought the horses in, they could not go into the pen so they scattered. He had to cut the wire, open the gate, and wrangle the horses again. The situation was getting serious. Peacock responded by getting some small nails and nailing the skirts of the men's saddles to the wooden saddle stands. He was careful to remove all the pliers and other tools that might be used to remove the nails. This was sufficient payback to stop the cycle, and the men declared a truce.

Sometimes the humor is impromptu. A cowboy who had been unpleasant to his coworkers one day got his payback later in the morning. The men had gone into a pasture to retrieve a cow that refused to be penned. The men roped her and tied her down. In order to load her, the men untied her legs and dragged her into the trailer. When they reached the pen, the driver of the truck backed the trailer to the gate; another man retrieved the rope around the angry cow's neck and dallied the rope around his saddle horn. The unpleasant man opened the gate and ran for the fence. The horseman doing the paying let the cow have just enough slack of the rope to "dust the mans pants" as the man did his best to get to the fence and safety, shouting obscenities and oaths at the laughing horseman. Nonetheless, the man on foot got the message. All of these tales live on in oral tradition among the cowboys, who tell them to new men as they come to work on the ranch or remind each other just for the sake of humor.

Occasionally a prank tests the mettle of the victim. Once Peacock and his friend Big Boy Mercer took a pair of mules to a remote ranch for the man who lived there to use pulling the feed wagon during the winter months. The ranch was quite remote and even to the present day does not have electricity run to the house on the property. The man who lived and worked there was named Tom Compton, now long deceased. Tom was, as the saying goes, "a few bricks short of a full load" but a good hand. As a joke George told Tom that someone had said one of the mules was broken to ride. George knew that Tom, an able rider with time on his hands, would have to try his skill at riding the animal. When George and Big Boy returned to the ranch a few days later, they noticed that Tom was limping a little and skinned up some. The men worked with the cattle during the morning and then broke for lunch. After lunch George suggested that the men go down to the corral and ride that mule. Tom drew himself to his full height and said, "George, those mules don't ride." George and Big Boy had to grin as they envisioned Tom trying one and then the other mule to see which one of them would accept the saddle. Of course, neither would because no cowboy in this country rides mules. Mule riding is more likely to be found in mountainous areas where the sure-footed creatures outperform horses.

Part of the oral tradition involves story telling, but some of the stories are not necessarily humorous. Sometimes the stories are instructive. Especially in my early days working alongside these men, I determined that some of the stories they were telling me had a purpose—how to do or not to do things, or what things could hurt me and/or endanger the stock. One was the story of the previous ranch foreman who was seriously injured when the stallion being used on the ranch locked his jaws into the shoulder of the man. His horse shook the man like a rag doll, tearing ligaments and severing muscles all the while. Once the man was freed, the owner shot the horse. Such an animal is just too dangerous to keep around. Another story involved a man who ran his horse over a slight rise into the trap near the pens and was seriously injured by the falling animal. At other times I was simply told how to grasp a calf's leg in the working table in order to avoid scraped knuckles, how to throw and keep down a calf to be dragged to the branding fire, and the like. Warnings on the use of the lariat were especially direct. George said, "A rope is like a gun; it is always loaded and can kill you."

Some of the knowledge of the folk is handed down in direct manner, especially those practices that may prove dangerous to man or beast. One of these is never use a tie-down on a horse's head when riding him in a pasture. This leather strap running from the horse's bridle to the front girth holds the animal's head down about level with his shoulders. The reason for this concern is simple—if a horse stumbles, he must raise his head in order to regain his balance. If the head is restricted, regaining balance is difficult for the animal to do and he is likely to fall. The men may use a tie-down in the roping pen but not in the pasture. Another involves the practice of resetting the saddle on the horse's back. Since these ranch saddles have front and back girths typical of Texas saddles, it is essential to undo, not just loosen, the girths. If the horse should spook with the girths loose, the saddle will likely slip under the horse, which will begin kicking at it to remove the "thing" under his stomach. Severe damage will result to the saddle, and the horse may well injure himself. It is also a good idea to lead the horse around a little after saddling him and before mounting. If something is not right, the horse will pitch in order to relieve himself of the saddle. The men are always careful to tighten the girths after a trailer ride and again before roping another animal. A horse inflates his lungs and swells up his abdomen to keep the man from tightening the girth too much, and the man must check the girth regularly to keep it tight enough to keep the saddle in place. Another danger is riding near two bulls that are fighting. When one of these bulls gets the best of the other, the loser will flee with little regard for what is in his way. These are just some of the ways a man can get hurt, and the oral tradition is a method of reminding those involved of these dangers.

Jobs on the ranch have long been traditional, especially those of the wrangler and the foreman. Peacock has been both. The wrangler also works as a cowboy, his wrangling chores just being extra responsibility. Fewer men make up the crews on ranches these days because mechanization has made the work possible with fewer hands and has also reduced costs. Although the pickup truck is essential to the work of the modern cowboy, the axis on which the cowboy's universe turns is still the horse. These are Quarter Horses with innate cow sense, an inborn instinct to work cattle. On most ranches, only geldings are used for cattle work. Essentially, the cowboy is a horseman who works with cattle. Since the early days, ranches have kept a string of mounts for each man to ride in rotation in the work. These horses were kept in the remuda and allowed to roam free in order to graze during the time they were not working. It has long been the job of the wrangler to bring in the horses for the men to choose mounts for the day. On trail drives, the wrangler brought the remuda in at first light. On modern ranches, the string of mounts is still a tradition, though the number in the string has dropped from as many as a dozen or so to three or four. With the use of trailers and less riding, the smaller number of horses is adequate. Horses are expensive to purchase and maintain. Now wranglers may pen the horses late in the afternoon after being told which ones the men want for the next day. In those cases, the horses are usually put into stalls to keep them from fighting and injuring each other in the pen overnight. Even in this circumstance, the wrangler still has to feed the horses and assure enough time for them to finish eating before the men show up to saddle up for the day. These men value their mounts, and I have heard cowboys who have left a ranch to go to another to inquire about the fate of their favorite mounts on the ranch on which they worked earlier.

The foreman is the director of the work in pastures and pen. The owner, or in some cases the manager, tells the foreman what to do and when to do it but not often *how* to do it. On large ranches like the Waggoner in North Texas, a wagon boss actually supervises the men in the work, while the foreman is more of a manager who remains mostly at the headquarters to handle the business of the ranch. On the smaller ranches, the foreman does all management chores. Peacock is the manager and foreman of the Nail Ranch and supervises the year-long cycle of work.

Discussion of the annual cycle of work reveals much of the demand on these men, and it is perhaps best to begin the discussion of this work on the Nail Ranch in January, when the cowboys begin to hold daily roundups to work the calves. Working the 2,500 head of cattle on the Nail requires several days since the herd is divided into small herds of about 150 head, the number the men can work conveniently in one day. The ranch is cross-fenced and the cattle kept in separate pastures. These days start early, and the Nail cowboys and those from neighboring ranches and any day workers slated for the day are at the headquarters well before daylight. The horses are saddled and loaded into trailers behind pickups for the trip to the pasture to be worked that day. On the Nail, that may be a drive of fifteen or more miles over rough gravel roads. The men unload in the half light, tighten girths on the saddles, and wait for George to direct each man on a path that will converge at the set of pens with the cattle in a herd by then. Getting the cattle together and in a herd mentality is not for novices, especially in the rough, brushy landscape. The roundup may be in a line or a circle maneuver, the choice being determined by the foreman based on the size and shape of the pasture and the number of men available, usually at least eight in the pastures with three or four thousand acres.

Once the cattle are in the pens, the men separate the calves from the cows, usually by driving the animals through a cutting chute with several gates opening into adjacent pens. Cowboys swing the gates to cause the cows to go into one pen, the calves into another. Once this step is completed, the calves are put down another chute onto the calf cradles or working tables and "worked." This "work" means each calf is vaccinated for potentially fatal blackleg, branded with the ranch brand, and dehorned. The bull calves are castrated. It takes less than a minute to work a calf, and the work goes on at a furious pace. On other days, the men may choose to rope and drag the calves to the branding fires, a tradition that goes back to the earliest days of ranching when no pens were available for the working. At this time the heifer calves and their mothers are separated from the steer calves and their mothers so that at marketing time this step will have already been taken. The steers are sold in July on the Nail. The heifers are soon after sorted and some are sold. Others are kept to become part of the breeding herd and given a year brand so that the females can be culled at the age of ten years, the end of a productive life for range cows. The cows are palpated to determine if they are bred, and culled if not. This is part of the economics of modern ranch life. The ranch cannot afford to keep a cow that is not producing a calf each year.

As fall approaches, the men ready the automatic feeders mounted on their pickup trucks. During the winter, the men feed range cubes at the rate of three to five pounds a day per animal, and do so every other day. Part of the process is checking the herds for problems such as sickness or injury. Also, during this time the new calf crop begins to arrive to renew the cycle. All of the calves arrive within a sixty to ninety day period because the bulls are left out with the cows for only that length of time nine months earlier.

The cowboys follow another traditional practice—neighboring. The men from neighboring ranches who help the Nail crew work their calves expect the Nail cowboys to come to the neighbor ranch to repay the favor. In this way a ranch has to keep only as much full-time help as is necessary for routine work. This practice helps curtail expenses.

The influence of a folk tradition is evident in the tack and other equipment that men in a particular area use and wear. For example, the saddles in this area have moderately swelled forks, rolled cantles, front and back girths or cinches, breast collars, and unpadded seats. The stirrups are usually two inch wood bound in metal and covered with leather. No tapaderos or toe fenders are found in the area as a general rule, if the cowboy is native to the region. The cowboy's rope is about thirty feet long, and he often ties hard and fast to his saddle horn, unless team roping, in which case he dallies the lariat. For securing the rope to the saddle horn, the cowboy may use a metal or rawhide honda. The bits are shallow port on older horses, snaffle on young ones. The reins are split leather, usually six to ten feet in length, and the headstall usually has a throat latch but no nose band or bosal.

Other gear includes hand-made high-top boots with two to three inch heels and a spur ridge to keep the handmade spurs from slipping over the heel. Predominant boot colors are black bottoms with red tops or brown bottoms with green tops. Other combinations will appear as well to show individuality within the tradition. The spurs are the work of a preferred artisan and bear the marks of the owner's name, the name of the ranch, or some other personalizing emblems. Newer ones lack the emblems from the deck of cards popular in the late 1800s and early 1900s. Although some cultures such as the vaquero of Mexico use a quirt in addition to spurs, the cowboy does not. The spur straps may sport buckles made by hand and ornamented like the spurs. The jeans will be blue denim, usually Wranglers. The belt may be plain but even if tooled will not sport the owner's name. Shirts are cotton with pearl snaps rather than buttons and Western cut with a yoke across the shoulders. The hats sport a rolled brim of from four to six inches and a high crown, which may be formed in one of several crushes. Chaps are the straight-legged shotguns with zippers to close the back and, more recently, the short chink chaps that drop just below the knee. These reveal the brightly colored and stitched tops of the boots. The men wear no pistols but may keep a rifle in the pickup to shoot varmints that threaten the cattle.

Living conditions have changed even since George has been in the work. The use of several bachelor cowboys on a ranch is far less common today than before. Now the men are usually married and live in a camp located at a strategic spot on the ranch. The Nail, for example, has housing for the wrangler and one of the cowboys at the headquarters and a camp some miles away at what is called the 7W. Here one of the men and his wife and children live and see after the pastures adjoining the house. The camp has a horse pasture, a set of pens, and a barn. On days that the men are to round up cattle, this man loads his horse into a trailer and meets the rest of the crew at a designated spot for the work. In the winter, the man sees after and feeds the cattle in the pastures assigned to him.

Entertainment for these men is predictable. On the Nail Ranch is a large roping arena where many a late afternoon is spent heading and heeling steers. This kind of practice keeps the men's roping skills sharp. For the last several years George's family gives him and his friends a birthday party that includes a lunch in the cookhouse and an afternoon of roping in this arena. The men also like to go to rodeos to watch and to participate. The Nail team is widely know as one of the best ranch rodeo teams in the world. George manages the team in such a way that it has won the title of World Champion on three occasions and been in the running several other times. For those who are unfamiliar with ranch rodeos, a description is appropriate.

Ranch rodeos are held in numerous small towns as well as some larger ones such as Fort Worth, Wichita Falls, and Abilene. In these contests teams of cowboys from ranches compete against other teams in demanding work situations such as the men face on the ranch. These include riding bucking horses with regular cowboy saddles, milking wild cows, branding calves, cutting yearlings from a herd and penning them (team penning), and other such chores. No rodeo cowboy could do these very well because all of these together require skills that the rodeo cowboy may never have developed. All events in this contest require teamwork by men proficient in the work, except for bronc riding, still an individual event. I once talked with a young collegiate bronc rider who could ride bucking horses but had a heck of a time riding a running horse around the arena to celebrate his winning the bucking horse contest.

There are schools for ranch management, roping, breaking horses, and palpating. People can get this training from books, videotapes, and compact disks. But putting the knowledge and skills together to function effectively is the test of a cowboy. The men did not learn in schools but in the school of experience under the supervision of someone who knows. This was brought to me vividly one morning on a ranch north of Abilene when almost twenty men gathered for a roundup. I commented to George as we rode off that we had lots of cowboys for the day's work. He calmly responded that we had lots of riders and that by noon we would know how many cowboys we had. He was right. Some had the gear and almost the look, but cowboys they were not.

Those who believe that the cowboy is dead and gone should go on an odyssey. Leave behind the concrete canyons in the cities, the creek crossings at the city parks, and the sterile ranchettes in the suburbs, and go to the still existing cattle ranges of the West. In Texas, these are in the countryside around such places as Albany,

Benjamin, Electra, Hebbronville, Carizzo Springs, Premont, Kent, Guthrie, Van Horn, Alpine, Gail, and dozens of other such small towns, mostly west of Interstate 35. There sometimes, if you are lucky, before daylight on a weekday morning you will see a four-wheel drive pickup pulling a stock trailer with saddled horses riding calmly on their way to work.

The men will be wearing wide-brimmed hats. The saddles on the horses will be worn and weathered, not the shiny, silver-mounted kind seen in parades. Lariats will be snugged to the swell of the saddles. If you follow the rig, you will see it turn off the highway and pull into a gate and disappear onto a dirt road miles from the nearest house. Late in the day you will see the cowboys head in after a hard day of riding and working cattle. In the cookhouse, and sometimes, on the weekend, at the "watering holes" of the area, these same men will gather to share the stories and memories that celebrate their lives. Even in the social environment, the men and their families will show the look of cowboy life, with jeans, boots that may still have the spurs strapped on, hats, and the like. If they have a telephone, do not try to call one of these men or women at their homes during night hours; they will be outside. Do not call after 9:00 p.m. because they will be in bed. Leave a message on their machine if there is one, and they might decide to call you back when they get up at 4:00 the next morning. This is cowboy life going on quietly and steadily, just as it has for centuries, but adapted to this day.

The best chance the city dweller has to share in this life is to go to one of the several ranch rodeos held around the state and see these men and women demonstrating what they do every day—work cattle while sitting astride an athletic cow horse. Baxter Black, the cowboy humorist who ably and humorously depicts the life of these folk heroes, advises in one of his poems—if you want to see a cowboy, go to where he works because he rides in remote pastures and is "hard to see from the road."[4] We could only wish that Jane Kramer had gotten off the road and met the real cowboys before she embarrassed herself and *New Yorker Magazine.*

Notes

[1]Jane Kramer, *The Last Cowboy* (New York: Harper and Row, 1977).

[2]Numerous interviews, early morning conversations, and pasture rides by the author over more than fifteen years.

[3]Letter to author, quoted in "Introduction," *Horsing Around: Contemporary Cowboy Humor*, ed. Lawrence Clayton, Kenneth W. Davis, and Mary Evelyn Collins (Lubbock: Texas Tech University Press, 1999), 3.

[4]"The Vanishing Breed?" in *Horsing Around*, p. 81.

TEN
The Peacock Brothers

Cowboying is a tradition that runs deep in some families. When people around Albany, Texas, discuss good cowboys, the names of the Peacock brothers almost always come up. These four West Texas cowboys are following traditions established by their father and grandfather. When their grandfather, Frank, cowboyed in the early days, he saw the end of the open range. When their father, Benjamin Franklin, served his stint as a cowboy, he saw his generation still following in the footprints of the previous one.

For many years, their father's wages were only $35 a month, which was certainly inadequate to raise the large family he had. But he taught his four sons—George, Troy, Dean, and Benny—a way of life they love and are still living.

They have seen cowboying evolve into the mechanized era with widespread use of pickups, horse trailers, calf cradles, and the like. But they are cowboys at heart, still following the outlaw steer, and building reputations among the very best who follow their line of work.

The oldest is George, presently manager of the 99 section Nail Ranch, north of Albany. Born on a ranch in Archer County in 1935, he lived on various remote ranches as a child. He says, "I'd never even seen a car until I was eight or nine years old. The ranch we lived on was so remote cars never came that way. We had horses to ride, but no cars. I was much impressed by the first car I saw going by in a cloud of dust on a nearby gravel road."

The Peacock Brothers

After graduation from Breckenridge High School in 1952, he worked on the Ross Sloan Ranch in Stephens County, north of Breckenridge, along with several other bachelor cowboys, including his lifelong friend, "Big Boy" Mercer, now foreman of a ranch for the Everett Brothers at Crystal Falls. George eventually married Sue Fonville, a ranch-raised girl whose father cowboyed with George. "She is an able ranch wife and a fine ranch cook and proves it on the days working crews gather on the ranch," George says.

Although George has more administrative responsibilities than he did when he was wrangler and later foreman of the Nail, he still rides with his four-man crew and tries to keep up with the daily workers on the ranch, focusing on oil exploration and production, leased hunting, and other activities. He even accompanies the crew when they swap help with other ranches such as Watt Matthews' Lambshead Ranch, which joins the Nail on the north.

"I like to ride with the men and know what they are doing and help them when I can," George says. "I also like to visit other ranches and see how things are being done there. I especially like to swap help on the Matthews Ranch because I enjoy visiting with Watt."

Troy, the next oldest brother, left school in Breckenridge, joined the Marine Corps, and later lived in California, where he went to horseshoeing school and then worked as a farrier. He didn't stay with the work, however. "It's a job that's extraordinarily hard on a man's back. I like riding horses a whole lot better than I do shoeing 'em. So I make it a point to ride as much as I can and not shoe any horses other than my own string," Troy says.

Troy was a longtime foreman at the Alexander Ranch, just north of Abilene, Texas. While there, he and manager Mike Alexander set up an annual cow camp on the Akers Ranch. There the men stayed for most of a week working the pastures around the temporary headquarters set up as men have been doing since the beginning of this work in North America. Today he is foreman of McMinn Estate Ranch, and he and his wife, Louise, live in a log house south of Anson.

Dean has worked on the Caldwell, Nail, Lambshead, Fish Hook, and on the Star Brand Ranch on Matagorda Island. He is currently foreman of the Blackwood Ranch in Nolan County, west of Abilene. A superb Dutch-oven cook, he led the way for the cooking at the Western Heritage Day at Blackwell, Texas, a small ranch community near the shores of Oak Creek Reservoir on the Nolan and Coke County line. He recalls, "I've eaten the food of some mighty fine wagon cooks, and I decided to become the best one I could."

He once grew philosophical during a conversation concerning the way cowboy work needs to be done, whether it is herding cattle or cooking. "It may take a little longer to do it right the first time, but that's a heap better than having to do it the second time. Part of what galls you the second time is knowing you should have done it right the first time and just didn't."

He is an outstanding cowhand and an exceptionally fine roper. Although battling cancer, he still keeps up with his work. "When I'm on horseback, my problems don't seem as big as they do when I'm not working," Dean says. "I hope to keep working and riding as long as I can."

Benny is the youngest and perhaps most colorful of the brothers. After graduation from Woodson High School in 1968, he worked on the vast Waggoner Ranch in north Texas for three years, breaking fine Waggoner Quarter Horses for cowboys to ride for ranch work. Later, he joined the cattle crew.

"I helped break out those horses from the late 1960s that were branded 8, 9, and 0 for a year brand. There were some awfully good horses in that bunch, and I was a great admirer of the Waggoner horses, but man, there were some rank horses the cowboys rode," Benny says.

"One time the foreman got a bunch of those rank horses and put them all in one string. Any time a cowboy came by looking for work, he'd give him that string to ride. If a man could ride the string, he was a good hand. Some of those horses would buck with you every day, but they had as much cow sense as any horse a man ever had between his legs."

Benny has worked on the Swenson, Pitchfork, 06, Triangle, and Muleshoe ranches as well as Lambshead and the Nail. He has been a longtime foreman for the Bob Green ranches near Albany, and for several years lived on the edge of Hubbard Creek Lake near Breckenridge.

Benny and his wife resided between Abilene and Albany on the 10,000 acre Merrick Davis Ranch, leased by the Greens. He is sometimes reminded of his early bronc-breaking days, especially if he wants to travel by air, because the pins and screws holding his bones together set off airport alarms.

Like the other cowboys they work with, the Peacocks still retain the old-time pride in gear, especially in boots, spurs, and hats. Handmade boots with fancy stitched tops seem to be preferred, even for riding the range. All the brothers wear spurs with medium-sized rowels, with their names and little other ornamentation on the spurs, a trait characteristic of West Texas cowboys.

Their hats are hand-shaped felt with high crowns. Troy has strong feelings about his hats. He says, "You can tell a lot about a man from the kind of hat he wears and the kind of crease he wears in it. A hat is a statement, as well as a necessary piece of apparel for a cowboy."

The saddles ridden by these men are characteristic of the

region—double-rigged models with swelled forks and rolled cantles. Tapaderos do not make up part of the regular gear of cowboys in this region.

Roping has long been an attraction to cowboys, and today's followers of the trade are no exception. Although these cowboys no longer rope calves to doctor screwworms, they still rope regularly in their work and may heel calves at branding time. They still gather on weekends in roping arenas to practice their skills, and George tells anybody who gets careless with his rope, "A rope is just like a gun. It's always loaded and can hurt you. Most people think the rope is a toy, but it's not. It's a tool and is as dangerous as any of the other tools a cowboy works with."

George recently constructed a roping arena on the Nail Ranch, and has a roping as part of his annual birthday party each March. During his days as foreman of the Alexander Ranch, Troy regularly had his brothers and their families out to practice team roping on Sundays. "I love to rope," Troy says, "and most cowboys these days don't get as much practice in the pastures as we did when we were kids roping out calves to doctor screwworms. I like to rope on weekends to keep my eyes sharp so when I do have to rope one in the pasture, I can get it done." Benny and George keep small herds of Corinte steers to practice roping.

George is still more conservative than the others, and ties his lariat hard and fast, and even when team roping, uses a shorter rope to keep the animal closer to his horse. The other brothers tend to dally in that circumstance. All enjoy periodically roping and dragging even though they think the calf cradle is faster in working the calves. "When I feel we have time," George says, "I like to let the boys rope and drag. They enjoy it, and it keeps them happy."

George helped organize the initial performance of the Albany Ranch Rodeo in 1988, and Troy helped plan early editions of the Anson Ranch Rodeo. Benny has been on the Green's team at these area rodeos, and all of the brothers enjoy the sport because they are interested in ranch rodeos, especially those in Abilene, Anson, Albany, and Breckenridge.

The brothers regularly figure among the high scorers at these events, and in July of 1990, George led his Nail Ranch team to the World Championship of the Working Cowboy Ranch Rodeo Association in Fort Worth's Windy Ryon Arena. George and his team claimed two national championships, one in 1993, another in 1994 in Stephenville, Texas. The Green Ranch team, on which Benny is a regular competitor, regularly scores high in the competition at the Western Heritage Classic each May in Abilene. The brothers are also regular, tough competitors in area team pennings.

Cowboys in Shackelford County also play roles in the Fort Griffin Fandangle, and take full advantage of this event held each June in the Prairie Theater west of Albany. They find the parade a big attraction for themselves and their cowboys. The amphitheater where the production is enacted is located on terrain astride the old trail to the railroad corrals on the now-abandoned Texas Central Railroad, the line that changed the area when it was built in the 1880s.

This outdoor show, originated by a Princeton-trained dramatist, Robert Nail, depicts the settlement of the region around Fort Griffin on the Clear Fork of the Brazos River. A large part of the development included the cattle culture, and Benny and his friend, Bud Leech, usually rope the calf for the branding that is part of one segment of the show. Benny says, "It puts some pressure on me to have to rope that calf in front of an audience, but I try to rope enough during the year that it is not unusual to have to snag one under pressure."

Benny also helps drive a herd of longhorn steers onto the stage, a frightening event for first-time spectators. He is one of the dashing flagbearers in the flamboyant figure-eight flag parade at the beginning of the show. Although occasionally two riders will collide during the race, Benny still enjoys it. "It's a challenge to see if we can keep those horses running full blast and still make the figure eight work. The audience loves it, and we love doing it," George says, noting he drives a team of horses pulling the hack carrying the narrators onto the stage.

The social side of the brothers' lives often centers around the

Texas Eatery and the Dairy Queen in Albany, frequent gathering places for these men as they swap stories on a Sunday morning or perhaps a rainy afternoon. As Morris Ledbetter, a rancher and oil field pumper from Albany, says, "There will be more bad horses ridden and wild cattle worked in these two places on a Sunday morning than you will see on the ranges around Albany in a year."

One thing that hasn't changed is the way cowboys tell stories about their adventures and events. George can recall the old days as being harder than those now. He remembers days as a bachelor cowboy on the Ross Sloan Ranch, when meals were simple, men cooked their own breakfast over a wood-burning stove, and the first one in that night started supper over the same stove.

Lunch was even simpler than that. Sloan bought canned goods by the cases, especially peaches, Vienna sausages, and other "portable meals." The men carried these canned goods in a boot top, cut off and laced across the bottom. Using a string around the top of the boot top, they hung lunch on the saddle horn and rode until the sun announced it was time to eat. They stopped and ate wherever the hour caught them.

The drafty bunkhouse in which the men slept allowed cold wind and even snow to blow through the cracks. George recalls, "That's why we kept a tarp on our beds. There was never any doubt how cold it was outside because it was just that cold inside. And it didn't do any good in the winter to get up and try to warm up before we got dressed.

"Many a morning I turned into that north wind and headed to the cookhouse to light the fire when I was still buttoning my shirt. I stood over the fire to stop my shaking and then fed it 'til it was a roaring blaze."

George also recalls driving a bob-tailed truck loaded with cattle and hogs from the Sloan Ranch to the Fort Worth Stockyards in the 1950s. He said, "I knew that truck would tip over if a bunch of those hogs, which ran back and forth under the bellies of the cattle, happened to get on one side of the truck as I started around a curve. I have made as high as three trips a day from the ranch to Fort Worth hauling cattle, and the roads weren't all that good in those days."

He also remembers when men on the Sloan Ranch drove their cattle to the railroad corral near Breckenridge for shipping. "We drove the herd across a swinging bridge that spanned the Clear Fork of the Brazos River. Two cowboys in the lead would each rope a calf and drag them across the bridge. The mothers of those calves would follow their calves, and the rest of the herd would follow along."

Driving down the road also had its disadvantages compared to driving across open range. George says, "We had to keep a rider in the pasture on each side of the road in order to turn back calves that slipped through the fence. It was a different kind of trail driving but interesting enough the way we did it."

More than once, the train sounded its whistle as the herd approached the railroad corral and scattered the frightened cattle. "I know that engineer enjoyed scaring those cattle that way, and I know he did it on purpose. We finally got to where we expected it. Today's method of loading the cattle on huge cattle vans at the ranch corrals is certainly am improvement over that system," George notes.

Modern life has not been without its problems for these cowboys, and examples are easy to find. One particularly appropriate one involves Benny when he was gathering cattle on the home spread of the Bob Green Ranch, part of which is covered by Hubbard Creek Lake.

What had formerly been a hilltop became an island when the lake level was high, but during a period of drought several head of stock migrated across the shallows onto the island and were trapped there when rains fell and the lake level rose.

All the cattle were eventually removed from the island except for one cantankerous crossbred bull, whose disposition did not lend itself to being easily driven off the island. Finally, Green told the cowboys to go get the bull off the island and back with the cowherd.

The cowboys finally succeeded in getting the bull headed out into the water. Benny recalls, "Just as we got that old bull going, a motor boat came by pulling a water skier. That guy used his skies to splash water in the bull's face, and of course the bull turned back to dry land. We like to have never gotten that bull back into the water, which was saddle blanket deep on a tall horse. We worked most of the day trying to get that old rascal out of there."

The cowboy's life is a reality for these four brothers and many of the other men who work with them in West Texas. Hard working, dedicated to their life on the range, the Peacock brothers are fine examples of what today's cowboys face—adversity, happiness, good times and bad. What separates them from others is that they still face their challenges mostly on horseback.

Benny says, "If you can sit on a good horse at the head of a draw or at the back of a pasture just as the sun begins to come up and know what's ahead and not feel good about life, then you must already be dead. It's sure something I look forward to doing every day."

ELEVEN
George Truett Self: Cowboy and Bronc Rider

If you find a cowboy who will tell you what a good cowboy he is, he is probably not near the cowboy he claims to be. The really good cowboys don't have to tell you. Someone else will already have told you who the best in the county are. George Truett Self is one of the latter type of cowboys.

I had heard of Mr. Self for many years before I finally got the chance to interview him at a cattle sale during the annual auction on the R.A. Brown Ranch in Throckmorton County on October 9, 1991. Mr. Self, then in his 80s and living in Mineral Wells in retirement, came back to the sale to be introduced and to see one more time the operation for which he worked for 47 years. Mr. Self was a cowboy, one of the best that ever rode the ranges in any part of the world, and he was a bronc rider who could ride the best or worst of them and did so while breaking horses for the Brown Ranch, a spread known for quality Quarter Horses.

Mr. Self, a second generation cowboy, was born in Throckmorton County on November 25, 1904. His father was a cowboy and horse trader who believed that his son should follow the same path. Mr. Self remembers, "He put me in a saddle when I was just a kid. Many a time he went off trading for horses and mules and took me with him." As the herd accumulated, the man and his son would tie pairs of animals together by a rope around the animal's necks. They allowed about six feet of distance between each one. The older man would ride ahead of the horses as they traveled down the dirt roads of that day while young George Truett followed along making sure that none of the animals straggled and became lost from the rest of the herd.

When he grew up, he married Helen Dawson on October 14, 1934, and they had two sons, George and Joe, as well as one daughter, Marina, whose husband, Don Welch, is a vice-president for West Texas Utilities. The boys have followed in the life of a cowboy, though Joe served a career of military service in the Special Forces and had extensive Viet Nam experience. George Calvin, a grandson, is a fourth generation cowboy.

Self began working for ranches at an early age. He has strong recollections of his years at the Long X Ranch of the Reynolds Cattle Company near Kent in far West Texas. For example, on the X Ranch many years before, he remembers feeding cake to the cattle during the winter or during droughty periods. The ranch hands would store feed in small houses scattered around the ranch, and when it was time to feed, the men would ride out on horseback, move the sack over onto the saddle, and then scatter the 43% protein cottonseed cake over a wide area so that the cattle could feed on it without fighting with each other. Self also worked on the Figure 6 Ranch, as well as the Bar X Ranch, run by Mrs. T.S. Richards of Throckmorton.

When R.A. Brown of Throckmorton County decided to marry and settle down to run a ranch, he hired Self and his brother Carl to work for him. He promised Self that he could run a few cattle on the ranch, and Self did as long as he worked for the ranch. Early in the operation the Browns started a Hereford operation with the purchase of four Hereford cows. They went on to become one of the leaders in Hereford breeding in that area before changing in 1965 to a cross-bred operation after R.A. Brown died. Then Rob Brown, his son, developed a reputation in breeding Simmental and Simbrah cattle, breeds for which they have now become widely known as suppliers of quality breeding stock. They also breed Red Angus. Self's initial duties included looking after the cattle and placing the bulls in appropriate pastures. Mr. Self spent many days living out of the chuck wagon, eating and sleeping there. He remembers the diet as pinto beans, steak, and sourdough bread. I asked him if they worried much about green vegetables, and he just grinned and shook his head. Self also remembers that the men would supplement their diet with wild hog meat. These feral hogs, which multiply freely on the range, had to be roped and penned and then put on feed until they got "the weed scent out." After that the animals could be killed and eaten fresh, or the meat could be cured for use during the winter.

He often carried a .30-.30 rifle in a saddle scabbard for shooting coyotes. He said, "I seldom got a shot. Coyotes seem to know whether you have a gun or not. They are pretty smart. If they know you've got a gun, they'll stay out of range."

He remembers seeing working tables come in the 1940s and '50s, when much of the mechanization that now characterizes cowboy life came into existence. He still preferred to rope and drag, and knew that men preferred to flank calves on the ground. He tied his rope hard and fast because, he said, "I could get off my horse anytime." He watches men these days as they dally when they head and heel and realizes the necessity of that, but he is still, in the true Texas fashion, one who ties his rope off hard and fast.

The Brown Ranch, prior to World War II, drove its cattle to the railroad corrals at Albany. They would drive the herd of cows and calves to the corral and spend the night wherever darkness overtook them. Then they would separate the calves and ship them, and then they would drive the cows back home. This is a trip of some twenty-five miles and took about a week. If the creek was up, he said, "We just swam it." It was in the late '30s and after the war that driving of cattle to the railroad corrals was replaced by hauling them in trucks. They shipped their fat cattle in these days to markets in St. Louis, and their less desirable animals to Fort Worth.

Mr. Self made quite a reputation as a hunter of outlaw cattle in 1920s and '30s. His technique was simple, to him, but was dangerous and demanding. These cattle were typically steers two or three years old or older that had managed to elude capture. He would rope one of these big steers and "put him to bed" by throwing him and tying him down. Then he would hunt another steer, drive him as close to the tied animal as he could, and then rope and trip him. Once the animal was tied up, he would drag the animal as close as possible to the previously captured steer, and with a piece of soft one-inch well rope, tie one end of the rope around each animal's neck in such a way that the animals could not choke. Then he would turn the two loose, and they could be driven out. If they were left singly, they would scatter and were impossible to drive.

The lariat rope that he used in those days was a grass rope, made up of thirty-six strands of fiber. But he said, "I broke lots of 'em. Those steers were big, heavy, and mean."

Mr. Self always carried a bullwhip when he was working cattle. One of its uses was to separate two bulls that might be fighting, a danger to the other livestock as well as to the men on horseback. These enormous animals, especially the bull which is defeated, will run over whatever is in the way of escape. He also said he killed many a rattlesnake with his bullwhip.

One of his principal duties, however, was breaking horses, and he was a bronc stomper as good as they come. He had accumulated plenty of experience working with horses on the Long X Ranch. These horses were the descendants of the famous Steel Dust, and most of them weighed between 1,000 and 1,200 pounds. They were legendary for their strength and stamina, though they were "sure rough" when it came to breaking them. At that time, each man on the Long X Ranch kept sixteen horses in his string and was responsible for shoeing his own horses. Self recounts that he did shoe his own, and a few for friends, but never shod horses for the public. He said the work was just too hard to do that.

Of his bronc riding days, he says, "When I was young I really enjoyed it. I didn't care if an old pony bucked or not." He goes on to say that no one can make a bronc rider if it's not built into the individual. His father was a good rider, as are both of his sons. Of his grandson, he says, "George Calvin comes by it honest. For example, he is currently riding a horse that was not broken until it was eight years old." His grandfather asked George if the horse ever tried to buck. The young man nonchalantly replies, "Not too bad."

Self's view is that horses today are bred to the point that they are not as tough as the old ones were. He remembers that it was all but impossible to ride a Steel Dust horse down. He says, "I can ride one of these horses today down in two hours or less even at my age." In the late 1930s and until 1943 Self broke horses out of a fine band of mares bred to a son of the famous Joe Hancock. Some proved to be remarkably fine steer roping horses. One, known as "Old Hadacol," proved to be an outstanding roping horse.

Self's technique for breaking the horses was to start them with a hackamore, and not just any hackamore. He has been making his own style of hackamore since he was twenty-five years of age. It takes thirty-six feet of rope to make the reins, and sixteen feet of rope to make the headstall. He broke the horse to ride and rein with just this device on his head, and he would use a bit later. He just would not use a bit in the horse's mouth until after the horse was broken and riding well. He said upon occasion he would let a young horse wear a set of bits for a good while just to get used to it. But he warned, "If you ever tear up a horse's mouth, he never gets over it." During many of his years on the Brown Ranch, he broke from eight to ten horses a year. If he did it well, and the horse sold well, which it usually did, Mr. Brown would give Self half of the selling price as a bonus for a job well done.

The saddles ridden by Mr. Self during his day included a Rope Spinner made in Denver. Slick Daws, a cowboy from Woodson, had a Rope Spinner and told Self about it. Self ordered one for himself and rode it for ten years. His next saddle was an S.D. Myers saddle from Sweetwater, and he rode it for many years. His last one was made by Carl Daar, a Paducah saddlemaker, who built the saddle with strap rigging so that it would hold up to the heavy roping that

Mr. Self often did. Self rode oxbow stirrups, but had his boots specially made with underslung heels so that they would not go too far into the stirrup. He hobbled his stirrup one time, but no more. He felt it was too dangerous, and he didn't need to. His best spurs were a pair made by Kelly Brothers. He has now given these, along with another pair of spurs, to his two sons.

Self has definite recollections of the advent of the radio in the 1920s. He said the earliest models that he saw had earphones, much like a telephone. He said some had only one earphone and others had two. For those who had two, two individuals would often share and listen through the small earphones to enjoy the programming. These radios were run on liquid cell batteries. This was, of course, long before the day when electricity was available in remote ranches. He also remembers in 1948 he saw his first television set.

When he was 25 years old, Self began making a hackamore to his specifications to use in breaking horses. In his retirement Self has made a name for himself as the "hackamore man." In addition to those he makes out of nylon rope, he also makes some from rawhide. He gets a cowhide and lets it age for three years during which he applies his own "treatment" to it. Before he uses it he runs it through a device to take the hair off. He uses only the back part of the hide cutting away the less desirable flank portions, and cuts the leather in a circle until he cuts the entire hide into leather string. He does not like to use hides with brands because he says, the brand ruins that spot in the hide, and he has to cut around it. He makes from 12-15 hackamores from each hide. Once he gets the strings cut, he has to stretch them and true them up. He says, "I have every tool I need," and some of these he developed himself. He also learned the techniques by himself.

Self remembers many of the experiences that he had; some of these were hard days and some were good. He says, "As long as the cattle were doing good, it was easy to work for a man, but if times got hard, it was hard to work for anybody." He remembers working with many good cowboys. He said, "I don't ask any of you to do anything I won't do." He said, "I never had any trouble, and always got along good with those boys."

TWELVE
Nig London, Throckmorton County Cowman

Anyone who thinks that all the old-time cowmen are gone has not met Nig London of Throckmorton. Mr. London has been a cowboy and cowman all his life and, he says, if he had it to do again, he would do it just the same way. He has operated a ranch of his own along with overseeing large leased ranches and herds of cattle, particularly steers, with a partner. At eighty years of age he still sees after his own cattle, rides his horses, and watches over a fine stretch of cattle country in Throckmorton County of West Texas, where he was born on a small family ranch along Hog Creek in 1910.

Mr. London can remember much about his days on the range. His most memorable experience involved a drive of 1800 steers from the Nail Ranch, just north of Albany in Shackelford County, back to Throckmorton County range in 1923. He was only thirteen years old at the time, but he remembers that his father gathered the saddle horses and a chuck wagon and made the two-day trip to the area along the Clear Fork of the Brazos. The outfit spent the first night near the site of old Camp Cooper, just north of the Matthews' Lambshead Ranch. George Wright had the land leased at the time.

The next morning they crossed the river and rode onto the Nail Ranch to the south. Francis Gober, who had worked for Judge J. A. Matthews for thirty-five years, led the party through the area because he knew all the crossings, gates, and natural barriers. As they crossed the river bottom, the horse herd went through heavy stands of cockleburs. That night as Mr. Nail looked at the night horses in the corral, he inquired about the cockleburs. He then told Mr. London's father to wrangle the entire remuda and get all the cockleburs out of their tails. Mr. London remembers that it took way up into the night to remove all the cockleburs, which were then burned. Mr. Nail had fought the pesky plants for years and did not want new seeds brought to his range.

The steers were gathered out of a large pasture, and Talmadge Palmer, mounted on a fine sorrel horse, cut out the 1800 head. These were cut out individually, and when a group of 400 was cut out, it was driven some distance to the north away from the herd so the danger of becoming mixed with the larger group was not possible. Mr. London remembers that the fine cutting horse had a technique that when each animal was cut out, the horse bowed his head to that animal before being reined back into the herd to select another.

As is characteristic of all cowboys, Mr. London has been interested in horses all of his life. When he was barely thirteen years old, he and his younger brother broke nine head of horses for the neighboring Davis ranch. The techniques employed by the boys, though differing noticeably from the more recently developed Ray Hunt technique, were nonetheless effective and widely used. Late in the afternoon the boys would rope one horse and snub it down to a post. Then they would put a hackamore on the animal. This rope hackamore, which Mr. London's father made by hand, was constructed of "nickel rope," a small grass rope, and included a nose band and brow band, and was securely attached to the animal's head. A lead rope some twenty feet long was then attached to a rock large enough that the horse could drag it, with considerable effort, but not so large that the animal would risk a broken neck by tugging against it during the night. By the next morning the animal's nose would be sore from pulling against the weight and his attention more easily gained by the lads. The youngsters would then take the horse to a round pen for the next step. To saddle the animal, the boys snubbed it to a post and tied a rope around the horse's neck and then got a rope around one of the horse's rear feet. By running that second piece of rope through the loop around the horse's neck, they could draw one hind foot off the ground, thereby incapacitating the animal for saddling. Once the saddle was in place, a task which might take considerable time, one of the boys would mount the horse and ride it. If pitched off, they had no choice but to get back on. They would ride the horse in a small pen, and then a larger pen, and, depending on the temperament of the individual animal, would eventually turn it out and ride it in the trap and later the big pasture. Through this process Mr. London and his younger brother spent an entire summer breaking and gentling nine horses. For this job, they were paid the sum of $5.00 per horse.

Nig London

He remembers when conscious efforts were made to upgrade the quality of horses available in the Throckmorton area. Mr. Davis, an area rancher, bought a high quality Yellow Wolf stallion from the Waggoner Ranch at Vernon to breed to his mares, many of which were of Spanish stock or mustangs. There was also a government breeding station at Seymour that kept two jacks, two Percheron, and two thoroughbred stallions. These sires were available to area farmers and ranchers, and represented an effort by the government to upgrade the bloodlines of horses available to people in a time when quality horseflesh was not a luxury but a necessity. The larger horses that resulted from this breeding program became work animals, and the smaller ones became saddle horses. Part of the motivation of the government was to secure remounts for the U.S. cavalry.

Mr. London recounts seeing numerous paint horses when he was younger and then seeing most of them disappear as selective breeding tended to favor solid colors—bays, sorrels, blacks, and browns. Now that cycle seems to be coming full circle because most ranch herds contain at least one paint horse.

Cowboy gear and equipment has not altered much in Mr. London's recollection. He can recall a good many saddles, old when he was a boy, that were slick-forked or A-fork saddles. He responded to my question about bucking rolls that he did not see them used on the old saddles, but many people tied a coat across the front of the saddle to pad them against the horn and to act as a barrier to being pitched off over the front of the saddle. Most of the saddles he has seen all of his life had at least some swell in fork and typically a rolled cantle. Two of the favorite makers were Turnsal of Miles City, Montana, and R.T. Frazier of Pueblo, Colorado.

The spurs he has been familiar with most of his life sported short shanks and small rowels. The chaps, in early days, were batwings, but he later saw a transition to the shotgun style. He said initially the shotguns were just sewn down the side and were not preferred by cowboys because whatever was on the cowboys' boots was smeared inside the leg as the foot passed through. It wasn't until full-length zippers were added to the shotguns that cowboys definitely came to prefer them over the batwings. Mr. London has seen the shorter chink chaps come in but has not seen them gain the popularity still retained by the shotgun style. In traditional cowboy fashion, he wore boots made by Bud Humphries, a longtime maker at Seymour.

Of other cowboy gear, Mr. London has strong recollections. He remembers that when he started out, most cowboys had only one bridle and used it on all their mounts. He said these days it sometimes takes a pickup to haul all the cowboys' bridles, since they still have several styles of headstalls as well as several different kinds of bits.

I asked Mr. London specifically about the length of lariat ropes. He said ranches kept a coil of rope, and when a cowboy needed a new lariat, the boss simply cut off 33 feet of rope. The typical pattern of roping cattle was to tie hard and fast, in the Texas fashion, and not to dally, a technique that has come to this region more recently, particularly with team ropers in arena settings. Some cowboys have adopted the technique for pasture work as well.

The working methods for branding cattle have not changed that much. Mr. London can remember the first working chute brought into the region by R.A. Brown for his large ranch in southern Throckmorton County around 1915. But Mr. London's early experience usually involved roping and dragging. The small calves were neck-roped; the larger calves were heeled. It was not uncommon to get smaller calves into a crowding pen and simply neck them down and work them, a technique still used by some today, and not unknown in some areas of northeastern Mexico, as recounted by one of my informants.

Mr. London agrees that World War II wrought the greatest change to the life of the cowboy. It was at this time that horse trailers became widely used for hauling horses from one ranch to another. Only later did the practice develop of hauling horses from the headquarters to the pasture to be worked. Cattle came to be more frequently hauled, rather than driven, even for short distances on the ranch during workings. Mr. London credits some of the change to welding techniques learned by men in the service and taught to veterans under provisions of the G.I. Bill. The effect is particularly apparent in areas where oil production has been prominent, because of the availability of pipe. Other forms of mechanization became common, and most allowed less manpower to run the ranching operation. The drives to the railroad corrals were also eliminated by the use of truck and large trailers. Several factors were at work in this change. Mr. London has seen watering facilities go from shallow tanks scooped out by teams of mules pulling fresnos to deeper, more efficient tanks dug by bulldozers.

The most significant alteration to cowboy life has been the eradication of screwworms. Mr. London remembers how ranchers changed their breeding cycle so that calves would be born during the cold months when worms were not a threat. But he also recalls how much gentler cattle became once cowboys could quit prowling pastures and roping calves to doctor screwworms. No one misses the ubiquitous bottle of Smear 62 or other such medicine tied to a saddle in a boot top cut off and laced up across the bottom.

The marketing of cattle has also undergone significant change. Mr. London remembers when all cattle were shipped to the Fort Worth yard. Later, regional auction rings opened. The first he recalls was in 1936 at Vernon. He said at first the auctions operated what he calls a "skin game," in which the sellers were manipulated by organized buyers. Later, however, as other auction rings opened in Wichita Falls, Munday, and Olney, the competition forced honesty on the part of the auction ring in order to attract buyers, and the shysters were soon driven out of business. Now ranchers can ship small numbers of calves to local markets, though they may choose to sell large lots of calves or steers to buyers for feed lots.

Mr. London is a perceptive cowboy, ranchman, and entrepreneur. He showed his good business sense in stating the qualities of a good cowboy. He said that some, of course, are better than others. He remembers that the only time he got into trouble was asking a man to do something that man couldn't do, or asking a man to do more than that man could do. That's a philosophy some managers these days might take a lesson from, one of many we might learn from studying the life of old-time ranchers and cowboys who not only persisted but thrived, during hard times and good, to take their place with the living legends of the American West.

THIRTEEN
Cowboys Keep the Tradition of Branding Alive

The old idea of heraldry of the range is not dead. Some of today's Texas cowboys still take quite seriously the idea of working for a brand, and that includes putting the ranch's identifying mark on the horses they ride. This feeling is definitely true on the J.R. Green Ranch near Albany in Shackelford County of West Texas. Benny Peacock, foreman of the ranch that sprawls along shores of Hubbard Creek Lake, has strong feelings about retaining this tie with the past. In early November he gathers some close friends to help him brand the year's crop of Quarter Horse colts by herd sire Bego Doc.

The work starts about 9:30 a.m. after the men have finished their morning chores on their home ranches and gathered for coffee at the cookhouse on the Green. When the propane-fired branding iron heater is set up and ignited, the first colt is turned down the cutting alley and trapped in the bronc pen. Once the colt is in the pen, two men enter. They work gently with each colt, which usually make several dashes around the pen before settling down.

The men talk to and soothe each animal as they reach for the halter each one is wearing. If that's not possible, a gently thrown loop of a lariat snares the colt.

Once the long lead rope is snapped to the halter, the gate is opened and the trip to the branding chute begins. As each colt bolts for freedom, the man holding the rope has to control the animal's lunges to avoid injury. When one of the colts is reluctant and pulls against the rope, a cowboy passes a loop over the back and hindquarters to urge the colt along. The colts fight the men on the way to the chute, but eventually each animal is trapped in the chute.

After one cowboy secures the lead rope to the side of the chute, another passes a soft nylon rope around the horse's neck, close to the withers, and draws the animal to the left side of the fence. Then the call goes out for the hot iron. A cowboy straddles the chute ahead of the horse and waves his hand to distract the animal. Another cowboy prepares to brand the colt and still another, who stays by the horse's head, twists the left ear of the colt. After the colt's tail is pulled out of the way, a puff of smoke signals that the colt has his first brand. Then the colt gets his year brand applied to his rump just beside the tail on the left side. Most of the animals make little sound, a positive comment on their heritage and character. More than once, a cowboy speaks to the horse as he applies the brand. "Wear it with pride," he says.

Once the animal is branded, the men remove the halter and let the colt walk down the chute toward the gate leading to the holding trap. When free of the chute, each colt runs to join the other horses. These animals are then put out to pasture to mature. It will be some months before they will be brought back in to be gelded and broken to ride.

All these horses are of registered stock and for good reason, especially these days. "If these were just ranch horses," Peacock said, "registration wouldn't be too important. But we may want to sell some of them. People who can appreciate a fine horse and pay what he is worth will want the papers to go with him. I can't blame them for that. It gives them bragging rights." One cowboy says he worked on a ranch where they branded several numbers on the colts.

Anybody who understood the system would know just by looking who the sire and dam of each horse was. Those numbers were in addition to the ranch brand.

Some ranchers prefer to brand colts at weaning time because the colts are easier to handle and are less likely to be hurt. It's common just to run the mare and colt into a pen, catch the colt by hand and let the mare out. Then the men simply hold the young animal against the fence and brand it.

Every effort is made to keep the horses calm, to reassure them, and to avoid injury. In addition, the men critique each animal's conformation, appearance, color, shape of the head, and other points that cowboys notice immediately. After the branding ends and the crew gathers in the cookhouse for lunch, the discussion of these horses and other outstanding animals the men have known dominates the conversation.

In their casual moments, these cowboys talk about cattle, bad horses they have ridden, wild cattle they have chased, and even the action in the ranch rodeo in Abilene, an annual event some of these men compete in against each other.

The registered colts will one day join the herd of working horses on the Green Ranch or be sold or traded for use on other ranches or in cutting and roping arenas or for pleasure riding. Whatever role they play, the colts will wear the brand of the Green Ranch. They have been initiated into the tradition by a group of men dedicated to a way of life that gives fine horses a special place in their lives.

FOURTEEN
Helicopter Cowboys

A new kind of cowboy is working some ranges these days. He doesn't wear cowboy boots, spurs, chaps, or even a Western-style hat. He may not own a horse, a saddle, or a lariat rope, yet he can round up a 10,000 acre pasture, cut with draws and brush, by himself, and sometimes he can pen more cattle than the rancher even knows he has on that stretch of rugged real estate. He can tell a land owner how many deer are on the ranch, what sex they are, and what condition they are in. He sounds like a contemporary "Pecos Bill," an emerging folk hero who rides the tornado. Not quite. Instead, he is one of a small but growing number of "cowboy" helicopter pilots helping ranchers manage their range more effectively.

It is exciting to watch these modern drovers swoop along mere feet off the ground or above the trees, darting behind a herd of cattle that emerges from the brush and heads for the pens in which they will be worked. These are not the gentle kind of cattle that can be drawn easily into the pen by a feed sack. Some of these are outlaws that haven't been in a pen in years, pasture-wise cows who will do anything to keep from going into the pen. But these men have the cowboy spirit and are dedicated to making cows do just exactly what the animals don't want to do.

One of these pilots is Aubrey Lange, who learned his helicopter flying at government expense, beginning in 1967. He repaid the training on two tours in Vietnam as a Medevac helicopter pilot, and is now making productive use of these skills. He has been using the helicopter to work cattle for over seven years now. He moved to San Angelo because the conditions there favor his kind of work: the big ranches, lots of cattle, heavy brush, and rough terrain. Any or all of these conditions must be present before Lange can make a rancher feel justified in using the kind of service that helicopters provide. Lange can work about 2,000 acres of rough terrain in about an hour. Terry Moberley, foreman on the Matthews' Lambshead Ranch north of Albany, estimates that Lange takes the place of seven or eight cowboys when they are working, but Lange says that in some West Texas terrain, he feels he can replace as many as fifteen cowboys. It depends on the roughness of the terrain.

Helicopter in Action at at Cattle Roundup

Lange first came to work on the Matthews Ranch in 1981 when Watt Matthews called him to help the cowboys who were unable to round up the herd in a particularly troublesome pasture that had the river on one side and heavy brush and draws on the other. Lange had done some work for people acquainted with Matthews and came at Watt's insistence. Watt rode with him on the first outing and, as Lange states, everything seemed to be going fine, the cattle were being gathered, but Watt said, " You'd better watch or they'll jump off into that river." Lange was unprepared for that, and the cattle managed to escape. Later Lange returned to the pasture by himself and drove the cattle on a route unfamiliar to them to a different set of pens and was able to pen them all—the first time that had been accomplished in that pasture in several years because the cattle had become pasture-wise; that is, they knew how to elude cowboys by using the terrain to their advantage.

The craft that Lange flies at the Matthews is a Robertson aircraft, a two-place helicopter which Lange says performs much better when carrying only one, himself. Lange owns two of them. He is of moderate size and weight, and he says that is much to his advantage in this particular helicopter because the weight certainly influences the amount of lift the craft has while dodging and darting to herd cattle by air. This is a crucial factor. Made in Los Angeles, this particular craft is economical to operate and very agile—two factors which Lange feels are important to this operation. This model also has far fewer moving parts than the third helicopter he owns—a Bell Company model. Lange is not a barn-storming daredevil but a proficient stockman who, as Watt Matthews testifies, knows how to handle stock and is, in addition, an excellent pilot. Lange has never had a crash but has had damage from parts coming off his helicopter, for example.

Lange works "a lot of cattle," but one of the most important things he does is deer counts. He said ranchers are discovering that the deer on their property are worth more than the cattle. On their counting jaunts, he carries with him a game biologist, and they cover the pasture in 150 yard swaths, recording what they see. They can give the rancher an accurate count of the game on his property, including bucks, does, and fawns. The biologist then recommends a kill level for the ranch for that year and in that way makes a major contribution to game management. In addition to that, they do some trophy counting management because they can spot quality deer among the herds on a ranch. Other information provided by the count is the condition of the deer. This information helps determine the amount of feed that must be put out in order to get the herd through the winter. He often carries the rancher along so that the rancher can see firsthand what the deer herd looks like. In addition to this activity, he also works a lot of Angora and Spanish goats, particularly in the heavy country around Del Rio, where the canyons are really so rough that men on horseback cannot work them.

The economics of the helicopter certainly argue well. Lange stated that on one ranch in West Texas a rancher was required to hire twenty men for a month and a half to do his roundups, and in that period of time they could gather eighty per cent of the cattle in the rough country on the ranch. Lange alone was able to accomplish the task in thirteen days. In that time he gathered ninety-nine per cent of the cattle, a feat which gained the rancher about one hundred extra calves to market. In addition, there were always men injured during the roundup—broken arms, legs, and other kinds of injuries—which caused high insurance costs. These are avoided completely by use of a helicopter. Lange is able to guarantee that he will get ninety-five percent of a herd to the pen.

Lange prefers to work cattle completely by himself, from gathering in the pasture to driving them into the pens. On the Matthews Ranch, however, he works with cowboys and likes that very well. He gets the cattle started and about halfway in, the cowboys pick them up, and they continue to work in unison. Some ranchers have asked Lange to get the animals close to the pen and then let the cowboys pick them up. He will not allow that because, he says, the cows have to readjust to a different system. It is very unlikely that the cowboys will be able to hold them if the men pick the cattle up here. This way—working in unison from mid-point in the pasture on—the system works very well. Lange is able to communicate with the cowboys on the ground through a loud speaker system attached to his aircraft. He gets the cattle going and then tells the cowboys where to go in order to keep them going. He said, "I'll be sure they get in behind them. If they don't, then it's my fault." The cowboys keep them moving. Lange spends his time hunting strays, and that makes everybody's work easier.

Cattle have to learn how to respond to the helicopter. The first time they are worked they have to be taught what the machine is, but after that they handle much easier. When Lange first started gathering cattle on Lambshead Ranch, it took about sixty hours, and he gets $130.00 an hour. Now that the cattle understand what he is, it takes hardly forty hours for him to help round up all the pastures.

The cattle do not get nearly so excited as they do when being chased by horsemen. When working in conjunction with mounted cowboys, Lange has found that if a cow gets by, the cowboys should let it alone, and he can go back and pick it up later. He admits that there is a level of excitability in driving cattle with the helicopter, but they do not become as upset as they do when being chased by mounted cowboys.

The practice of helicopter herding is not new; it started in Texas about twenty-five years ago in the southern part of the state where there is rough country and lots of brush. The Waggoner Ranch in North Texas has been using the practice for years. Up 'til two years ago, Lange was the only one from San Angelo on to the western boundary of the state. Now four or five others are doing the same kind of work. When he first started, especially out in the Pecos region, ranchers were reluctant to try the service. He stimulated business by making a deal with the ranchers. If he did not gather the cattle, it did not cost them anything to try. In some of the very rough pastures, Lange was sometimes able to bring in twice as many cattle as the rancher thought were in the pasture at all. Some of these cattle were outlaws that had eluded cowboys for ten years or more. And that makes Aubrey Lange plenty valuable these days when the profit margin is slimmer than a drought-stunted yearling.

Ranch Histories and Their Significance

For Lawrence's friends, his plans to retire in a few years to the J Lazy C Ranch on the Clear Fork, which he and Sonja had bought several years before his death, was a frequent topic of conversation. The ranch, part of the Irwin family heritage, beckoned him every weekend, when he left academic life for working his cattle and training his horses. His love of ranch life led naturally to his frequent visits to neighboring ranches, often in the role of a working cowhand. He took great pride in his initiation of Western Heritage Day at Hardin-Simmons University, where he treated the crowds to his famous chuck wagon biscuits. He participated in the ranch rodeo in Sweetwater, a cancer benefit honoring his late friend Dean Peacock. Most influential as inspiration to record the histories of Texas ranches was his close association with Watt Matthews, who shared his ranching knowledge and the Lambshead Ranch past generously. Lawrence then knew firsthand the value of preserving the history of the families and life of Texas ranches, and his primary concern was the history of those ranch families in his region. Collected here are the stories of three major spreads in the Fort Griffin area, as well as an essay tracing the adventures of the region's Reynolds brothers and the establishment of the Long X Ranch at Kent. Lawrence felt strongly the heritage of this culture must be passed on to the generations to follow.

FIFTEEN
The Importance of Collecting Histories of Texas Ranches

One of the sadly neglected areas in the study of culture in Texas and other areas of the West is the founding and operating of ranches. It is true that some of the larger ranches have been the subject of research and writing, for books are available on such large spreads as the King Ranch, YO, Pitchfork, and others. The segment of ranching culture which has been ignored is what may be termed the "smaller ranches," although some of them are quite significant in size. Several examples of such ranches will be included later.

The stories about ranches contain information culturally and economically significant in the development of the state because these business ventures provided, in many cases, the framework in which families grew up, developed, and contributed to the communities near which their ranches were located. In addition, a great deal of folklore and legend is found in these stories. This information contributes to the so-called "myth of the West," and involves stories about hardship, heartbreak, sorrow and joy, and stories of man against man, as well as man against animal or nature. In short, these are, in many cases, remarkable stories revealing the drama of human existence.

Lawrence Clayton and Watt Matthews

Although Frederick Jackson Turner, in his famous frontier thesis declared the frontier closed many years ago, the remnants of that experience are still evident in the stories involved in founding and operating ranches. In fact, to people outside the state, ranching is still considered part of the native element of Texas, and that belief is, indeed, a reality. Agriculture Commissioner Rick Perry recently confirmed that Texas produces more beef cattle than any other state in the United States. A large number of ranches are still being operated in the state and will be for a long time to come because the land currently in ranching is suitable for little other activity.

Texas culture is not easy to characterize accurately. The state has several large metropolitan areas, including Houston, San Antonio, and Dallas-Fort Worth, but it also has a number of other cities that are home to 100,000 or more inhabitants. Such cities as Amarillo, Lubbock, Midland, Odessa, Abilene, and a host of others are significant centers of population, with all the services one expects to find. And many of them contain more than a slight element of polite culture. I recall being asked by a representative of a major news network, who was planning a trip to Abilene to film a story, if Abilene had an airport and motels. I was quick to reply that we had not only those ingredients of modern life, but three small universities, two local dramatic groups, and a symphony.

Texas has enormous amounts of farming, particularly on the High Plains, in fertile East Texas, and on the Coastal Plains, and is blessed with the lush, warm, lower Rio Grande Valley, which produces delicacies for tables year around because of its almost tropical climate. Although oil is not as crucial as it once was to the Texas economy, the state still provides a major portion of the petroleum produced in the United States.

This brief synopsis of Texas's diversity does not include all elements of Texas life, for Texas also has significant heavy and high tech manufacturing. In contrast to this modern kind of life, however, ranching still survives as a major part of Texas life. It remains one of the last bastions of traditional family life to be found in the state.

It might be helpful to define what is meant by the term "ranch" for the purposes of this discussion. I think it appropriate to define a ranch as a piece of property upon which livestock is raised—be it cattle, horses, sheep, or goats. That operation constitutes at least a major portion of the work activity and is a principal source of income for the individuals involved in the operation. I am reluctant to set a minimum number of acres, although the small tract upon which an individual or couple might live in retirement, even if they have a horse or two and a few head of livestock, would not qualify for this definition. Rather, a ranch must be an operation upon which the breeding of cattle, horses, sheep, and goats, in order to raise them for market, is typically conducted.

The percentage of income derived from ranching operations may run less than 50 percent, but will still constitute a major concern when the operators are preparing the ultimate accounting of the year's financial position for with the Internal Revenue Service. The label "ranch" does not preclude some farming on the property but, if the growing crops are the major portion of the income derived from the operation, then it would more likely be called a farm that also keeps livestock. Exceptions occur. The King Ranch on the Texas coast derives more income from cotton than from cattle, but most of its 825,000 acres are devoted to raising cattle and horses.

There is no geographic limit to the application of the term, because some fairly small stretches of property in the better-watered portions of East and South Texas, where, for example, a large number of cattle may be run on a relatively small number of acres. The physician, lawyer, or some other highly paid professional may also own a legitimate ranch, but likely will not participate in the operation of the ranch on a day-to-day basis. A ranch it is, nonetheless.

Lawrence Clayton and Doris Miller, Bluff Creek Ranch

I feel a sense of urgency in gathering this material. Just as folk songs were once widely known and disseminated, and have now disappeared as the cultural context changed and singers directed their talents in other areas, so the stories about the founding and operating of early-day ranches in the state are disappearing as the second generation of operators gives way to the third or fourth generation within the next decade. As time moves away from those early days, many of the anecdotes and stories, as well as accurate details of the founding, will be lost. It has been said that when an old-timer dies, a library burns, and this truism is correct with respect to the history of ranching in Texas. The basic purpose of gathering these stories is to record for posterity the material related to founding and operating ranches that have been important to the economic and social development of Texas culture and economy. Without detailed written information, inaccuracy and other discrepancies will likely rise. Although the tendency toward myth may well take over, it is still best to tie stories as nearly as possible to what actually took place. Additional benefits include recording a part of the history of the state that is being radically altered by a number of factors affecting Texas life generally. Included, of course, are concerns about ecology, economics, and a number of other matters. It is particularly necessary to pinpoint the influence of various ethnic groups on ranching practices in the state.

It is also beneficial to establish what practices have been used in ranching in various parts of the state. In some areas, gathering cattle is still done by cowboys on horseback while in others men on horseback, are assisted by trained dogs. In still other parts of the state, where the ground is particularly rough, using a helicopter has become common. Use of the helicopter, however, does not extend to actually working the cattle or other livestock once the animals are in the pen. Providing men and mounts to cope with that final phase of gathering cattle is also a challenge to the economics of ranching.

There are always problems collecting such material. One of the reasons many of these stories have not been told is the intense desire for privacy on the part of the families involved. Many people drawn to ranching are private people who just do not want their stories widely publicised. In addition, in this day of environmental concerns, most ranchers do not want outsiders probing into the nature of their operations. Some environmental groups are currently trying to take over ranch properties in various areas of the state, held by families for more than a century. The properties are then taken over by the federal government and operated as parks. This kind of takeover amounts to little more than taking the lifeblood away, not only from a working person, but from a family, depriving them of the roots from which they came.

In any story there is always material family members would rather not see in print. This kind of information will surely be excluded from these accounts. Such stories are not found exclusively in ranching life, of course, but fall into the category of "skeletons in the closet" found in the backgrounds of virtually every family, and included will be family squabbles, infidelity, and even crimes such as murder, sometimes over contested boundary lines. There are also the inevitable family squabbles that emerge over the division of an estate.

As examples of the kinds of stories that are available, however, I would like to offer some briefly developed examples. First is the Nail

Ranch in Shackelford County, north of Albany, a 64,000-acre spread currently held in trust by a bank in Fort Worth under the direction of a trust officer. The ranch, which has been in the family for two generations, is run by an on-site manager hired by the bank to oversee the day-to-day operation. J.H. Nail established the ranch in the early decades of this century and passed it on to his son, James, Jr., widely known as Jim. Respected for its production of quality Hereford cattle and Quarter Horses, the ranch prospered, due in part to the production of oil on its many acres. In the 1950s sixteen full-time cowboys worked the cattle on the ranch. Now, three full-time cowboys and the manager handle the day-to-day operations and, on days when cattle are to be worked, day workers are hired or cowboys from neighboring ranches come to trade help or "swap help." This tradition of neighboring goes back perhaps as far as the history of ranching itself. Cowboys on the ranch still lead a fairly traditional life. All are married and live in houses scattered around the ranch: two live near the headquarters, and one lives at the 7W Camp some 20 miles away. The men are responsible for a specific number of pastures which they must oversee, checking cattle during the year and, in the wintertime, feeding the cattle in those pastures.

Lawrence Clayton and Leonard Stiles, King Ranch

Numerous stories can be told from the history of the Nail Ranch. One of these stories came from Nig London, a Throckmorton County cowboy and rancher, who, as a youth in the 1920s, accompanied his father and a crew of cowboys from

Throckmorton County across country to the Nail Ranch. There they took control of a herd of 1800 Hereford steers and drove them back to the London's property in Throckmorton County. Although major trail drives to market ended in the 1880s, smaller drives of this sort persisted until after World War II, when hauling cattle by truck/trailer became common. This change from driving cattle came about because of the development of large tractor/trailers (18-wheelers) which could haul large numbers of cattle at one time. In the 1920s men had no choice but to drive cattle across country, even if they herded the animals down the road between fences bordering the roadway.

The trust in which the Nail Ranch is held will expire in another decade or so, and the ranch will once again be in the hands of family members. At that time, decisions will be made whether to sell portions of the property or make other changes in the operation of the ranch. Breaking up the property will radically alter its operation, and ties to the past will be lost.

The Brown Ranch in Throckmorton County is in a somewhat different phase of development. A family-owned operation now in the hands of the third generation, the ranch has diversified its productivity by breeding registered stock and outstanding Quarter Horses. The ranch is home to Rob Brown and several members of his family, as well as four to six cowboys, including one of the few female cowhands working in the area. It is a ranch, but details of its operation make it unique.

A third example is Chimney Creek Ranch, located about a dozen miles southwest of Albany in Shackelford County. This ranch has been in operation since before the turn of the century and has been in the hands of the Davis family since the 1920s. Mary Frances Driscoll, who inherited her portion of the ranch, is the present owner of Chimney Creek and two other ranch properties. Chimney Creek is one of three ranch properties that she controls. Chimney Creek is currently leased to Robert Waller and his son Robert C., and is operated as Waller Cattle Company.

On this property are two historic sites identified by markers from the State Historical Commission. One is a set of corrals or pens built many years ago to load cattle onto railroad cars for the Texas Central Railroad. The pens, which otherwise would have rotted away by now, have been restored twice and the original sign returned to the location. This major historical site is important to the history of ranching in the area.

Numerous stories are told by those familiar with the corrals, including many short drives of cattle herds from neighboring ranches to the pens for shipping. One story, told to me by Florene Smith, concerns a herd of buffalo driven to the pens in the 1930s and loaded onto rail cars to be shipped to a now-forgotten destination. The humorous part of that story involves the efforts of the buffalo to completely destroy the rail car into which they were loaded. The conductor, a man who himself had some experience in handling livestock, urged the cowboys to get the animals loaded quickly so the train could pull out. He feared the buffalo would tear the car apart if it were left standing still with the animals in it.

A second, much earlier site is a stop on the Butterfield Overland Mail Route, which dates back to pre-Civil War times. The stone structure which once stood on the site was demolished and the stone crushed to provide gravel for the roadbed of Highway 180, which runs across the northern half of the ranch.

A similar narrative, the kind of story that is apt to slip through the cracks of even a reasonably dedicated effort to collect ranch histories, is the history of the Ledbetter Ranch. The property, along the banks of the Clear Fork of the Brazos River in northern Shackelford and southern Throckmorton counties, was settled just after the Civil War by William Henry Ledbetter, later a Throckmorton County judge. As generations passed, it was split repeatedly among heirs. One portion, an 850-acre tract containing a number of acres along the river itself, is in the hands of Morris Ledbetter, a descendant of the original settler. Ledbetter, principally an oil field operator and pumper, takes care of the work ordinarily done by a cowboy, that is, he sees after the stock, checks them for injury or disease, and, during the winter, sees that they are fed. When it comes time to work the animals, however, he hires help, often a cowboy in the area named Dick Hash, and, in recent years, Dick's grandson, "Boogie" Deaton. The three-man crew, along with help from Ledbetter's grandson Chris, handles the chore of working the calves. Hash's services are also required when it is time to gather the animals for shipping.

Ledbetter's ranching operation also exemplifies a pattern growing in prominence in some areas of the state. He has leased additional acreage from an uncle whose health has deteriorated to the point that he was no longer able to operate his ranch property. This man, J.C. Irwin, Jr., inherited 250 acres as his part of a larger family operation, and after his retirement, lived on the place with his wife Lee Ita and "ran some cows." This expression has come to be applied to small operators who have a few head of livestock they see after, but do not have an operation large enough to be dubbed a legitimate ranch. Properties such as the Ledbetter and Irwin places are also beneficial for the production of game birds and animals, but, because of the absence of subsurface water, will likely never be useable for other kinds of operation or dense habitation by humans.

Although the Nail Ranch is still characteristic of larger operations, as is the Brown, Chimney Creek is becoming a more common size and type for someone who is in full-time ranching. In this region of the state it generally takes at least 10,000 acres to carry on a legitimate ranching operation and make a living at it. A large number of cattle that eventually reach the slaughter markets, however, are grown on ranches such as the Ledbetter-Irwin operation. Here, people who perhaps wish they could ranch on a larger scale but do not have the resources to do so, content themselves with "running a few cows" and earning a living in some other fashion. They keep their families in town, where many wives and children are typically better suited, but the histories of their ranches are part of the cultural context.

The collection of stories from principally oral tradition, such as the kind hinted at above, provides a major addition to the ranching history of Texas. These stories may not be as exciting as those collected in Hunter's *Trail Drives of Texas* and other such volumes of early day range life, but they nonetheless constitute a valid storehouse of history, legend, and lore connected to the ranching industry in Texas. Along with the stories of the ranches come stories of cowboys, interesting events, historically important developments, and other such tales that make us better able to understand how this segment of Texas life fits into American culture.

SIXTEEN

The Brown Ranch: A Family-Run Operation in Throckmorton County

While it is true that some of the large historic Texas ranches, such as the XIT and Matador, were founded purely as business ventures, many ranches in the state were begun as family-run operations. Even such large ranches as the King, Wagoner, and 6666 were started by ambitious, strong-willed men who became land and cattle barons. Their ranches continued to be run by members of the family for years thereafter. Although ranch organizational style has changed through the decades, with some formally organized corporations managed by non-family members, others have remained in operation by descendants of the founders.

Such a family-run operation is the R.A. Brown Ranch, headquartered west of the town of Throckmorton, located between Abilene and Wichita Falls. Current owner and operator of the ranch is Rob Brown, the third generation of the Brown family to run the ranch. He and his wife Peggy, along with their children, currently manage this very productive cattle and horse operation in some of the best ranch country Texas has to offer.

Brown Ranch Livestock Sale

The story of the founding of this ranch actually begins in neighboring Jack County where Robert Herndon Brown had his -O- Ranch, which he sold in 1903. Brown then moved his family to an elegant, Victorian-style house in Fort Worth, and managed Evans, Snider and Buel Commission Company at the Fort Worth Stock Exchange. Still interested in ranching, however, he started buying ranch land in Throckmorton County. His partner was W.A. Page, who lived near the town of Woodson in southwestern Throckmorton County. The two amassed sizeable holdings, which they later had to divide.

The man who took over the ranch and really promoted it into one of the best livestock operations in the state was R.A. Brown, son of R.H. Brown. R.A. was born December 7, 1902, on the -O- Ranch and later moved with his family to Fort Worth. As a child, he began spending time at the ranch, especially after his father developed cancer in 1919. At the age of fifteen, he moved to the ranch permanently. In 1922 he enrolled in Texas A&M University, but was forced to leave after a year and a half because of his father's illness.

When R.H. Brown died in the late 1930s, R.A., his mother, and his sisters inherited the ranch. His mother and sisters elected to turn control of all of the property over to R.A. in hopes he would be able to save it from being repossessed. During those Depression days, debt was almost impossible to pay off. R.A. was warned there was little way to save the ranch, but he consolidated the properties, began borrowing more money, and started operating the ranch. All of his activities were not rewarding. On one of his early ventures he bought a string of steers one fall. The animals made it through the winter, but just as they were about ready to market the next spring at a profit, a number of them were killed by lightning.

R.A. married Valda Thomas on November 14, 1931. She was the daughter of Mr. and Mrs. D.B. Thomas of Throckmorton. Part of the land currently in the Brown Ranch came from Valda's inheritance from this prominent ranching family. The young couple had two children, Marianne and Rob. Marianne was born in a small house on ranch property between Albany and Throckmorton, and still controlled by the Brown Ranch. Life on the ranch was difficult and demanding for Valda. She remembers relying on kerosene for cooking and lighting her home. There was a fireplace for warming the home on cold days, and she also had a gasoline heater, which she was afraid to light. She relied on ranch hands to perform that task whenever possible.

R.A. established the Brown Ranch as a breeder of quality Hereford cattle and fine Quarter Horses. He brought some of the earliest Hereford cattle to the area and carefully watching the breeding to supply both better beef and breeding stock. Although he would be instrumental in cross-breeding later, throughout his life R.A. strongly preferred the virtues of the Hereford breed.

His interest in Quarter Horses was very serious. During his years of management, he kept about eighty broodmares, many of whom were descended from the stock formerly at the cavalry remount station in the area earlier. R.A. also bought excellent bloodlines to bring into his herd. He acquired Black Hancock, the offspring of the famous Joe Hancock from the 6666 Ranch. Later he traded for Blue Gold, a gray horse by Flue Rock out of a famous Hollywood Gold mare. He added to his bloodlines Joe Bailey Rickles, a double offspring of the famous Weatherford Joe Bailey.

R.A. was instrumental in helping form the American Quarter Horse Association in 1941, and later served as vice president of that organization. When he died, an article in the *Oklahoma Quarter Horse Breeders Association Magazine* stated that few, if any, had ever "tried to do more for the betterment of the American Quarter Horse Association than the late R.A. Brown."

R.A. gained prominence as a breeder of quality hunting dogs

because of his interest in greyhounds, coon dogs, and bird dogs. He used the greyhounds to run coyotes and had a special built truck with cages with quick-release doors to allow the dogs to overtake coyotes as he was driving through the pastures.

In the 1950s R.A. became a leader in sound land management. He began the practice of grubbing mesquite trees and clearing prickly pear cactus, the two predominant parasitic plants in the area. This practice was uncommon at that time, but got to be very popular later. R.A. left only one large mesquite tree in on pasture near the road as a conversation piece.

R.A. died in 1965, and management of the ranch passed to his son Rob, a 1958 graduate of Texas Tech University with a degree in Animal Science. With the help of his wife, Peggy Donnell Brown, they moved the ranch into a modern mode by adopting a number of operational changes. Peggy, herself a aughter of early pioneer ranching stock, was of great assistance. Rob was also strongly influenced by his association with Dr. Dub Waldrip, manager of the Texas Experimental Ranch, located between Throckmorton and Seymour. Rob began actively cross-breeding cattle, continued to improve the horse program, became active in range management, and started the public Brown Ranch Livestock Sale.

By 1965 Rob had begun cross-breeding Herefords. He worked with Brown Swiss cattle to develop a mother cow that would give more milk to grow a stronger calf. When he discovered that he was being penalized because of the brindle or sometimes strangely colored offspring, he brought in the Simmental, a breed whose coloration is closer to patterns of the Hereford. He began cross-breeding with Simmental and, in 1974, became president of that group. The organization added more than three thousand members during his tenure. The Simmental now ranks as the third most prevalent breed of registered cattle in the United States. The Browns also breed Black and Red Angus, Simbrah, and Senepol, and have become respected suppliers of excellent bulls.

Rob has actively continued the horse breeding program, which has ranked among the top twenty-five producers of fine horses in the United States since the late 1960s. Although the ranch did not compete in cutting, halter competition, or racing, their stock sold to participants in these activities brought the Brown's this high degree of success. Rob reduced the number of brood mares from thirty-five to thirty because his mother warned him that his father spent too much time with his horses. Sales of Brown Ranch horses have remained strong, and Rob is very proud of their history. He continues to travel widely in support of the work of the American Quarter Horse Association, and currently serves as second vice president of that group.

A good working horse requires not only good breeding, but good training as well. Rob has an agreement with his cowboys: if they do a good job training a horse and agree to sell it when it is seven or eight years old, the cowboy receives twenty-five percent of the sale price. The cowboy then starts over with another young horse, training it to do demanding ranch work.

Rob became very active in range management, and in 1974 received the Outstanding Range Management Award for the Texas area from the American Society of Range Management. He has used careful grazing practices, controlled burns, pasture rotation, and parasite brush removal to increase and improve the grazing capacity of the ranch.

Rob began having annual sales of bulls and horses each fall in order to more effectively market his livestock. These social and business events have grown in popularity over the years and are well attended. Early in October bulls are gathered, pastured close to the headquarters west of Throckmorton, then sorted into pens on sale day to be available to be available for examination by potential buyers. Here, buyers inspect the animals, and carefully examine blood lines and performance data documented in the sale catalogue.

One of the unusual highlights is the display of weaned colts for sale. The colts are haltered and tied to overhead cables in a large pen. Admiring spectators move freely among the suspicious, young animals to examine and enjoy them. At six months of age, these delicate, intelligent creatures, bred for cattle work in the cutting arena or pasture, promise careers as brood stock or working animals. They are sold to buyers in Mexico, Hawaii, and all across the United States.

Operating a ranch involves more than just the activities and efforts of the rancher. Excellent help is necessary to run a successful ranch, and that means good cowboys mounted on good horses. The Brown Ranch has been especially successful in this respect because they have worked hand-in-hand with members of the Self family for many years. George Truett Self, and his brothers Carl and Pete, started working with R.A. Brown more than sixty years ago. Truett's sons, Joe and George, continue helping on the ranch today.

Rob and Peggy's children assist in running the ranching operation: two daughters—Betsy and her husband, Jody Bellah, and Marianne and her husband, Todd McCartney—and two sons—Donnell and his wife, Kelli, and Rob A. and his wife, Talley, are actively involved. The Brown Ranch is a quality, family-run operation which continues to diversify and improve through sound family management and help from qualified cowhands. Ranches such as this that affirm the notion that ranch life in Texas is alive and well.

SEVENTEEN

Chimney Creek Ranch: An Historical Account and Personal View of a Shackelford County Ranching Heritage

THE BEGINNING

Southwest of present-day Albany the land rises on limestone hills where, especially in rare wet spring seasons, the rolling landscape is covered with waving grasses and wildflowers. Even in the more frequent dry years rich grasses sustain wildlife and livestock, although in some places the land is choked by mesquite, prickly pear, and other thorny brush. Before the white man came, this then almost treeless plain was the range of buffalo and Comanche Indians, lords of the South Plains, who trailed the migrating herds, and from the backs of their fleet horses, took from the moving brown masses what they needed for life—food, clothing, and shelter. Legend says one of the nearby canyons was a commonly used route over which the Indians traveled as they moved in their annual migration. It is an eerie feeling to look over these panoramic landscapes from the high ground at the junction of State Highways 351,

180, and 6, and imagine those horsemen of old riding past.

Cattle Car at the Chimney Creek Ranch

Today, this is cattle country. It has been since the great buffalo hunts in the 1870s eliminated the shaggy bisons from the Plains and, in 1874, Col. Ranald Mackenzie ended the threat of Plains Indian hostility. This was unfenced range in those days, but adventurous men came, tamed the wild cattle, and dug in deep to make homes here.

Ranches in this area today are well fenced and cross fenced. Cattle drink from carefully monitored stock tanks. Modern grazing practices prevail and blooded cattle roam where once longhorns grazed almost as freely as buffalo had. How this land was brought under fence can be illustrated by several of the area ranches, but an excellent example is the Chimney Creek Ranch, located west of Highway 351 about fourteen miles west of Albany. Highways 180 and 6 run across the northern part of the ranch.

When this was open range, the land and its rich grasses belonged to whoever controlled it. No thought was given to ownership. As the frontier became settled, this feeling changed; people began to homestead or buy property at very low cost. The formal ownership lineage of the property on which Chimney Creek Ranch and a Butterfield Stage station rest is somewhat detailed, and characteristic of many ownership changes. Joe Blanton's research of the records indicates that the first owners of part of the property were George B. and John F. Horsful. They conveyed it to A.W. Rhode on June 19, 1883, and he sold it to Joseph Kite on August 15, less that two months later. Nearly six years later, on February 28, 1889, the property was patented by Governor L.S. Ross to R.B. Thompson, a trustee of the estate of the late Joseph Kite. J.M. Kite, a descendant of Joseph Kite, and his wife transferred ownership of the land to Virginia A. King on January 12, 1903.

The most historic portion of the ranch, however, was that which Frank Conrad came into control of on December 19, 1888, including surveys nos. 220 and 221 of the East Texas Railroad State School land in Shackelford County, Texas. Running across this part of the property is a small creek flowing from the northwest to the east and then south. Called Chimney Creek, it is thought to have been named, Joan Farmer says, "because of the old chimney still standing from the Overland Mail Station established there." A.C. Greene in his classic *A Personal Country*, ponders the reason for the name because when he visited there he found no trace of chimney or cabin.

One of the principal historical attractions on Chimney Creek Ranch is the site of Smith Station, a stop on the old Butterfield-Overland Mail Line, whose coaches once charged across the prairie. John Butterfield's Overland Mail Company began service on September 16, 1858, when the initial coach left St. Louis, Missouri, headed for San Francisco, thus linking the still sparsely settled area along the Mississippi River with the pockets of civilization on the West Coast. The line cut its way along the 32nd parallel across vast stretches of territory still hostile from the threat of Indians, weather, and geography. It was indeed a bold step.

In order to accomplish the trip of 2,700 miles in just over twenty days (the first trip took twenty-three days and twenty-three hours), the stage needed fresh mules at regular intervals. In the area near Chimney Creek, these were obtained at Fort Belknap, on the Brazos River in present-day Young County, near Graham. Later, Franz Station would be built between there and Clear Fork Station on the banks of the Clear Fork of the Brazos. Then the stops were Smith Station and Fort Phantom Hill, the old military fort by this time abandoned and burned. The road continued to Abercrombie Pass and Fort Chadbourne, then on to Horsehead Crossing on the Pecos River, and eventually to San Francisco.

Waterman L. Ormsby rode this first coach as a newspaper correspondent and describes the area of interest. At Clear Fork Station, later Stribling Station, he says, "A log hut and corral were under construction." At Smith Station, twenty-three miles south, the line's employees lived in a tent, and a corral of brush was "nearly finished." Ormsby notes there was no timber nearby to use in constructing a pole corral. The chinks in the brush corral were filled with mud. For supper, Mrs. Smith offered "cake cooked in the coals, clear coffee, and some dried beef cooked in [her] best style." Little other record of Smith Station remains. A station house was eventually constructed of the useable chunks of limestone found in the area, and it stood unnoticed for decades. When historians and archeologists began searching for the structure, however, no trace could be found. It was later discovered that it had fallen victim to "progress." The stone had been sold to be crushed by a contractor who used the resulting gravel to form part of the base for nearby State Highway 351. Later, removal of mesquite brush by dragging a heavy chain across the area scattered any remaining evidence. The landmark is irretrievably lost, but in 1992, an archeology team from the Texas Archeological Research Library began studying the site to determine the accuracy of the location and to find any remaining artifacts.

During the late years of the 1870s or early '80s, a house was erected on the property by persons presently unknown. What is certain, however, is that the structure was adapted to the needs and potential dangers of the frontier setting. This original dwelling is today part of the north side of the main house on Chimney Creek Ranch. Built of native limestone quarried from near the site, the square house consisted of a bedroom and a living room with a fireplace all on one level. Legend has it that Confederate arms were once cached here, in case there was a need to fight the Yankees during the Civil War, but the probable time of construction, the 1870s, likely makes this account legendary rather than factual. Up about five steps was another level, which included a second bedroom with a screened-in porch. A separate kitchen stood away from the house, and the privy was down the slope from the kitchen. Between the house and the privy stood a springhouse, a small structure covered in the summer by trumpet vines, and naturally cooled by spring water flowing through it.

The coming of the railroad eliminated the need for trail drives to markets. This expanding rail system brought the demise of bypassed towns and gave birth or new life to others. This was the case for Fort Griffin and Albany. When the fort closed, the buffalo were all killed, and the railroad passed Fort Griffin by in favor of Albany, Frank Conrad and other citizens left the banks of the Clear Fork in search of a better life. The Texas Central Railroad made Albany a far better choice for a businessman, so Conrad reopened his mercantile business there in early 1882. Conrad ran a successful business. In her application to the Texas State Historical Commission for a marker for the Bud Matthews railroad pens, Joan Farmer quotes one of Conrad's advertisements in the Albany News: "We were here in Indian times, we sold goods in soldier times. We did a little business here in buffalo times. We went slow here in hard times. We handled wool here in sheep man's times. We boomed things in booming times." Indeed, Conrad had seen the boom and bust of the frontier economy. Conrad sold his store in 1891 to devote full time to ranching. For unknown reasons, he committed suicide on May 4, 1892, the day he turned fifty years of age. He left Ella, his wife, with five children between the ages of two and ten. Following her husband's death, Mrs. Conrad relied heavily on the advice of her brother, John A. Matthews, area rancher and prominent county judge. His son, Watt Matthews, can recall traveling by buggy and wagon to visit his Aunt Ella. He remembers that his father and mother sat on the front seat because his father drove the team, and the children sat in the back. They followed the rutted trail of the Butterfield-Overland Mail, which provided the most direct route across their Lambshead Ranch to Smith Station on Chimney Creek Ranch.

No doubt with the encouragement of Matthews, Mrs. Conrad granted a right-of-way to the Texas Central Railroad Company to lay railroad tracks through her property, to move the line toward Stamford in 1900, and then on to Rotan by 1906. A set of cattle pens and a loading chute, to enable Mrs. Conrad and her neighbors to load cattle into railroad cars for shipment to market in the northern and eastern outlets, was designed and constructed by Mr. Matthews, and named "Matthews, Texas," by Mrs. Conrad. When she learned that the name "Matthews" was already used by the railroad to designate another site, she added her brother's nickname to make it "Bud Matthews, Texas." It was located at Texas Central Milepost No. 201.9, a number meaning the distance of this point from Waco, Texas. Farmer notes that many ranchers are known to have used the facility over the following years, including the Monroe Cattle Company, which controlled about 30,000 acres of range nearby; George W. P. Coates, whose ranch was southeast of the pens about five miles; Reynolds Cattle Company; W. I. Cook; Dawson and Company; and the Rafter Three Ranch.

On July 20, 1909, Mrs. Conrad purchased additional property from Virginia King to swell the acreage of Chimney Creek Ranch to 14,000.

G.R. DAVIS—THE LEGACY BEGINS

In 1920 the ranch was purchased from the Ella Conrad heirs—John N., Louie B., and George Reynolds Conrad—by George Robert Davis, a member of one of several families already established in ranching east of Breckenridge. G.R. was born July 18, 1869, one of eight children of John Love Davis and Loiza Crawford Davis. The family came to Stephens County in 1890 from Kaufman, east of Dallas. These early families made an impact on the area. G.R.'s sister Alice married Breck, actually Breckenridge, Walker, regarded as the first white child born at a settlement in Stephens County. The town of Breckinridge is named for him. Today it is the county seat of Stephens County and is an important trading center.

G.R. married Hattie Collins (born January 19, 1870), remembered by her granddaughter, Mary Frances "Chan" Driscoll, as "a delicate, sensitive, pretty school teacher." G.R. himself she recalls as a hard-working, intelligent, personable, honest rancher, who soon became the village druggist as well. Davis sold ranch property east of Breckenridge to pay for the Chimney Creek Ranch, and enlarged the original house by adding first a dining room and then a makeshift kitchen. Later, Mr. Davis bought another house and moved it to the site, where he joined all the units together to form a single dwelling. This latter section provided room for a spacious kitchen and pantry, and allowed the old kitchen to become a dining room. In the 1920s he arranged construction of a rock wall around the yard and, north of the house, a small bunkhouse for the cowboys. A large barn constructed of sheet iron on a wooden framework, which stands to the northeast of the house, served to store feed and shelter animals and wagons. Built around the turn of the century, it has been strengthened and modernized, but it still has the flavor of an old ranch barn. South of the house stood a carriage house that sheltered the Davis's car until the structure was torn down because of damage by termites and habitation by skunks.

Mr. Davis granted an easement to the Missouri-Kansas-Texas Railroad Company and agreed to construct "stock pens and cattle concentration yards." From these pens cattle continued to be shipped, especially by the Davis family, to pastures operated by Glen Hawthorne in Eureka, Kansas. There the stock was pastured and then shipped to feedlots, or to market in Kansas City. Later shipments went to Fort Worth by rail and truck. The MKT agreed to an annual payment of $9.65 for a period of fifteen years, and further agreed to negotiate the contract on an annual basis for as long as the agreement was beneficial to both parties. Farmer notes that these new pens were enlargements of the existing pens at Bud Matthews switch. The MKT evidently used the existing rails for access because only one set of tracks has ever crossed the ranch. The agreement later terminated at an unknown date, and the rails have since been removed.

G.R. Davis ran the ranch from its purchase in 1920 until his death on December 31, 1955. The operation produced quality Hereford cattle and horses trained for cattle work, not for the show ring or racetrack. During many of these years he was aided by the efforts of his son, Louie.

As G.R. grew older, Louie's role in runnung the ranch became significant, especially during the middle fifties when a terrible drought gripped the area. Frugal by nature, Louie kept a tight grip on the operation and saw it through the trials of a time when many ranchers went broke and gave up. The ranch was his life, and he was uncomfortable any time he was away from it. He was both a good cowboy and a good rancher/businessman, and he devoted his life to Chimney Creek Ranch.

On days when the ranch conducted its annual roundup and shipping, the work began early. Cowboys from other ranches had risen well before daylight, saddled their horses, and ridden in to help. No trailers were available to haul horses in those days. Pastures were large and required many riders spreading the dragnet to assure gathering all the cattle, a chore which usually required until nearly noon to accomplish.

The lunch of chuckwagon food typically included roast beef, pinto beans, cole slaw, sliced tomatoes, lightbread, and coffee. Peach pickles or homemade pies served as dessert. Mrs. Davis herself prepared this food and had it ready for the crew when the appropriate time came.

After the men had lunch, they separated the stock into desired groupings, and those animals to be shipped were loaded aboard rail cars and started on the long journey to Kansas City, Fort Worth, or some other distant market. A problem that regularly caused difficulty around railroad shipping corrals was an apparent requirement that the train crew had to sound the whistle on the train at given times. This whistle blowing often interfered with gathering the cattle. Unaccustomed to this sound, cows became extremely frightened and tended to bolt wildly into stampede when the whistle surprised them. More than one crew of cowboys had to repeat rounding up the cattle after an engineer had seen fit to sound his whistle.

After many years living on the ranch, the Davis family moved to Abilene to a house which they had built at 718 Victoria Street. Mrs. Davis had longed for a prairie mansion in town, and Mr. Davis built a fine one, with three floors, a basement, and servants' quarters over a two-car garage. After years of heavy labor, Mrs. Davis had a maid to help with the hard work, and the family assumed the lifestyle of the cattle baron, alongside such other ranching families in Abilene as the Guitars, Caldwells, and others. Mr. Davis also purchased other ranches; the Throckmorton County ranch, part of which is now called Comanche Crest, earlier known as Box Springs, was bought in the late 1930s from Reynolds Cattle Company. In the 1940s, Mr. Davis purchased a ranch located on FM 1492 between Midland/Odessa and Crane in Upton County. He knew the land was of little use in ranching, but its potential for mineral income would later be important to the family. The part of the Box Springs Ranch inherited by Mary Frances Driscoll has been named Comanche Crest by the family. Her portion of the Upton County ranch is known as Buffalo Basin.

During this time, oil was discovered on the Davis property. Near Chimney Creek Ranch, on a draw southwest of the headquarters, a large power "station" was constructed in the 1930s to help pump some of the oil wells in the area. Referred to by the family members as "The Power," it was a device featuring a large wheel to which several cables were attached. The cables ran exposed over the top of the ground, and were kept out of the dirt by threading them through holes or "eyes" cut in pipe set upright in the ground. These cables provided the power to pumpjacks of six to eight oil wells in the vicinity. The entire unit was run, Louie Bob Davis remembers, by a very noisy pumping unit likely fueled by natural gas from one of the wells. The device was certainly an awesome sight on the rolling prairies of Shackelford County.

Once the family had moved to town, G.R. regularly came to the ranch to supervise its operation. Louie had primary responsibility for much of this work, with the help of a man whose efforts at Chimney Creek and other Davis ranches came to be appreciated by the family.

Grady Smith began working for the Davises in the spring of 1924, first on a ranch near Chimney Creek, formerly owned by the Cauble family. Later Smith moved to Chimney Creek, living and working as a foreman on the ranch for several years. When the Davises moved to Abilene, the Smith family moved into the main ranch house, and two of the Smith's children were born. Florene, one of the Smith's daughters, recalls sleeping on the screened-in porches during the warm months. She has very fond recollections of playing outdoors around the back of the house during the summer when the weather was simply splendid. She also remembers sleeping in the north bedroom during the wintertime. Her principal recollection of the large basement underneath the house is that on more than one occasion her parents heard rattlesnakes there. Since snakes have long been a problem in this part of the country, it was not unusual to find them in such a setting. She does recall that her father killed snakes in that basement. Mr Davis also left a loaded Colt .45 caliber pistol for her mother to use against snakes when he was gone. On one occasion, Florene remembers, her mother saw a snake not far from where the girls were playing. After she had moved them safely into the house, she emptied the gun into the snake and literally shot it to pieces.

Florene's recollections also include going to Albany to school. On the neighboring Buck Nail Ranch, a family named Meadows had a daughter who joined her on the school bus. Also on an adjacent ranch was a family named Harris, whose children made the bus ride from the ranch country into Albany to school.

Smith's routine work on the ranch ran as did that of most other cowboys—sunup to sundown, seven days a week. He spent many hours riding horseback, checking cattle in the pastures five days a week, usually Monday through Friday, and then Saturdays and Sundays were spent building or repairing fences, or performing other tasks required to keep the place going during those depression years when everyone was strapped financially, and had to carry the load regardless of the imposition.

Florene has strong memories of the people who visited the ranch, especially those from the Swenson Ranches, one of which was located near Lueders. In addition to Eric Swenson, one of the family members was a man whose reputation lives on, "Scandalous" John

Selmon figured prominently in Swenson Ranch history for many years, and his role in the Texas Cowboy Reunion at Stamford is fondly remembered by those who attended during the long time he was active.

Smith's role with respect to the Bud Matthews' pens is also noteworthy. Around 1930 Smith undertook the task of rebuilding the pens. He made a deal with Parker Sears, who ran a lumber yard in Albany, to purchase pine lumber for the project. The lumber, as Florene recalls, was beautiful pine that did not warp when left out in the sun and was free of knots, certainly a remarkable condition considering the inferior quality of contemporary pine lumber. Smith hauled the lumber from Albany to the site in a new 1929 Ford truck which, characteristic of motor vehicles of the day, could not carry much weight but finally accomplished the task. During these depression years, cash payment for the lumber was supplemented by a number of swine raised on the ranch. Sears took the hogs in trade and sent them to East Texas, where members of his family had a great deal of corn available to feed the hogs. For many years thereafter, Sears humorously reminded Smith how disastrous the trade had proved for him because he ended up selling the hogs for less than he had allowed Smith on the trade. The posts, used in the repair of the pens, though of poor quality because the bottom ends were so much larger than the tops, were purchased by Louie Davis and Mr. Smith in Palo Pinto, a community in a cedar growing area between Albany and Fort Worth. Smith's efforts, however, kept the pens from falling into complete disrepair for many years.

One amusing incident related to the use of the pens involves the time when persons, whose identity Florene cannot recall, drove a herd of buffalo into the pens with the intention of shipping the animals out by rail. Buffalo are very difficult to manage, but the cowboys finally succeeded in penning them in the corrals, which held up to their battering. Once the rail cars were in place, the men began loading, but the buffalo, distressed at being confined, began bursting boards off the sides of the rail cars. The conductor, a man who had some ranch experience himself, encouraged the men, "You men need to get these animals loaded and gone before they tear up those cars." Florene recalls that the project succeeded, but barely, and only because of the strength of the lumber used in the construction of the cars.

Another amusing anecdote from the above story involved Eric Swenson who, like many a cowboy, had a desire to rope one of the buffalo bulls. Grady Smith wisely declined the opportunity, but when Eric said, "If I head him, will you heel him?" Grady responded in the affirmative, but was relieved when Eric changed his mind and decided not to rope the bison.

Later, Smith was moved to the Goodwyn Ranch, adjacent to the Cauble, when the Davises bought it in 1937. In all, he worked for the Davis family for nineteen years. He left ranch work in 1945 because he had not fully recovered from an injury sustained earlier when, as he stepped up onto a horse, his foot slipped and he pulled the horse over onto himself. Smith felt he could no longer contribute to the workload on the ranch. He purchased a store in Hamby, between the ranch and Abilene and operated it for many years. The Davises were good customers. Grady Smith died December 16, 1986.

Other cowboys who helped run the ranch over the years included Clarence Holt, and Lewis Burfield, and Duncan Leech. Leech lived on Chimney Creek Ranch when G.R. Davis passed away.

THE CHILDREN OF G.R. DAVIS

The family of G.R. Davis consisted of three children—Louie, Robbie, and Oma Frances, whose nickname was Pet. Louie and Oma remained at home and took care of the parents until late in the lives of these children. Louie married Ouida Beavers in 1938, and they had one son, Louie Bob. Louie died March 29, 1966, and his wife died June 24, 1987. Oma married Claude Touchstone. She died tragically in an automobile accident near Merkel in the summer of 1941 while still a young woman, on her way to visit the new infant, Louie Bob Davis.

On July 18, 1921, on Chimney Creek Ranch the second child,

Robbie, married T. Edgar Johnson, a lawyer trained at the University of Texas and Oxford University. The ceremony was held under the large pecan tree in the backyard of the main house. Johnson practiced law in Breckenridge but, in those depression days, his clients were often unable to pay for services rendered. With the help of his father-in-law, Johnson purchased a Ford automobile agency in Vernon. He added a Ford tractor distributorship and other outlets, for not only for Ford products, but for Lincoln and Mercury as well. Mr. Johnson came to bill himself as the oldest car dealer in North Texas.

On April 20, 1922, Robbie gave birth to Mary Frances. Because of Robbie's many physical problems, Mary Frances spent a great deal of time on Chimney Creek Ranch with her grandparents, and grew to love it. She spent every summer there in her early years. She recalls seeing bob white quail and other game, but especially clear are her memories of Uncle Louie using string to harness two large grasshoppers to an empty match box for a make-believe stagecoach to go along with his stories of the Butterfield Stage stop on the ranch.

Mary Frances recalls that the regular meat choice for Sunday lunch was chicken in those early days. She can still remember watching her grandmother wring the chicken's neck. The flock of chickens from which this Sunday lunch regularly came had to be penned up at night to keep predators from killing them.

Other memories are strong. Like many families in similar situations, they made lye soap in the washpot, with lye leeched from the ashes of the fireplace and cooking fires. There was an outhouse, with a half moon cut in the door, featuring facilities for two people, thus being called a two-holer, complete with the Montgomery Ward catalog. The ranch had no electricity, so lighting came from kerosene lamps. Butter was churned from cream which rose to the top of the milk from a cow kept for the purpose, and canning provided vegetables during the winter. There was a smokehouse where pork was cured. Mary Frances remembers that her grandmother taught her to cook and sew, and "Mamaw," as she was called by her only granddaughter, patiently pieced quilts to provide colorful coverings for the family bedding. This kind of life was normal for many families of this period. Cattle and horse operations continued in much the same manner with shipping still done from the Bud Matthews Switch.

Upon the death of G.R. Davis on December 31, 1955, Robbie Davis Johnson inherited Chimney Creek Ranch from her father. Mrs. Johnson knew that she would be unable to operate it, so on July 1, 1957, Mrs. Johnson leased the ranch to C.B. "Charlie" Waller and Robert and Ruby Waller, operating as Waller Cattle Company. Thus began the period of absentee landlords on Chimney Creek Ranch.

Waller Cattle Company has been productive. Charlie, along with his wife Ella, ran the ranch in partnership with their son, Robert, and his wife. When Charlie died December 28, 1973, Robert, a Texas A&M University graduate, continued operating the ranch, and later formed a partnership with his son, Robert C., a graduate in Texas Tech University. Together, they have worked to improve the ranch in various ways. When Robert and his father first took over the ranch, the fourteen thousand acre spread was still in very large pastures. One pasture contained eleven sections. Ever since they have taken over, however, they have been cutting the pastures up into smaller, more manageable tracts. For example, on the southwest corner a four-section pasture has now been cut into four single-section pastures. Early fencing on the ranch was done with barbed wire and cedar posts, but in more recent times, five-wire construction on steel posts, with four-inch pipe corners set with braces has been used. Now, about two-thirds of the ranch is fenced in this more contemporary and longer-lasting fashion.

Water for the cattle comes from surface tanks, supplemented by water pumped from a well not far from the house into twenty-two knee tubs scattered across the ranch. These were originally metal tubs, but as the metal began to deteriorate, cement linings were placed in the tubs. Water is pumped by a one and one-half horsepower submersible pump, which in addition to keeping the tanks full, also provides water for the house. The pipeline is of plastic pipe, either the kind glued together in sections or soft-laid plastic pipe.

Only five or six geldings trained for working cattle are kept on the ranch by the Wallers. When new horses are needed, the Wallers buy desirable animals rather than raising their own. Mr. Waller felt that ranchers raising their own horses have trouble getting the animals broken to ride and trained to work, and then face the dangers inherent in riding unpredictable young horses.

The Wallers' cattle operation includes about five hundred mother cows, a hundred and fifty replacement heifers, and about forty bulls, continuing the commercial cow-calf endeavor begun by the Davises. Originally, the ranch stocked Hereford cattle, but by 1973, the Wallers were using Black Angus bulls on first-calf heifers and keeping these cross-bred offspring as replacement heifers. Gradually, the Herefords were phased out in favor of the Angus crosses. Still later, looking for additional new blood to cross-breed with, the Wallers selected Chianina and black Maine Anjou bulls. They have also used Charolais and Limousin bulls. Although they keep a hundred registered Angus cows on the ranch, the Wallers buy Angus bulls from the R J Ranch at Briggs, and Chianina bulls from Black Champ at Waxahachie. The Maine Anjou bulls come from Billy Dillard and Herman Boone.

Shipping on the ranch is still done from the Bud Matthews pens. From the beginning of their time on the ranch until the early 1970s, the Wallers shipped on the railroad. In the early '70s, however, the tracks were torn up, and the Wallers began shipping by truck. On a typical shipping day around the first of June, nine or ten day workers are hired to help. The cattle are shipped out on large cattle vans provided by the contract buyer. The Wallers will congregate the cattle in one or two pastures close to the pens and, on shipping day, push them into the pens for separating and shipping. The pens have recently been restored and the original sign, rescued years ago by Watt Matthews and kept safely for the occasion, was returned to the site. Robert Waller can remember during his tenure shipping on the railroad that such ranches as Bluff Creek, Cook, Dawson Conway, and McComas also shipped out of the pens. He thinks more cattle were shipped from the Bud Matthews pens than from the rail shipping point in Albany.

The cattle shipped from this area typically go to pasture, often wheat fields in Kansas and Nebraska, to condition and toughen them before going into the feedlot. Waller indicates that the calves coming off the cows are "juicy," with a low tolerance for disease. The animals need time on pasture to be ready for the feedlot.

One exception to this pattern occurred during the early 1970s when a government program caused large numbers of dairy cattle to be put on the slaughter beef market. The buyer contracted for that year declined to take the Wallers' cattle, and they were put into a feedlot. It was not a good experience because the calves were easy victims of disease and other ailments, and just did not grow off well. The government program helped dairy farmers but proved harmful to those raising beef cattle.

Ranches bordering Chimney Creek include the Newell Ranch across part of the east and the Merrick Davis Ranch on the south. About four miles of fenceline is shared with the Akers Ranch and the Buck Nail. Schkade Brothers, Pete Baker, and Dawson Conway touch the ranch on the west and part of the northwest. Bluff Creek Ranch covers the north boundary. About 1700 acres of the ranch is north of U.S. Highway 180 and State Highway 6.

Leasing of hunting rights for deer and quail on the ranch is handled by the owners. There are two hunter's cabins—a trailer house on the southern part of the ranch and a hunter's house on the northern part.

When Watt Matthews had the Buck Nail Ranch leased, he transplanted nineteen antelope onto the ranch. These later migrated to Chimney Creek Ranch. Rather than prospering, however, the group has shrunk to a small herd of six or eight antelope. Coyotes and poachers take too many of the animals. Waller has noticed that if any big bucks grow up in the herd, they soon disappear, probably victims of poachers. He also said that recently no buck had been with the does on the ranch until the great range fire in the 1988 destroyed the net wire fencing and burned about 3,000 acres. Then a buck from the Akers Ranch came over. Net wire had been an effective barrier against antelope, because their tendency is to crawl under fences rather than to jump over them, as deer do.

Waller and his son, Robert C., are still running a prosperous ranching operation and providing an opportunity for Robert C. and Carolyn's children, Rob and Will, to grow up in a ranching atmosphere. Carolyn is a librarian in the Albany school system, and she and Robert C. live in town rather than on the ranch. This is a more convenient arrangement since children tend to be involved in school activities and unnecessary travel is required to get children to and from the ranch, especially since some of this must be done at night.

THE NEXT GENERATION

In 1973 the ownership of Chimney Creek Ranch passed to Mary Frances "Chan" Driscoll, the only surviving child of Robbie and T. Edgar Johnson. Robbie Lou, Mary Frances' sister, had died in infancy.

Mary Frances recalls clearly many of her adventures on the ranch, but one of those uppermost in her mind is her abortive career as a horsewoman. When she was small, her grandfather bought her a Shetland pony, and proudly outfitted it with a black saddle trimmed in white with silver mountings. On her first ride, the cankerous horse pitched her off and stepped on her stomach, a tactic requiring X-rays to determine that no serious damage had been done to her. From then on she rode only in front of her grandfather on his horse, if she rode at all. He enjoyed her company as he rode the pastures of Chimney Creek, checking stock, grass, and water. She never became an avid horsewoman, and later discovered she was allergic to horses. She still remembers that at summer girls' camps, especially the Glen Rose Girl Scout Camp, she was always expected to be an expert horsewoman because she was "a ranch girl." She never lived up to that expectation, and came to accept her non-equestrian preferences.

Under Mary Frances' ownership, Waller Cattle Company has continued to operate under a lease agreement. She maintains a small home on the ranch, a building constructed in the early 1980s just south of the main house, on the site of the old smokehouse and chicken coup, designed to be a very nice, modern, rural retreat or weekend cottage. There is a two-car carport on the north side, a stone fence around the yard, and an area for pitching horseshoes, playing baseball, croquet, badminton, as well as for target shooting. The décor features old wagon wheels. No all-night guard lights interrupt the serenity of the nights on Chimney Creek Ranch. Care is taken to watch for rattlesnakes, and many of them have been found and killed in the house area. Mary Frances often remarks, "This is my heaven on earth. Chimney Creek Ranch is a peaceful spot."

CONCLUSION

Today, Chimney Creek Ranch remains a working operation under the careful management of Robert and Robert C. Waller. In many ways it is unchanged. The waving grasses have flourished in the wet years of the early 1990s, and in the spring and summer sleek cattle and horses graze on the hillsides where the buffalo and Indians once roamed at will. The winter winds still whip across the land in the cold months, and the wild game flourishes. Admittedly, contemporary life has made its impression on the ranch in the form of improvements in watering facilities, fencing, brush and cacti control programs, and buildings. But the land still stands in mute testimony to its original condition, with its nourishing forage on the limestone enriched soil and its history stemming from the Butterfield Overland Mail and the other historical figures who once traveled the area: Waterman Ormsby, Robert E. Lee, and others.

Two historical markers on the ranch witness to the part played by the shipping pens at Bud Matthews Switch and by the Butterfield Overland Mail. The descendents of G.R. Davis are a credit to themselves for reserving for the rest of us these remnants of a past that reinforces our hold on the future.

APPENDIX

Two historical markers have been erected on the ranch property. The first, for Smith Station, erected in 1982, reads:

Smith's Station

From 1858 until the outbreak of the Civil War in 1861, a station of the Butterfield Overland Mail Route was located here. Despite a brief existence, it was an important stop on the early stage line that reached from Missouri to California. Stages made the trip in under 25 days, a marked improvement on earlier communication links with the rapidly developing West. Located on Chimney Creek between stage stops at Clear Fork (26 Mi. NE) and Fort Phantom Hill (12 Mi. SW), Smith's Station was the only Butterfield stop located in present Shackelford County.

The second marker is for Bud Matthews Switch, erected in 1993. It reads:

Bud Matthews Switch of the Texas Central Railway

In 1900 the Texas Central Railway extended a line Northwest from Albany across this portion of Rose Ella (Matthews) Conrad's cattle ranch. Ella and her brother John A. "Bud" Matthews, for whom this site is named, promptly constructed cattle pens and a loading chute at this location. Surrounding ranchers soon were shipping their cattle from this switch to markets in Fort Worth. As many as 105,000 head of cattle were shipped annually until the railroad ceased operations in 1967. Since that year local ranchers have continued to load cattle onto trucks from this site.

EIGHTEEN
THE EVERETT BROTHERS: BOUND BY BIRTH TO THE RANCHING TRADITION

In the pale glow of two kerosene lamps, the men bent over their plates of sausage, eggs, biscuits, and coffee on the rustic pine board table. Outside, the faint glow in the east announced the coming day. One of the men rose and carried his plate to the sink, his spurs jangling as he walked. He donned his large brimmed felt hat, pulled on his leggings, and spoke to his friends: "I'm going out to get those horses in." One of the other figures followed him out, pulling on his chaps as he went. The others rose, cleared the table, and got their gear together. The last one to leave blew out the kerosene lamps.

A scene that likely occurred a century ago in this same setting, the early morning cowboy ritual was repeated as it had been for more than a hundred years in this same house along Paint Creek, in Throckmorton County of West Texas. The date was April, 1993, on what was known for many years as the Reynolds Brothers' X Ranch at Round Mountain, now called the Everett Brothers' X Ranch at Round Mountain. This ranch is not to be confused with another famous Reynolds ranch, the Long X Ranch near Kent, in far West Texas.

Carl Everett performs the job of cook with unusual skill, a rite still enacted on the property three or four times a year when the Everett brothers bring in a crew of cowboys for several days of work required to keep up with the annual cycle of chores on the ranch. The use of propane gas helps with the cooking, and an old Servel refrigerator serves as that modern necessity. Water from the metal cistern catching runoff from the roof still provides suitable drinking water.

The brothers also come here to hunt in the fall, and find large-rack whitetail deer and feral hogs plentiful. In fact, leased hunting of deer is an important part of the business enterprise of the ranch, and hunting of hogs is getting a serious look because of possible income and the destructive nature of the animals, which are all too plentiful along Paint Creek.

The everyday activities are carried out by Sonny Vincent, a cowboy from Throckmorton. On this day, the crew consisted of Vincent; Carl and Jim Everett; Big Boy Mercer, a long-time employee of the family; and Trey Robertson, himself a descendent of an early-day Texas ranching family.

Also participating was George Peacock, now manager of the Nail Ranch in Shackelford County. As a young man he was one of the hands who, along with Mercer, worked for Ross Sloan on this ranch in the late 1950s. They stayed in the bunkhouse with Tom Compton, who lived full-time on this remote ranch for years.

Peacock and Mercer had stayed there mostly when work was to be done, and moved to other ranches owned by Sloan when necessary. Peacock still recalls sleeping in the unheated bunkhouse in the winter and racing into the north wind in the early morning to go light the fire in the kitchen of the house, so the men could have a little warmth with their breakfast.

One thing that separates the X Ranch from others in the same area is the wonder of electricity has not yet penetrated. The remoteness and relative primitiveness are two attractions to the men who work here, and to Jim and Carl Everett and their sister, Julie Sloan Watson, owners of the ranch.

When William D. and George T. Reynolds, famous shakers and

movers in the early day cattle business, began establishing ranches across the West, one of these ranches was very close to the home range of the Matthews and Reynolds families, present-day Lambshead Ranch, along the Clear Fork of the Brazos River in current Shackelford and Throckmorton counties of West Texas. Lambshead, still run by 95-year-old Watkins Reynolds "Watt" Matthews, a descendent of the Reynolds-Matthews families. Matthews is considered the dean of Texas cattlemen and was honored with a Wrangler Award from the National Cowboy Hall of Fame at the 1990 Western Heritage Award ceremonies.

This nearby property was first controlled by Thomas Lambshead, one of the earliest settlers in the region, and by 1880 was in the hands of the Matthews and Reynolds families. Three years later, the Reynolds brothers gained control.

In 1892, the brothers erected their headquarters: a spacious two-story house, large two-story barn, stone smokehouse, and, eventually, two bunkhouses and a cookhouse. The steep banks of Paint Creek plunge off just behind the house, running close to the smokehouse, cookhouse, and bunkhouse, not far from the stream's confluence with the Clear Fork of the Brazos.

Recently modern corrals made of pipe and net wire, with a modern working chute, have been added to replace older ones. Standing starkly against the sky to the northeast of the house is well-known Round Mountain, the site where Captain Randolph B. Marcy, an early military explorer and mapmaker, held talks with Sanaco, leader of a band of Comanche Indians.

Another notable landmark stands on the property. Sitting atop Round Mountain is a cement water tank bearing the date 1928. Legend says that Work Projects Administration labor helped construct the facility, which held water pumped from the creek by a windmill now standing in ruins nearby. From the tank, water was gravity fed down to the house and other watering places at headquarters.

The roofs of the house and barn, as well as the top of the mountain, are visible from high ground on Lambshead Ranch to the east, but access to the property is circuitous by way of County Road 2584 near Throckmorton, then on a gravel road for several miles through more than half a dozen cattle guards and gates. The road ends in the yard of the X Ranch headquarters.

This ranch made up part of the empire of the Reynolds Brothers, but as days stretched on and times got hard by the end of the Great Depression in the late 1930s, the family sold the property to invest in other ways and to pay debts. In 1940, Stephens County rancher Ross Sloan bought the property, although he did not take possession of its 24,000 acres until 1941. Sloan's ancestors had pioneered the area around current day Breckenridge and Crystal Falls before the turn of the century.

The ranch acquired from the Reynolds already had a proud heritage, but the Sloan family era was just as rewarding. Sloan passed a major portion of the X Ranch on to his daughter, Jenny Sloan Stanley, who is proud of her link to the early day ranching culture. Her sons, current owners Carl and Jim Everett, with her guidance, have dedicated themselves to obtaining more land and leaving it in better condition than when they received it, as a legacy for their 10 children.

These owners are, indeed, interesting individuals. Carl graduated from high school in Breckenridge, attended New Mexico Military Institute, and then transferred to Texas Tech University, where he earned a Bachelor of Science degree in accounting. "I knew at the time I was not really interested in accounting, but I seemed inclined in that direction," he related.

His brother, Jim, followed a similar path after graduating from high school in Breckenridge and from New Mexico Military Institute. He attended Texas Christian University, earning a Bachelor of Business Administration degree, and later a degree in law from Southern Methodist University. Although he is licensed to practice law, like his brother, Jim has had no interest in working in the traditional business world.

That the Everett brothers ended up in ranching is not unusual. Jim remembers his mother often told her sons about helping her father on the ranch, so it is no surprise that she groomed her children to take over the operation at the appropriate time. And they did so with a pride of profession and ownership. They run this ranch, along with the Crystal Falls Ranch, north of Breckenridge; the Drummonds Ranch, northeast of Albany; the Talley Ranch, in Throckmorton County near Woodson, Texas; and the Colmor Ranch, near Springer, New Mexico.

Why do these young men prefer this rustic life to that of the professions for which they trained? Jim says, "I think it's a love for this way of life. Carl and I know that we could probably make more money in those professions, but this way of life is in our blood. I'd rather be here than in a courtroom or in an office wading through books." College was only a necessity for them in case things did not work out well in ranching. But they say they are bound by birth to this way of life.

The Everetts began operating the property in 1978 in partnership with their mother, and ended up with almost 24,000 acres, part of which was the more than 12,500 acres belonging to the headquarters portion of the X Ranch. They have added an additional 4,000 acres to their holdings since 1978.

The ranch is characterized by hills, steep draws, and heavy brush, and the Everetts run mostly steers on the ranch. About 220 acres in the flat, fertile land along the creek is given over to winter grazing of wheat and oats.

One of the pastures borders property on the Lambshead Ranch where Robert E. Lee, a commander at Camp Cooper, staked a new site for the military post and ordered bake ovens built to help feed his troops. Today, only the ruins of the ovens silently attest to Lee's effort. For some reason, the land was abandoned and the troops moved back to the original site.

The Everetts' property was seriously damaged in 1978 by the devastating Albany-area flood. At the height of the deluge, water rose halfway up in the second story of the ranchhouse. Although moved slightly off its foundation, the house survived and has been restored to its frontier simplicity. A large screened-in porch was added on the south. The stone smokehouse, constructed originally from stone taken from the site of Camp Cooper, withstood the flood without any apparent damage. The cookhouse, blacksmith shop, and bunkhouse, however, were washed away. The bunkhouse settled in a field nearby, but was completely ruined and had to be destroyed. The original wood barn, now covered with sheet iron, withstood the flood and stands as it did when first constructed in 1892.

On that day in April of 1993, before the men rode off to finish gathering cattle, Geoge Peacock led a walking tour of the property. It was a nostalgic trip for him. The sparsely furnished rooms of the house show only men's preferences. Walking through the reconstructed bunkhouse and the land around the headquarters, Peacock recounted numerous incidents of good times he had experienced on the ranch.

After lunch, the men recalled old stories and added new ones to the body of oral lore that makes up part of this ranch's history. They told tales of Tom Compton's futile efforts to ride a team of wild mules, his efforts to capture feral hogs by himself, his mistrust and lack of understanding of the world outside the ranch in the 1950s. Carl says of these talk-swapping ventures down memory lane: "It seems like the recounting of cowboy tales has always taken place on the old porch—after eating—and all of the day's adventures are reenacted. This has been a special place for me, first as a young boy and now, as the manager. The closeness of God's earth and the camaraderie of men are two vital ingredients to the history of this ranch." It may be difficult for those sitting in offices, or even in fairly remote locations with the benefits of electricity, air conditioning, and the like, to imagine a situation such as this exists on the X Ranch today. But it does.

Carl recollects that, following the flood of 1978 when they were in the process of rebuilding the structures on the property, they made an effort to get electricity to the ranch. "But it is just too far from any other electricity," Carl says. "Now I'm glad we didn't secure the service because it would take something away from the aura of the property. We love coming here. It's like a breath of fresh air for us, and it is something we look forward to doing every year."

NINETEEN

The Reynolds Brothers and The Long X Ranch

When George T. and William D. Reynolds established the Long X Ranch in the Davis Mountains of far West Texas in 1895, they had no way of knowing that, a century later, a direct descendant of William D. would still have a large portion of the original Long X working and prospering. Not that the founders lacked perseverance, hardiness, or vision. George T. and William D. Reynolds, had a long history of frontier activity, trail driving, and cattle ranching over a vast part of the American West. Their story begins in 1847 when they came with their mother, Anne Marie Campbell Reynolds, on a steamboat from Alabama to Shreveport, Louisiana, and then on to Texas to join their father, Barber Watkins Reynolds, who preceded them to make ready for their coming.

On their way to west, the Reynolds family stopped for a time in Shelby County in East Texas. Water and timber made the area attractive, and the customs were much like what they were used to in the Old South. Logs existed for cabin construction, water was readily available, and rainfall was sufficient for growing crops. However, the family felt the call of the open plains, where cattle ranching was more promising than in East Texas.

On August 3, 1859, the Reynolds family loaded up in wagons and headed to the town of Galconda (later Palo Pinto) in Palo Pinto County, west of Fort Worth. After a short stay, they moved to the Cantrell Ranch on Gonzales Creek, near the present-day town of Breckenridge, then in Buchannan County, later renamed Stephens County, which it remains today.

Within a year, the Reynolds clan was part of a loosely organized community of hardy pioneers who had settled in the area along the Clear Fork of the Brazos River in what would prove to be excellent cattle country, now divided into Stephens, Throckmorton, and Shackelford counties. By this time the Reynoldses had eight children: John Archibald, who died in childhood; George Thomas; William David; Susan Emily; Glenn; Benjamin Franklin II; Phineas Watkins; and Sallie Ann.

As years passed and the children grew, George and W.D. began working on their own. George's first job outside the family was to carry mail from Galconda to Weatherford, some twenty miles to the east. Because Indians were a problem at the time, he often rode the route in darkness to avoid detection. At age eighteen he enlisted in Company E, 19th Texas Cavalry, to fight under the leadership of Col. Nat Buford on the Confederate side in the Civil War. When his service ended, he returned home.

W.D. remained in Texas during the war and served in the Frontier Battalion, a paramilitary Texas Ranger force that helped protect settlers on the Texas frontier from Indian depredations. The Indian raiders had apparently decided they were winning in their efforts to purge the area of whites, because the regular troops had been transferred out to fight on battlefields in the South, far from the Texas frontier. The Frontier Battalion was spread thin over a wide area, but it was the best protection available for settlers at the time. Once the war was over, the brothers returned to their ranching interests and became active in the trail driving that led to the establishment of ranches across the West. Both men later found their military training useful, because over the following years they would face more than one life-and-death situation.

Entrance to the Long X Ranch

In mid-October of 1865, George put together a herd of about eighty steers, drove them to Mexico, and turned a profit. On this trip, he traveled over what would become the first stretch of the Goodnight-Loving Trail, which followed the Pecos along the Butterfield Overland Mail route. This segment of the route was well planned and laid out, had available water, and was well marked in many places by the ruts of Butterfield coaches. On his drive George followed the stage line as far as Horsehead Crossing, that famous landmark on the Pecos River, and then pushed into Mexico. At this point the trail bearing the names of Goodnight and Loving turned upstream, following the water source and the inherent good grazing along the river's course into New Mexico. Only later did Charles Goodnight and Oliver Loving, both famous trail drivers and cattlemen, become associated with the route. He returned home by mid-January of 1866 a committed and experienced cowman and trail driver.

The Reynolds brothers had numerous brushes with hostile Indians, and lost friends and stock to the raiders. Consequently, the brothers never missed a chance to trail the pillaging band of raiders in hope of finding lost stock, particularly their own. This practice led to one of the most famous—and dangerous—incidents in the life of George Reynolds. South of the Double Mountain Fork of the Brazos River on April 3, 1867, several men of the community along the Clear Fork found themselves in pursuit of a band of Indians taking advantage of the green grasses of spring to launch a raid on the white settlements. George, W.D., and eight other men rode up on the Indians as the raiders were skinning a buffalo. The band of some thirty braves immediately showed their willingness to fight. One of the Indians who could speak some English started toward the group of whites, making threats and firing his two revolvers, which George noticed were aimed too high to strike the white men. George restrained the other members of the group as the bullets whistled harmlessly overhead, until the Indian had emptied both his six-shooters and reached for his bow and arrow. George then fired his revolver and hit the Indian, who turned to run, only to be cut down, his neck broken by a second bullet from George's pistol.

The whites charged the camp. The Indians mounted their ponies and fled in several directions to make pursuit more difficult. George and Si Hough, a friend, were riding together in pursuit of several Indians and gaining on them, when one of the raiders fired an arrow at his pursuers. The arrow struck George just below the belt, and he fell from his horse, sorely wounded by the arrow sunk deep in his abdomen. He removed the wooden shaft, but the steel head was lodged securely in the muscles of his back.

Hough rode up to see the extent of his friend's injury, and was Hough to press on in the pursuit. Hough asked if George could identify the Indian who shot him, and George did: the one in the red shirt. Hough spurred his horse in pursuit of the Indian who had wounded his friend. In about fifteen minutes, Hough returned with the Indian's scalp and the silver-mounted bridle from the Indian's mount.

The band of men carefully carried George back to his home at Stone Ranch near the Clear Fork, and sent to Weatherford for a doctor. Five days later when the doctor arrived, George was out of danger from the wound, but the doctor was unable to remove the steel point of the arrow. Years later in Kansas City, as trail driver Shanghai Pierce stood and watched, a surgeon made an incision in George's back to search for the arrowhead. As the surgeon proceeded, Pierce is said to have remarked, "Doc, if you cut that man any deeper, you will cut him to the hollow." At this point, the doctor stopped his probing and George sat up. Only then did the point, which George had carried in his body for fifteen years, become visible in the incision and was removed. This metal arrowhead, the pistol Hough used to kill the Indian, and the silver-mounted bridle taken from the Indian's horse are displayed at the National Cowboy Hall of Fame in Oklahoma City.

In 1867, when he was twenty-one, W.D. Reynolds accompanied the famous cattlemen and trail drivers Oliver Loving and Charles Goodnight on a trail drive into New Mexico. In a letter dated 1917 to Harry Crain, an official with the Wyoming Stock Growers Association, Reynolds recounts that he was a member of the trail crew taking two herds of cattle, one about two or three weeks ahead of the other, up the Pecos River and into New Mexico. Some of the cattle were to be sold in New Mexico, and the rest of the herd taken on to Colorado. After several days traveling with the first herd up the Pecos, Loving and a companion, Billy Wilson, left the herd to go on to Fort Sumner to sell some of the cattle in this outpost that was to become famous in the Lincoln County War. Near the confluence of the Black River, which flows out of the Guadalupe Mountains, and the Pecos, Indians attacked the pair and wounded Loving in the arm with an arrow. The two white men hid in canebrakes along the river and escaped the Indians, but lost their horses and saddles to the raiders. Painfully wounded and reluctant to travel in that condition, Loving convinced Wilson to swim down the river to escape the Indians and walk back to the herd with news of the wound and the loss of the horses.

Wilson, exhausted from his ordeal, was asleep along the route of the trail herd when discovered by Mose Cooch, a member of the trail crew. Apparently, the crew did not believe Wilson's story and drove on to Fort Sumner, where they found Loving, who had tried, despite his wounds, to walk to Fort Sumner. On the way, he encountered a group of Mexicans headed in that direction, and they loaded him into an ox cart and carried him the rest of the way to Fort Sumner. Loving's luck ran out, however, and he died of blood poisoning from the wounded arm.

W.D. arrived some few weeks later, after helping drive the second herd on into southern Colorado. In February, when the herd had been sold, the crew began the trip home. Reynolds recounts in his letter that he helped exhume Loving's body, load it into a wagon, and haul it to Weatherford, where it was re-buried. He does not mention the names of any others on the trip, but most accounts of this event include Charles Goodnight and several others. It is likely that Larry McMurtry borrowed heavily from this incident for one of the scenes in his novel *Lonesome Dove*.

Nor was this the only dealing the Reynolds brothers had with the Loving family. In 1870, George began to put together a herd of cattle for a drive in the spring. These were gathered at Lost Valley in Jack County, near a ranch belonging to the Loving family. George bought some steers from Charlie Rivers, the son-in-law of Oliver Loving. The night the deal was closed with Rivers, however, Indians raided the camp. In the fight Rivers suffered a fatal wound. He sent for his brother-in-law, J.C. Loving, who had camped nearby, and informed him of the sale of cattle to Mr. Reynolds. Rivers died a few weeks later in Weatherford, where he had been taken for treatment of his wound. The steers were received on schedule, a positive comment on the bargain-sealing handshake legendary in the West.

The Reynolds brothers figured in the founding of the forerunner of the Texas and Southwest Cattle Raisers Association, an organization that still checks brands and wages war against rustlers. The first meeting of the group had been held in Graham on February 15, 1877. In the summer of 1878, a second meeting of the Cattle Raisers Association of Northwest Texas was held at Fort Griffin, the town named for the military post erected on the hill overlooking the Clear Fork just after the Civil War. Phin Reynolds, a brother of George and W.D., recalls that a very large crowd came to this second gathering, so large that the two hotels in town were filled to overflowing. To accommodate the crowd, the four stores in town, owned by Frank Conrad, E.P. York, Charley Meyers, and E.E. Frankel, converted their businesses into temporary sleeping quarters, with men sleeping on the floors and counters on blankets loaned by the merchants. The meeting was held in the Masonic Hall and was well attended. The Reynolds brothers figured significantly in the meeting, as did most of the early-day cattlemen in the area, including Goodnight and W.D. Waggoner of the famous Waggoner Ranch.

The exploits of the Reynolds brothers, as well as their brother-in-law, John A. Matthews, who established Lambshead Ranch north of Albany, are the stuff of legend. Matthews's wife, Sallie Reynolds Matthews, sister of the Reynolds brothers, carefully detailed life during the period in her book *Interwoven: A Pioneer Chronicle*. The brothers established ranches in several Western states, including North Dakota, Montana, Kansas, Colorado, Utah, Nevada, Arizona, and California. The Reynolds brothers were traders, trail drivers, Indian fighters, and founders of many western institutions. George was even instrumental in establishing banks in Albany, Texas, and Oklahoma City, Oklahoma.

The brothers were survivors as well, and managed to live through one of the sternest tests for cattlemen all across the American West. In the winters of 1886, '87, and '88—in what Phin Reynolds later called the "Die-Up"—record cold temperatures and unusually heavy snowfall cut cattle off from water, which froze even in the bottoms of wells, and denied the animals access to the scant forage on the drought-stricken ranges. In some cases, the losses in the herds ran to seventy percent or more.

In the spring of 1887, after the first year of bitter weather, the ranges turned putrid with rotting carcasses of dead livestock. Polluted water made streams undrinkable. Scavengers could not take care of the glut of death on the ranges. The next summer was little better, nor was the following winter. The open range cattle industry was obviously doomed. Fortunes had been made speculating on the increase in grazing cattle, but ample evidence now existed of the negative outcome that could result.

This wholesale hardship demanded a dramatic change in ranching practices. Cattlemen saw that three things had to be done. First, they would have to cut and store hay, and have other feed available to get their herds through the winter storms. That lesson was amply clear. Next, they would have to cross-breed the longhorn, long the cow of choice for open range grazing. The longhorn's ability to walk long distances to market and still gain weight was no longer an important asset in a time when cattle were being shipped to market by rail. The longhorn's beef characteristics were sadly lacking when compared to Herefords and Durhams, both vigorous British breeds. Bulls imported for crossbreeding with longhorn cows proved capable of producing a vigorous crossbreed that provided a better product to consumers, so ranchers made the switch. The third major development resulted from the decision to upgrade breeding stock. In order to keep scrub bulls away from their herds, ranchers would have to control access to their ranges. This step required fencing. Barbed wire proved the fencing material of choice, and barbed wire fences went up across the West, to the distress of many who had no home range and owned little or no property. Many cattle raisers found they had been fenced away from water sources.

These traumatic conditions affected the Reynolds brothers the same as they did other ranchers. During the "Die-Up" Phin Reynolds says bad weather hit the North Dakota ranch, where he was at the time, in the form of two feet of snow that lay on the ground for two months before it thawed briefly and then refroze. Like other ranchers, the Reynolds brothers had no feed for their animals. Even the "native" cattle, those which had been on the range for several seasons, suffered as badly as those brought in recently. Jimbo Reynolds recalls the devastation on their ranges north of the Big Missouri in Montana, where Reynolds Cattle Company lost 90 percent of the 11,700 cattle they had there. They had 12,000 head on the Little Missouri in North Dakota and lost seventy percent of them. The Hashknife Ranch, another Texas-based operation with range located in North Dakota, had driven up 30,000 head and lost ninety percent, although their loss of native cattle ran only about twenty-five percent. A ninety percent loss was not uncommon on many of the northern ranges.

When the range cattle industry emerged from the transition forced by the extreme weather conditions of 1886-1888, it was a much different business, one based on economical concerns, sound breeding, range management, and market strategies. Because of the severe problems they had experienced, ranchers were forced to move toward more contemporary methods.

In Texas the brothers founded the Reynolds Brothers X Ranch at Round Mountain near the Clear Fork, north of present-day Albany; the 7 Triangle, south of Albany; the 9 R near Snyder; and a dairy farm near Fort Worth. In 1895 they also established the Long X at Kent. They chose for their brand, not the traditional letter X, but the "long X," drawn like the letter in the flag of the Stars and Bars of the Confederacy.

The property that made up the Long X ranch was not purchased in a block, but was instead bought and homesteaded over a period of several years. The original purchase in 1895 was made by a partnership of five men, three of whom were members of the Reynolds family. They purchased from Tom Newman of El Paso a ranch containing fifteen sections of land and a house. The next year they bought an additional 6000 acres from neighboring ranchers. By 1916 or so, state school lands in the area were made available for homesteading. By this time three of W.D.'s sons were of age, and filed to homestead eight sections each. Joseph Matthews Reynolds homesteaded the part known as Rincon, and his brother Will secured Rock Pile, a stretch of mountainous country known by its famous landmark. Soon after this, the company began buying land homesteaded by others. By 1920, the company controlled some 430 sections, or 275,000 acres, of cattle country, including some of the desert-like land surrounding Kent and the rugged mountain terrain south of the small town.

The Long X also accumulated about 100 sections of land in the Texas Panhandle near Dalhart. This property was formerly part of the famous XIT Ranch that covered much of the Panhandle. The Kent property and the Dalhart property together certainly made the Long X one of the "big" ranches in Texas.

The extensive holdings of the Reynolds Brothers Cattle Company were operated as a single unit, with headquarters in Fort Worth. This city offered all of the facilities the company needed, and had the additional advantage of being close to the primary market at the Fort Worth Stockyards.

Operation of the ranch continued to draw heavily on members of the family during the first six or so decades of the present century. The generation following that of the founders included the eight children of W.D. and one adopted daughter of George, who had no children of his own. W.D.'s children were George Eaton, Ella (Silsby), Will, Joseph Matthews, Merle (Harding), Watkins Wendell, John, and Nathan. George, Ella, Nathan, and Will had no children. Joseph fathered only one child, Mary Fruzan. Merle had two, Susan and Bob. Watkins had one son, Watkins, Jr., who died at thirty years of age. John was the father of one daughter, Susan.

When the founders turned the actual running of the ranch over to the second generation, things continued along traditional lines until after World War II. Few records exist from that period, but two men who knew the operation during the 1930s remember typical cowboy work, and daily life that harkened back to the days of the open range. And for good reason. The ranch at the time had very little cross fencing, except for a few large fenced traps with a section or more of land in each one. The ranch had one pasture north of the highway and another very large pasture to the south. The men saw no need for pens, because crews branded on open range, and drove the cattle to the railroad for shipping. Sick animals or cases of screwworms were doctored on the range after the animals were roped and thrown by the cowboys. It was a grand day for cowboys of the time because this ranch offered many of the freedoms of the open range, enjoyed throughout West Texas decades earlier. Jack Pate, an Albany-raised cowboy, who worked on the Long X and went on to work for decades in the mountainous parts of New Mexico, says that on the Long X, a cowboy "could let down his feet and ride."

The two men who recall this period are Jimbo Reynolds and Glenn Leech, both typical cowboys of the day. Leech was born September 23, 1913, on a ranch near Albany, and graduated from Albany High School. He learned ranch work on his family's home ranch south of Albany. Reynolds was born on a ranch in Stonewall County, August 6, 1913, and grew up around Albany doing ranch work. When he was thirteen, he spent the summer working on the Matthews Lambshead Ranch north of Albany. When he and Leech graduated from high school in 1931, they loaded their gear—saddles, bridles, spurs, boots, bedrolls, and other cowboy accoutrements—into a Model T Ford Coupe and drove over sometimes difficult roads to the Long X to work as cowboys. Leech remembers it as one of the greatest adventures of his life.

Upon arrival at the ranch, the young men found a well-organized operation. Will Reynolds was manager of the ranch, and worked through foreman Doc Kannedy. Reynolds and Leech also remember Berry Hart, an outstanding cowboy and bronc rider.

The two teenagers were sent to Rock Pile, one of the permanent camps on the southern part of the ranch, to assist a crew of men in building a strong corral to pen a herd of buffalo that roamed the ranch. This work was accomplished mostly by Mexican hired hands who went into the high mountain country and cut the largest trees available, pulling them to the site using mules. The Mexicans also dug the holes, and Leech and Reynolds assisted in raising the corral.

When that time the chore was completed, it was time to begin the late summer and early fall branding. The two young men joined the crew of cowboys living with the chuckwagon as it moved across the ranch. Preparation for the roundup was predictable. Each man was responsible for shoeing the ten horses designated as his "string" of mounts. Since there were ten cowboys in the working crew, the remuda was made up of well over a hundred horses, including some extras brought along in case a man injured one of his mounts in the rough terrain. The hands worked seven days a week, and depended completely on the services of the cook and the chuck wagon for their support.

The wagon was resupplied periodically with goods brought from ranch headquarters by truck or car. The wagon moved at least every other day to a new section of the ranch, so the men could gather the cattle that ordinarily grazed that part. The men slept in traditional soogans—bedrolls made up of a large tarpaulin intricately folded to provide protection from both cold and rain. Leech recalls that the men put in these bedrolls as many quilts as they could get, with an equal number under the sleeper and on top. In addition, they had a pillow, but no mattress of any kind. On nights when rain threatened, the men erected "tepees," small peaked rectangular tents designed to accommodate two men. Food consisted more of fresh beef than anything else. Anytime the cook ran short of beef, the crew would find a fat, mottled-faced heifer calf and slaughter her for food. This diet was supplemented with pinto beans, Dutch oven bread, and, very often, Leech remembers, a dish the cook labeled "bear sign." A dessert, it depended upon canned tomatoes as its principal ingredient.

When it was time to move the wagon to another part of the ranch, the cook served breakfast, then loaded all of his equipment into his wagon. The men loaded their bedrolls into a smaller trailer hitched behind the chuck wagon, which was pulled by six mules. Home that night was at a different spot on the range. By moving often, the men were close to their work, and the fresh ground was usually less dusty than the spot trampled for a day or two by the men and their horses.

The work routine smacks of old-time cowboy life. Since there were no pens for the horses overnight, the night wrangler kept the herd together within easy distance of the chuckwagon, and by daylight brought the remuda in to the wagon. There, the men would hold a long rope to form a makeshift pen and enclose the herd of over one hundred animals. Leech recalls the animals cooperated readily, and he never saw any of the horses try to bolt past the handheld single rope making up the enclosure. Horses learn the lesson of the rope during the training process and do not forget it. Each man was expected to ride every horse in his string, in rotation, to distribute the work evenly among his mounts. Once the remuda was gathered, a man would go into the rope pen, rope the horse he was to ride that day, and saddle up for the day's work. Then the horses not being used were released to the care of the day wrangler to graze for the day. The horses had to forage for their keep: no feed was provided.

For the roundup, the cowboys rode a wide circle in a designated stretch of country, and by noon had the herd on that part of the ranch gathered. Once the gathering was completed, part of the men would go to the wagon to eat while the rest of the crew held the herd in check. When the first men returned from the wagon filled with beef, bread, coffee, and whatever else the cook had ready, the other men would go eat. Then began the feverish activity of roping and dragging the calves to the branding fire as the men rushed to finish branding all the calves in this herd before dark. This work usually involved two ropers per ground crew of three men to do the branding and other operations of the calves. The roper rode into the herd, roped a calf, and dragged it to the ground crew. Once the calf was thrown to the ground, the rope was released, and the roper returned to the herd. Once the crew on the ground worked the calf, it was released to return to the herd.

It was dangerous, demanding work, but the men, living in the open air and eating the hearty food, got along fine. Leech remembers very few injuries to the men and, considering the roughness of the work, surprisingly little damage to the stock. Reynolds recalls it was not uncommon to lope a horse ten or twelve miles a day in one of these roundups, a feat which would devastate contemporary horses, because they are not conditioned to that kind of work schedule.

The routine was not without a break. Reynolds recalls that one day during a roundup he saw the wrangler leave the remuda and ride into the herd to talk to the foreman, something that was just not done unless there was some emergency. Reynolds saw the foreman and Berry Hart break from the herd and shake out their loops, so he followed along. He soon discovered that the wrangler had spotted a small black bear crossing the range, and the first two riders had decided to follow their cowboy instincts and rope the animal. The men were thwarted when their horses refused to get close to the bear because of their natural fear of the predator. Reynolds, mounted on a three-year-old, green-broke bronc at the time, forced his horse in on the bear and roped it. Within minutes, Hart managed to get a second loop on the bear, which the men then killed, intending to provide a break in their beef-only diet. Reynolds said that once he saw the bear's carcass hanging up, it so resembled the skeleton of a human he was unable to eat any of the meat.

Other breaks were less entertaining to the individuals involved. It was not uncommon, in these colder months, for the horses themselves to provide some comic relief, as they often tried their riders' skills early in the mornings. Since these horses were not ridden regularly during the year, it was customary each spring or fall, before roundup time, to re-break many of these excellently bred and spirited animals belonging to the Reynolds Cattle Company.

Once the branding was completed that fall, Leech remembers the men were sent to gather a large herd of Angus cattle on the southern part of the ranch, and then drove the animals to Kent to ship by rail to the buyer. Since the drive took several days from the south part of the ranch to the railroad corral at Kent, the men had to hold traditional night guard over the herd and perform other chores common to trail drives. Reynolds states that those cattle were "wild as deer."

Gathering and shipping cattle was an intricate job that required careful planning. Cattle sent to market each season were yearling steers that had ranged an assigned part of the ranch, but they sometimes drifted off that range in the course of storms and natural wandering when grazing. No fences were present to keep them in an assigned area. Therefore, when the cattle were gathered for branding, any of the steers found with the cows were kept in a separate herd, often in one of the large fenced traps on the ranch, until the entire herd could be collected. Then all the steers were driven to Kent and loaded on rail cars for shipment to market in Fort Worth. Following the fall branding, the calves were separated from the cows for weaning, and later the steers were driven to an assigned range to begin the cycle anew.

Once the cattle were loaded on the railroad cars and shipped, the crew occupied itself with the annual chore of reworking the pastures, and gathering maverick bulls to brand and castrate Many of these animals were two or three years old and had never been captured before. Another recurring task came in warm months when men on horseback prowled the range doctoring cases of screwworms, that devastating threat to livestock.

During this period ranching continued to depend heavily upon the horse, and the Long X ranged between three and four hundred brood mares on the northern part of the ranch. Because the mare band grew quite large, the management traded more than one hundred mares to a horse rancher in Mexico, who returned one gelding for each of the mares. Gathering the mare band was quite a chore, with much racing after the wild females in the rocky country. Once the mares were gathered and the ones to be sold separated, a crew from the ranch in Mexico took charge of the mares and drove them across the border.

Breaking horses for use in the remuda took place during the winter months, and was restricted to geldings selected for work on the ranch or destined to be sold. Jimbo Reynolds recalls hearing about one of the famous bronc riders on the Long X—Jose Guerrera. He came to the ranch as a fifteen-year-old boy and bet his only possessions, a pair of gloves and $15.00, that he could ride any horse on the ranch. The foreman picked a particularly bad bucking horse and let Jose try. The horse won the contest, but the lad's effort made such a good impression that the foreman refused his gloves and money, and gave him a job breaking horses for the ranch. Jose remained in that job for the rest of his life, and died on the ranch an old man.

Life was good, for the most part, but the Great Depression and the severe drought that spawned the infamous Dust Bowl had negative effects. Hard times made it necessary for the Reynolds family to sell off various properties, in order to keep the ranch going financially. They sold off the Round Mountain Ranch, the 7 Triangle, the 9 R, and the dairy farm, and most of the out-of-state properties. The Long X was kept intact, however, and after conditions got better in the early 1940s, the family began to improve the facilities at the headquarters and at several camps, located at strategic points around the ranch.

When the Reynolds Brothers founded the Long X, the headquarters was located near a strong spring south of Kent, where it remains today. A small adobe house stood on the site, and other buildings were added. At the headquarters, the main house, incorporating the original structure, has been expanded and improved, and stands today as a brilliant white stucco house with large shaded hallways open to the prevailing winds. A patio with a unique screened roof provides a comfortable shaded, but insect-free, setting. Two houses for ranch hands stand south of the main building, and to the northeast is a stone house made up of four rooms with private baths, two other houses, a slaughter house, two saddle houses, barns, and a set of pens. The living quarters are air conditioned for comfort, although at this elevation air conditioning is not needed as many months of the year as it is at nearby lower elevations. To the west of the house is a shop constructed of stone, which has been recently expanded to include an enclosed storage shed for wagons and other conveyances. The houses at the camps, like those at the ranch headquarters, are painted white with red trim, the two colors used by the ranch, and very often are marked on the roof, chimney, or some other place with the Long X brand.

Social life on the ranch during the early days included horseback riding, picnics at favorite places, hunting, and visits with neighbors, such as the Means, Cowden, and Jones families. The election polling place was at the Long X headquarters, so election day brought families from over a wide area to the ranch, where many stayed for a meal and a time of visiting.

Family members, especially women and school-age children, lived in Fort Worth, and traveled to the ranch by train. It was convenient to catch the train in Fort Worth at ten P.M. and ride out to Kent, arriving about eleven the next morning. Travelers took their meals in the dining car, and slept in the Pullman. When passenger train service was discontinued, the family had to travel by car, or to fly to Midland, the closest airport, and drive from there.

Following a division of the estate in 1986, Mary Fru Reynolds Pealer was joined by her daughter, Mary Joe, and together they operate one hundred and fifty sections of the original Long X Ranch. Other major divisions were made to Betty Cornell, George's heir; and to Bob Harding, who took the property in the Texas Panhandle as his part. The current operation of the outfit continues in the vein established by the founders.

The ranch, operated by the Long X Cattle Company, lies on both sides of Interstate 10, surrounding the small town of Kent. In 1985, for about six months, cattle all over the property were gathered, sorted, and counted as part of the settlement of the estate. Since then, Mary Fru and Mary Joe have spent much of their time at the ranch overseeing the day-to-day operation of such a complex business venture, although both women maintain homes in Fort Worth. Mary Fru, a frequent visitor to the the ranch since childhood, says, "I love this ranch. This is where we always came, and there are lots of family memories here."

The two women have continued the Long X tradition of raising fine Hereford cattle, but they have begun about twenty-five percent cross-breeding with Red Brangus. This mix retains the basic red coloration of the herd, although the cross-bred calves usually have red necks and mottled faces. Also, as part of the cross-breeding program, longhorn bulls are bred to first-calf heifers. A small herd of longhorn cattle is maintained on the ranch, partly for breeding purposes, and partly as a reminder of the historical importance of this breed. The ranch figures one bull for each ten cows, because the country is extremely rough and most of the pastures are large, some containing as many as 10,000 acres. The bulls are put with the cows in March, and left out from 90 to 120 days. Under normal circumstances, the longhorns are put out in February, to allow more time with the first-calf heifers.

The ranch currently keeps five full-time cowboys in camps on different parts of the ranch. A camp on the Long X is as it is on most other ranches; a house for the cowboy and his family to live in, a barn, often a set of pens, and, in many cases, a pasture for keeping the horses assigned to that particular cowboy's string. The cowboys are assigned pastures adjacent to their camps to check daily.

Foreman Bill Evans is a seasoned cowman originally from the Matador Ranch but with experience on other large Texas ranches. He gives orders to the cowboys in English, but it is, as one would expect, English strongly interspersed with Spanish terminology, reflecting the flavor of the region. Spanish is typically the native language of several cowboys on the ranch.

Transportation over long distances on such a large ranch is a concern. As is typical in cowboy country, pickups and trailers are standard equipment, and horses are hauled to the particular pasture to be worked, thus saving both cowboys and horses the long rides to the working area. Using trucks and trailers, the cowboys can drive back and forth to their routine work, cutting down on the number of horses needed for a cowboy to do his job. One of the laments of modern cowboys, generally, is that, because horses get so much less working time than in former days, a thoroughly trained and conditioned horse is hard to find these days. The dozen miles of loping daily, recalled by Jimbo Reynolds, is not required of these horses.

The chuckwagon still plays a role in the routine on the Long X. During the busy branding and shipping season of the year, the ranch takes out the chuck wagon whenever work in a given area will stretch over several days. In mid-April the wagon is carried out for about two weeks, because working calves takes up much of the time during the spring. Calves are still roped and dragged to the branding fires, as they always have been. The men use no working tables. This is a practical approach as well as a historic one, because using the tables would require transporting them to the various sets of pens, then bringing the cows to these points.

Marketing is no longer handled by rail. Instead, a buyer either visits the ranch to make a deal for the cattle, or more often, in the case of remote ranches such as the Long X, a video marketing company sends a representative videotape the cattle being sold. On a prearranged day, the company airs the footage via satellite to prospective buyers, bids are received by telephone, and a deal is struck. Then, on a day convenient for both parties, the buyer arranges for trucks to be at the ranch. The cowboys gather and sort the animals to be sold. Then the stock is weighed on scales at the ranch's shipping corrals, and loaded into the trucks. No longer must the herd be driven to some distant point; truckers have become modern-day trail drivers.

In addition to the five cowboys, the ranch also keeps a cook, now Juliana Valeriano, whose husband José is one of the cowboys. Currently, Carmen Navarrete, whose husband Noberto is also a cowboy, comes in to do some cleaning once a week. Norberto has the additional responsibility of seeing after the band of brood mares and their colts. He is an excellent horseman and cowboy, whose skills are valuable wherever well-trained cowhorses are essential. Frank Escobedo, whose tenure on the ranch goes back to 1952, making him the employee with the longest service, handles the chores that require the skills of a mechanic or a carpenter.

One of the main tasks of cowboys today, as it has long been, is seeing that the cattle have plenty of water, since sources of fresh water are scarce in this country. Well water is unavailable in most areas. The characteristic method is to trap water at a high elevation, and gravity feed it through a network of underground pipes to tanks scattered across the ranch, sometimes miles from the original source. Each one of these "waters," or watering sites, has a low cement or stone trough. Nearby, in a round cement cylinder topped by a metal plate, is a float device keeping the water in the tank at a usable level. This method of watering cattle requires almost daily checking, because the small tanks do not hold enough water to satisfy the needs of the cattle for very long. Cattle also sometimes damage the devices and cause malfunction. Daily checking of the water system is one of the unique demands of ranching in this arid part of the country.

Cowboys must also ensure that cattle have ample forage. Since the ranch keeps a series of roads passable in each pasture, the men are able to check the quantity and condition of the grass from their pickup trucks, which the ranch furnishes. Roads are graded once or twice a year, after the rainy season, to keep them able to support traffic.

A third essential task for any cowboy is seeing that the cattle receive supplementary feed during the winter. Currently, this feeding is done by making a liquid supplement available in a container allowing free choice access to the sweet liquid. The men must also check for signs of sickness or disease, as well as occasional breaks in fences, caused by bulls fighting or by the buffalo wanting to go from one pasture to another. Buffalo disdain fences, and their strong bodies and short, sturdy horns can destroy a fence in short order. Thankfully, cowboys no longer have to check for screwworms during the warm months, since that threat has been eliminated by modern science.

Most of the ranch retains the original net wire fencing with two strands of barbed wire on top, attached to cedar posts. This fencing, erected decades ago, is a good indication that the land behind that fence is currently, or formerly, Reynolds property.

As many other ranchers have discovered these days, the owners of the Long X have learned that guided game hunts are profitable undertakings. Cowboys guide hunters in the search for oudad sheep, whitetail deer, mule deer, antelope, javelina, and blue quail. Meals and lodging are furnished for the hunters, typically professional men from areas far from the mountains, who welcome the challenge in landscape and game.

Today the ranch keeps a remuda of forty saddle horses. This number allows each man to have about six horses in his string. These animals are short-bodied, medium-height Quarter Horses, adapted to breathing the thinner air in the higher altitude, and working in the rocky, steep terrain, two qualities necessary for successful cattle work. These traits are not often found in horses not raised in the area. Adaptation of horses from other geographic areas is possible, but often requires a year or more.

The ranch also keeps a herd of about a dozen brood mares. In recent years, the stud was a gray Quarter Horse named Stranger, that had in him the breeding of Doc Bar and Poco Bueno, both famous Quarter Horses. This horse was sold at the Western Heritage Classic horse sale in Abilene in 1992, and replaced by a paint stallion, Skip A Star Junior. A colt is halter broken by tying its lead rope to a harness on a donkey, one of the accepted ways to teach a colt patience and obedience to the lead rope. In some years the colts are sold, but often one or two fillies will be kept for brood mares, and an equal number of male colts are kept, to be castrated at two years of age and trained for use by the cowboys.

Following the tradition of the founders, the Long X still keeps a herd of thirty buffalo. Ranch personnel maintain that size by selling off or slaughtering excess animals. The herd stems from five buffalo originally acquired from Charles Goodnight.

The town of Kent is almost completely a Long X Ranch operation. The store, warehouse, and post office are run by the ranch, and, in effect, the store serves, as it has for decades, as the supply house for the ranch, currently stocking some grocery items, hardware, windmill parts, essential items of tack, beer, water pipe fittings, wool blankets, cold drinks, candy, gasoline, and feed. The walls of the store are decorated with period décor items, such as a scythe, various kinds of hand tools, a horse collar, and the like. In this remote region, it is surprising to learn that almost 8,000 vehicles a day pass by on Interstate 10, which runs just south of the store. In fact, gasoline is the principal item of sale. More than one uneasy traveler has, no doubt, been attracted by the Chevron sign standing above the store, because it is a long way between gas stations in this part of the state. The post office is at the rear of an adjoining building, and functions as a sub-station of the U.S. Post Office in Van Horn, some forty miles away. The brick warehouse, originally constructed as a wool shipping point, now serves as storage for ranch supplies, such as feed and salt, and unneeded equipment. A railroad siding on the north side of the building has been removed. The café that once stood nearby no longer exists.

Operation of the Long X Ranch has continued in the proud tradition established by the Reynolds brothers, it is a family-run business reflecting the combined efforts of fine cattlemen for more than a century. Mary Fru and Mary Joe have proved good stewards of the resources of the ranch, and have kept a traditional and historically accurate viewpoint while upgrading operations to take advantage of available technology.

The Fandangle and Oral Tradition

Nowhere has the oral tradition resulted in a more colorful pageant than the annual Fort Griffin Fandangle, staged in an outdoor amphitheater near Albany every June. Based on the history, legend, and lore of the region, the musical drama traces life in the area from the days of the Native American to the arrival of settlers and the establishment of families and homes. Included first here are several essays on events and personalities that have provided the community with the lore necessary for production of such an ambitious show. Lawrence includes as well the history of the Fandangle itself, and a summary description of the entire show. Featuring live longhorns, agile horsemen and horsewomen, many citizens of the area, and colorful costumes and sets, the musical draws large crowds from across the state every year. This variety of stories and personality sketches, which have long been a part of the legend and lore of this region, makes a fitting conclusion to this last gathering of essays by Lawrence Clayton, dedicated folklorist and collector of regional history.

TWENTY

J.R. Webb, Historian, Author, Archivist

Without the work of J.R. Webb, much of the history of the Fort Griffin Country would have been lost to posterity. Through interviews of numerous pioneers, and his unceasing search for and careful filing of material, Webb contributed much to the history of the area. A quiet, unassuming man, Webb is largely unknown to us today.

James Richard Webb was born in Waco, Texas, on November 19, 1884. He was the third son of Sam and Ella Downs Webb. The family ranched in eastern Shackelford County, and moved to Albany in 1883.

J.R. developed an interest in ranching as a young man, and worked during the summers on the Hadley Roberts Ranch. He chose Baylor University for his undergraduate education. After graduating from the School of Law at the University of Texas in 1907, he began practice in the firm of his uncle, J.R. Downs, in Waco. Ill health forced his retirement in 1914.

By 1919 he had recovered enough to return to Albany to ranch. He ran the Russ brothers ranch southeast of Albany, as well as the

Watkins Pasture owned by his brother-in-law, Leon F. Russ. In 1933 the property was sold and he stopped ranching.

Webb's greatest contribution was in the field of history, especially local history. He interviewed many old timers still alive at the time, and was quite active in celebrating the state centennial. He authored several entries in the early edition of *The Handbook Of Texas*. He was active in the Texas State Historical Association and the West Texas Historical Association.

In the files of Webb's correspondence are letters from the notables of the day: J. Evetts Haley, J. Frank Dobie, and others. He also collected newspaper clippings and historically important notes. He was the right man for the hour, and much material exists today because he saw fit to record and save the information.

TWENTY-ONE

"Buckskin" Bowden Recalls His Frontier Adventures with Bad Nell and Billy the Kid

In the papers of J.R. Webb, Albany, Texas, historian and rancher, rests a brown tattered newspaper clipping, the work of Frank P. Hill and credited to *The Lynn County News*. It was published in the *Albany* (Texas) *News* in November of 1932. From the content of the article, one gathers that Buckskin Bowden was an adventurer who bordered on being a scoundrel, typical of the frontier period. At the time of the interview from which the article stems, Bowden was eighty-four years of age. Of principal interest are his dealings with a cross-dressing woman named Bad Nell, and later with Billy the Kid.

Bowden's first visit to Fort Griffin came in 1868. He came first to Dallas in 1867, when he was nineteen years old. He remembers the now-massive city as "a little berg with just a few houses." He caught a ride to Fort Griffin on an ox-drawn wagon loaded with lumber and flour. The trip lasted "several weeks" and included sighting two bands of Indians, but no conflict with the Native Americans. The recently established fort consisted of "a few wooden and adobe huts housing a handful of soldiers." He remembers that the town on the flat below the fort became "worse morally than any gold mining town ever in the West." And Bowden saw several of those because he later left Griffin and followed the gold booms. He characterizes the people who drifted into town as "desperados, wild women, and other scum." Thieves attracted to Griffin were mostly fleeing from the law back east. Fights and killings were common in the town, despite the presence of the soldiers, who had to keep careful watch on their supplies and horses to prevent their being stolen. The soldiers also did not wander out except in groups to assure their safety.

Bowden remembers three saloon keepers: Nat Buckham, Poker Jack, and Tol Bowers. He said they were "all desperadoes." Nat Buckham supposedly had killed several men, and one night he killed a Tonkawa Indian man and "beat a naked Indian woman to death with a mesquite limb." Even in Fort Griffin, however, justice could be as swift as crime. The next morning, Buckham was found dead in his tent "with his stomach cut out." Tol Bowers was killed later in Oklahoma. Poker Jack played into Bowden's life later.

One of Bowden's main recollections was a female outlaw he called Bad Nell. He describes her as "an outlaw and a thief and a poker player, a good shot with a pistol and as good a horse rider as any man." She worked alone, with no "confederates," either male or female. Other than these flaws, he said, she was "a nice gal morally and had nothing to do with the hundred or more tough women around Griffin."

Bowden first met Nell in 1874 when she hired on at a ranch where he worked. The job of the crew on this ranch was to see that strays from passing trail herds found their way into the owner's herd. Nell went by the name of Neil, weighed about one hundred thirty pounds, and dressed as a man. She shared a room with Bowden and three other men for six months without revealing her true sex.

A few days before Christmas, Bowden and Nell rode to Griffin to celebrate, and went to Poker Jack's saloon. They had a drink, and then went to the dance hall in the saloon. There both Bowden and Neil (Nell) danced with women. Later the two drifted back to the bar for another drink, whiskey, straight. This time the bartender was Poker Jack himself, and he recognized Nell. He asked, "Bad Nell, what the Hell are you doing here?"

Nell responded with gusto: "Breathe that name again and I'll bore [shoot] you." She drew her gun to emphasize her resolve. "I'm a man now, can't you see, and if you ever tell anybody different but Buckskin, I'll bore you." She then confessed to Bowden that she had known Jack in Kansas. Bowden kept his promise not to reveal her true identity until after she had left the Griffin area.

Bowden related one of Nell's adventures that occurred about this time. About ten o'clock one night, Nell announced her intention to go to Griffin, about three hours away on horseback, and refused Bowden's offer to go along. About two hours later, she returned, with the excuse that she had decided not to go to town. Bowden knew it was only about two miles over to the main trail, and learned later that the trail was her real destination. The next morning, Nell took him out to the corral, where she pulled up a post to reveal $600 in gold. Later, the story spread that a single horseman had pistol-whipped a trail wagon boss, and taken the money from the sale of his herd. Then Bowden had the full story of Nell's midnight ride.

Jack may have broken his promise to keep Nell's secret, because her true identity soon became known. One night in Bowers's saloon, a group of men confronted Nell with the question of her identity. She readily admitted she was Nell, but proved why she was called "Bad Nell" when one of the men insulted her. She promptly shot his kneecap off. Bowden was standing in the door of the saloon when the shot was fired, and he was trampled by the mob of men and women getting out of danger.

Nell confronted Poker Jack with his betrayal, and reminded him of her promise to "drill" him. Jack turned pale, but Nell relented, and decided instead to take Jack's money at poker. She had Bowden and two friends look for Jack's hoard of gold. They found it, $300.00 worth, and Nell promptly won it all, in what Bowden called the biggest poker game in Fort Griffin.

After that night, Nell decided it was time to move on. She demanded her pay from her ranch boss, who refused to pay up. Nell promptly pulled her pistol, and took his gun and the few dollars he had in his pocket. She was not through. That night she single-handedly robbed the crew in a nearby cow camp, but got only about $20. She went to Jacksboro, and then to the Indian Territory, where she settled on a farm with a man she had married. He never knew she was an outlaw.

Bowden survived the Fort Griffin flood of 1876, which washed away many of the town's buildings. He said Griffin was not as big or as wild after that, and he lost his desire for the outlaw life. He worked for a man named Overall, and for Andy and Frank Long. Then, in 1880, he decided to go to the gold fields. Trouble seemed to follow him.

Bowden rode by himself to the Goodnight-Adair JA Ranch in Palo Duro Canyon. After he left the JA, he came upon a group of six men, driving a herd of horses. He accepted their invitation to ride along, but discovered belatedly that the horses were stolen. As the men neared Tascosa, the Texas Panhandle town with a reputation much like that of Griffin, five of the men hid with the horses in the Canadian River breaks, and Bowden rode with the leader to a saloon in Tascosa. Some men came in and talked with the leader. One of the men bought drinks for everyone, and then all of the men left. The leader of the other men was identified as Billy the Kid.

At the insistence of the leader, Bowden returned to the horse herd, and Billy the Kid showed up and took delivery of the horses. Bowden discovered the leader of the thieves and Billy were old friends. Billy left with the herd, heading to New Mexico. The thieves insisted Bowden ride with them until daylight, and then they allowed him to go his own way. He rode back to Tascosa, but never revealed the identity of the Kid. Bowden rode on to begin prospecting for gold, a hunt that took him to Colorado and Arizona, a quest that lasted until 1906. He remained single, but had accumulated little fortune by the time he told his story.

Bowden appears to be a picaro of the frontier, someone just short of being a criminal, who lives by his wits. He was one of many who found, on the frontier, the challenge and freedom that made life worthwhile. His tale was real to him, if only in his mind.

TWENTY-TWO
THE RETURN OF ALLISON DUMAS'S HORSE

On the frontier, where horses were essential for safety and transportation, stories of lost and found mounts abound. Few, however, are more surprising than the tale of a horse stolen from Allison Edgar Cebron Dumas, a young Frenchman on the northwest Texas frontier in the early 1870s.

The story begins at Weatherford, the seat of Parker County, west of Fort Worth. There Dumas met Joe McComb, who was to become one of the greatest buffalo hunters in the West. The two were looking for work and wandered west, stopping first in Eastland and then moving on to Fort Griffin, the military post on the Clear Fork of the Brazos River. Perhaps work awaited them here in the town that had grown up on the flat between the fort on the hill and the river.

Griffin Flat was one of the wildest towns on the frontier. Here thrived every vice known to man, especially in the numerous saloons and brothels. The town was an outfitting point for hunters, who slaughtered the vast southern buffalo herd almost to extinction. Gunpowder and lead were important commodities, and the stench of drying buffalo hides in season hung in the air.

One night in 1874, the town of Griffin became unusually rowdy and the two young men, having found no work, determined to seek their fortunes elsewhere. Fate had other ideas. They crossed the river at the ford north of town, and rode about a mile north on the road to Fort Richardson. Alongside a slough that held water much of the year, they hobbled their horses and turned into their blankets, which they had spread in high weeds to help conceal themselves. During the night, the two heard horses passing by and saw Indians in the pale moonlight. The two did not pick a fight, and were relieved when the shadowy riders passed. In the morning when the men awoke, their horses were gone, the hobbles cut with a knife. The two were afoot. Enraged by their loss but glad to be alive, they made their way to the fort and reported the theft.

General George P. Buel, commander of the fort, sent out scouting parties who determined the raiders were Comanches, but were unsuccessful in catching the raiders or retrieving any of the stolen stock. Then Colonel Ranald Mackenzie enters the picture. Adjacent to Fort Griffin, he established a staging area for a large punitive raid against the Comanches. Mackenzie's expedition of Buffalo Soldiers and Tonkawa scouts rode from Fort Griffin to the high plains, and eventually to the canyon of the Palo Duro, or "Hard Wood." There the cavalry dealt the Indians a crushing blow.

When Mackenzie's troops attacked the camps in the canyon, the surprised Indians fled. The troops burned winter supplies, tepees, and gear, and captured more than 1,400 horses and mules, many stolen from settlers and the army.

Mackenzie had previous experience with captured Indian horses. He had seized a large herd from McClellan Creek, a tributary of the Red River, in the Texas Panhandle in 1872. The Indians had stampeded the horses out of his control, and he had no intention of letting that happen again. He knew dismounted Indians would have to come into the reservation, and he determined to deny them access to horses.

His men first cut out the horses needed to supply the military. Mackenzie then let his Tonkawa scouts pick out some horses to carry back the booty they had seized from the plundered camps. Finally, he ordered the troops to shoot just over a thousand of the screaming animals. The nomadic Plains Indians were afoot, a devastating blow that ended life as they had known it. The slaughter left piles of bones, later picked up and sold to become fertilizer.

The troops and scouts continued to hound the Indians, in an effort to drive them onto reservations and end the fighting. By December, with the mission accomplished as much as possible, the foray ended. The scouts returned to their homes near Fort Griffin, with their horses. Dumas must have been astounded when he saw his horse among those brought back by the scouts. He recognized the mount despite its mutilation by the Indians. They had cut off its tail and one ear.

Dumas recovered his horse, and determined to leave the area. His friend McComb elected to stay, and became one of the great buffalo hunters. Tragically, as Dumas crossed the Clear Fork, his newly recovered horse drowned. The mutilated horse, that had been spared death in the Panhandle at the hands of the soldiers, met a watery fate. The incredible part of the story is that, on the vast frontier, the paths of a stolen horse, a wanderer, some Tonkawa scouts, and the command of the "most promising young officer" should cross in so bizarre a fashion.

TWENTY-THREE
Russell Young Gilbert, West Texas Frontiersman and Scout

Many a young man drifted to the Western frontier in search of adventure and fortune and disappeared, never to be seen or heard of again. Posterity has little notion of the feats and accomplishments—or losses and early deaths—of many of these people. One of these young men was Russell Young Gilbert, a young white man who decided his destiny was in West Texas. Fortunately, his son, James R. Gilbert, wrote an undated, ten-page chronicle citing some of the more noteworthy accomplishments of his famous father. Without this chronicle, details of Gilbert's life would be largely lost.

The manuscript found its way into my hands from Sam Webb, nephew of J.R. Webb of Albany, Texas, a lay historian, who collected documents of life along the Clear Fork of the Brazos River in Shackelford and Throckmorton counties. This region has an extraordinary amount of history connected with it. Particularly important are stories dealing with Camp Cooper, the pre-Civil War post where Robert E. Lee commanded elements of the Second Calvary, and Fort Griffin, the post-Civil War post and town, widely known for rowdy civilian life and the great buffalo slaughter. Military life and Indian depredations make this area one of the most intriguing in Texas, from the 1850s to the end of the trail drive era and the coming of the railroad. Gilbert's life was integrally involved in this rich period of frontier history.

James Gilbert recounts that his father was born on a farm in Mississippi on November 7, 1841, of English and French parents. The family moved to Alton, Illinois, in 1846 or 1847. Shortly thereafter, Gilbert's father died, and it fell young Gilbert's task to help his mother, sister, and brother make a living. This he did by working on a farm. The notable problem with his job was that the Mississippi River stood between him and the farm. He had to swim to work each day. He was fourteen years old at the time.

When his mother remarried and freed him from supporting the family, Gilbert decided to try his fortunes out West. According to the narrative history, Gilbert bought himself "a good horse and a fine silver-mounted rifle," and tied to his saddle the new clothes his mother and sister had made. He left Ohio and, as his son later wrote, "he never stopped . . . until he reached Old Camp Cooper, Texas."

Camp Cooper served two roles: to help control lawlessness on the frontier and, principally, to oversee the Comanche Indian Reserve located adjacent to the post. Both responsibilities proved burdensome during Gilbert's stay on the Clear Fork, but the post provided him with employment. His first job was for the Quartermaster, who put him to work cutting hay for the cavalry horses. His next job was slaughtering wild beef to feed the soldiers. "He would send to the post all the hind quarters, and the rest the Indians would take," said the son. He befriended the Indians, who helped him round up the cattle. He came to spend all of his free time in the Indian camp, "practicing shooting and learning their singins [sic] and ways and their language." He also had, the son recalled, "a buckskin suit and some fine painted buckskin rugs, painted by the Indians." The son also recounts that there was relative calm on the reservation at this time—1857, 1858, and 1859. Soon, however, this situation would change, and Gilbert would be in the middle of the trouble.

During these years, Gilbert was hired by the army to carry dispatches, on a route that took him from Fort Belknap in present-day Young County to Fort Chadbourne in Coke County. Other posts on his route were Camp Cooper and Fort Phantom Hill, north of present-day Abilene, a distance of more than sixty miles. The experience familiarized Gilbert with a large part of the Comanche hunting range, something that would be invaluable later. During this time, Gilbert had the good fortune to capture "a fine blooded horse out of a band of mustangs." This young sorrel horse, with one white stocking and a star on its forehead, stood sixteen and a half hands high. He had apparently escaped into the wild, but he proved very useful to Gilbert. He trained the horse to follow him around "like a dog," and to come to Gilbert's whistled command. James Gilbert recalls his father's use of the horse: "He was a very fast animal. [I] could start the horse upon the course . . . at night to take dispatches . . . to the other forts [and on] the darkest night, . . . he would keep the course." If the route were unfamiliar, Gilbert would guide on the North Star, if the sky were clear. When it was cloudy, Gilbert would wet his finger to determine the direction of the light breeze, and set his direction in that way. He never whipped the horse or ran him, except in pursuit of Indians.

One of Gilbert's most arduous and dangerous missions occurred when John R. Baylor, a noted agitator of the Indian problem at Camp Cooper, killed nine Comanche Indians while they were camping south of Camp Cooper on the Clear Fork. This action caused the Indians to go on the "warpath," and threaten to break out of the reservation at Camp Cooper. Gilbert was ordered to take a dispatch to Dallas, one hundred and fifty miles away, in order to forward the dispatch to the War Department in Washington, D.C. The pressing question was what to do about the Indians, who seemed determined to leave the reservation. The son wrote: "Gilbert rode night and day with the dispatch and returned with the answer to move the Comanches and Kiowas to the Indian reservation" in Indian Territory. To recruit soldiers to handle the move, officers sent

Gilbert to Fort Chadbourne, Fort Phantom Hill, and, the narrative says, Fort Concho. The last post was not established until after the Civil War, and is an obvious error. Likely, he was sent to Fort Belknap. When all the soldiers had gathered, the officer in charge wanted to wait until the next day, but Gilbert recommended leaving immediately: "You are never too soon for an Indian," the son recalled his father saying, "for they know your moves and plans and always have out spies. . . . The Indians are there now, but in the morning the Indians may not be there." So the commanding officer took Gilbert's word and marched on into the Indians' camp, and "told the chiefs that they [the soldiers] had come with orders from Washington to move them [the Indians] to the Indian Nation to Fort Sill." So Gilbert's words saved the day and probably a big Indian fight as the chiefs told Gilbert and the commanding officer, "Good thing you came this afternoon; if you had not come, tomorrow would be a big fight." The chiefs explained further: "They were going to send all of the women and children out that night and in the morning when the soldiers came to move them, they intended to give battle, but they would not fight now on account of the women and children."

When the Indians and soldiers left for the Indian Territory, Gilbert remained behind as bodyguard for the family of Matthew Leeper, the agent who had been in charge of the reservation since March 1857. Gilbert served for three months before Leeper's family left to join him at his new post. In all, Gilbert had nine months' pay coming, but the Civil War broke out before he got his wages. He never collected the money.

During the war, Gilbert served with what James calls the old Dragoons, Home Guards, and then Old Belknap Rangers. Most sources call the force Texas Rangers. He scouted for the group for four years, and participated in several battles. One, which the record places on Mule Creek, a tributary of the Pease River, in Wilbarger County, was particularly noteworthy. The writer correctly gives the date as December 18, 1860. The Rangers, with Ross leading and Gilbert scouting, caught up with a band of raiders after following the trail all day in "a cold and drizzling rain." As darkness approached, Gilbert warned that he "could tell that the Rangers were near the Indians" because some of the horses "were dragging their feet." Gilbert advised Ross to keep the men behind a ridge, out of sight in some tall grass, and not allow a regular camp because of the noise. The next morning, the Rangers charged the camp just as the Indians were "rounding up their horses getting ready to go." The description of the next action is the most significant in the narrative: "Gilbert took two men with him and charged off to the left to a little fire in a wigwam. There was an old woman and an old Indian buck inside and a boy about sixteen and a white woman with a child. Gilbert and the other two men commenced shooting as the old woman and the old Indian and boy were shooting. Gilbert and the two men killed the old Indian man and the old Indian woman and the boy. When the white woman held her child up at arm's length above her head, Gilbert stopped the other men from shooting." Then the men rode up to the wigwam and captured the woman, who proved to be Cynthia Ann Parker. Gilbert scalped the old Indian, believed to be Peta Nacona, the husband of Cynthia Ann. This reported scalping, if true, lays to rest the notion that Cynthia Ann continued looking for her husband, if the man Gilbert shot and scalped was indeed Peta Nacona.

The captive was not cooperative. The narrative records that "she would keep falling off her horse," so Gilbert tied her on her horse with his "horn lariat.". Some sources indicate Parker was taken to Camp Cooper, and kept until her uncle came for her, but this narrative indicates she was taken to Fort Belknap, and cared for by a Mrs. Peavley, mother of one of the Rangers. Mrs. Peavley gave her some clothes other than her Indian clothing. Gilbert includes the anecdote of Cynthia Ann identifying herself as Cynthia Ann to her uncle, John Parker. Identifying the uncle as "John" is probably a slip of memory. Other sources call him Isaac Parker.

John C. Irwin recounts in his life story, recorded by J.R. Webb, that the party came back through the Camp Cooper area and that he saw Cynthia Ann there.

Bill Tackett and other Rangers told James of some of Gilbert's experiences. One day a group of the Rangers surprised some Indians, led by one who "looked like a big chief." This Indian attempted to escape, and Gilbert raced in pursuit. A second Indian started in pursuit of Gilbert, and one of the Rangers raced after the second Indian. A third Indian, pursued the second Ranger, so a third Ranger, Bill Tackett, rode after the third Indian in what must have seemed a bizarre race for life. The first two Rangers killed the Indians they pursued; Tackett failed to kill his Indian, but did recover from him a blood-stained blanket with a bullet hole in it. Another time, a projected ten-day patrol stretched to twenty, and the men were forced to rely for food on what they were able to kill between Indian fights.

Gilbert scouted for the Rangers until 1864. During this time, he went on "furlough" to a farming area on the Brazos River, some fifty miles south of Fort Belknap. He accompanied two of the Rangers, named Littlefield, there on one trip, and he met Susan Williams. After that first meeting, Gilbert visited often. In 1864 he quit the Rangers, married Miss Williams, and began farming, apparently in the same community where the Williams family lived. He "did not do any good," James wrote. In 1866 he moved back to the vicinity of Camp Cooper, his old original home in Texas, and began farming in a "bend of the Clear Fork River, one mile northeast of the fort." He became a scout for the army when Fort Griffin was established in 1867, and continued until the spring of 1870. That October, while gathering his corn crop, he suffered a heatstroke and died on October 30. It is unclear from the narrative whether this was in 1870 or 1871. James recounts that Gilbert was buried in the soldiers' cemetery southeast of the fort. His grave was marked with a wooden marker, but a fire later swept through the cemetery, and the gravesite was lost. The fort closed in 1881, and the remains of soldiers who died while serving there were moved to San Antonio. Presumably Gilbert's remains were among them.

The narrative of a grateful son is one of the few remains of a man who lived the frontier experience during the early days of settlement in the Fort Griffin area. He is in many ways typical of the period. He was born in the Old South, and came west seeking his fortune. He lived a life of high adventure as a scout and Indian fighter, and died prosaically, the victim of a heatstroke rather than of an Indian arrow, tomahawk, gunshot, or even a riding accident. This last is a real surprise, considering his long hours in the saddle under dangerous conditions. No record exists of his faithful "blooded horse," but the calm that reigns over the Clear Fork today belies the fevered action there in the days of Russell Young Gilbert.

TWENTY-FOUR
The Death of Charley Rivers

The tragedy of death, especially at the hands of Indians, was no stranger to western settlers. In post-Civil War Texas, the Loving family was particularly well acquainted with such sorrows. Trail driver and pioneer rancher Oliver Loving died in 1867 of complications from a wound suffered in an Indian attack while on a trail drive from Texas into New Mexico. His long-time friend and associate, Charles Goodnight, and others returned his body home to Weatherford, Texas, for burial in one of Southwestern history's most famous actions.

Less well known is that an Indian attack in northwest Texas also caused the death of Loving's son-in-law, Charley Rivers. That action occurred in June1871, in what is now Jack County, some forty-five miles from Weatherford.

As with his father-in-law, Rivers' death involved a cattle drive. J.C. Loving, Oliver's son, and Rivers were in the process of gathering a herd of cattle to sell to George Reynolds, a cattleman whose family ranched along the Clear Fork of the Brazos River near Fort Griffin, in current Shackelford and Throckmorton counties to the west.

Reynolds was himself an experienced trail driver, and had

crossed paths with the Loving family before. In fact, his first drive, in October of 1865, headed west along the Butterfield Stage route, past Fort Phantom Hill and Fort Chadbourne, and then on to Horsehead Crossing on the Pecos River, the same route Goodnight and Loving followed when Loving was fatally wounded. That trail came to bear their names—the Goodnight-Loving Trail. Instead of turning north into New Mexico and Colorado, as the Goodnight-Loving Trail did, Reynolds drove his herd into Mexico and sold at a profit. By January 1866, he was back home. He had found his niche on the frontier, and remained a trail driver for decades thereafter.

In another tie between the Reynolds and Loving families, W.D. Reynolds, George's brother and frequent partner in cattle and ranching deals, was with one of the two herds Goodnight and Loving were driving toward Colorado when Loving was wounded in New Mexico. He was among those who later accompanied Loving's body back to Weatherford.

By June 16, 1871, the cow hunt beginning Rivers' fatal venture had successfully accumulated a herd. Cowboys of the Loving and Rivers outfits, as well as those with Reynolds, held the herd on Dillingham Prairie, in Lost Valley on the Loving Ranch. As darkness approached, Loving camped with his fifteen to twenty men about a quarter-mile from Rivers' camp, which had a crew of about the same size. Reynolds' somewhat smaller crew camped about a hundred yards from Rivers. Reynolds and Rivers bargained on the price of the herd, and sometime early in the evening agreed on the deal. Probably because of the hour or, perhaps, just for the companionship, Reynolds decided to spend the night with Rivers' group instead of traveling back to his own camp in the dark. During the night, however, disaster struck, in the form of a slashing Indian raid.

The area had long been subject to Indian attacks. In fact, just a month earlier, the infamous Warren Wagon Train Raid took place in a nearby pasture once belonging to Loving. In that tragedy, Kiowa Indians led by Satangya, Satanta, and Big Tree killed several teamsters. Satanta and Big Tree were later tried and convicted for the crimes in civilian court in nearby Jacksboro. The old man, Satangya, purposely hastened his death in a confrontation with soldiers at Fort Sill.

Now, on the night of June 16, Indians swooped in under cover of darkness and drove off both Reynolds' and Rivers' remudas, more than fifty saddle horses. Fortunately, the noise did not stampede the cattle grazing some distance from the camp, and the Indians had no interest in them. The action was brief but furious as the cowboys exchanged shots with the raiders, who soon disappeared, leaving behind only a cloud of dust.

Hearing the noise and correctly guessing its cause, the men in Loving's camp, only a quarter-mile away, expected a rush on their animals as well. They hurriedly gathered their horses into a tight circle to protect them, but the assault never came. The Indians apparently were satisfied with their booty and beat a hasty retreat. No pursuit was launched, and the perpetrators were apparently never identified.

Once they realized the raiders were gone, the cowboys took stock of their situation. They were afoot, a disastrous state for cowboys, especially on the eve of a trail drive. Gravely dispirited, the men did not know how to proceed.

Then they discovered Rivers, grievously wounded in the left lung by a gunshot. A messenger hurried to Loving's camp, and summoned him to Rivers' side. Rivers told his brother-in-law that the deal with Reynolds had been made, and should be honored. Loving agreed, and preparations continued despite Rivers' condition.

As soon as possible, Loving dispatched a rider to Weatherford to summon a doctor. Rivers was later carried to Weatherford, and kept under what medical care was available at the time.

For the crew, one pressing need had to be met: horses. Fortunately, Loving had other saddle horses available on the family ranch not far away, so Reynolds bought enough animals to launch his trail drive west. To provide each man with a suitable string of mounts, Reynolds may well have picked up other horses on the home ranch, some fifty miles to the west, as he traveled through the area along the Clear Fork of the Brazos.

The drive was successful. Reynolds pushed on to the Pecos over his familiar trail, and then, according to one account, on to Nevada, where he sold the cattle. That account says he went on to California and bought a herd of horses, which he sold at a profit in Colorado on his way back to Texas. Another account maintains that he simply sold the cattle in Colorado and returned to Texas. If he did, he would have used the Goodnight-Loving Trail.

Whatever the case, Reynolds avoided disaster in Jack County and went on to prosper. He established ranches in Nevada, Colorado, New Mexico, Arizona, Wyoming, and Texas. He later established banks in both Texas and Oklahoma.

Meanwhile, Rivers languished through the hot Texas summer, and died in August, 1871. Whether he was wounded by Indians or by one of the cowboys' errant shots will never be known, but it is irrelevant. No malice was ever suspected in the matter, because Rivers was an upright, honest, and respectable man, as was Reynolds. Charley Rivers lost his life pursuing a dream of ranching in the West. He belonged to a legendary cattle legacy and in that way helped bring civilization to the Southwest.

TWENTY-FIVE

Benjamin Franklin Reynolds, Texas Pioneer

Benjamin Franklin "Ben" Reynolds was one of eight children of Barber Watkins and Ann Marie Campbell Reynolds, early pioneers in West Texas, especially in Shackelford and Throckmorton counties. Four of his brothers—George, W.D., Phin, and Glenn—are well known by students of the history of the time. The life of Ben is no less interesting than that of his better-known brothers. Indeed, he accompanied them on many of their adventures, and had not a few of his own.

Born in Shelby County, he accompanied the family to Galconda, now Palo Pinto, Texas, when the family settled there in 1859. Only months later, the family moved to the Cantrell Ranch in Buchanan, now Stephens, County. In 1860 the county was organized in a meeting in the Reynolds home.

While living on the Dawson Ranch, also in Stephens County, Ben and his brothers had a close call with raiding Indians. The older boys had killed a panther, and the three younger boys—Phin, Glenn, and Ben—were cutting into the tail to get some sinew to fix some arrows. The cowboys and older boys had gone, and with them all the weapons. Indians dashed close to the house, cut the hobbles on two horses grazing nearby, and drove the stolen animals away. The boys called their father out of the house, but he was armed only with an old gun that would not fire. Fortunately, the Indians were not looking for a fight, and fled with their booty, but not before Ben recognized one of the horses, ridden by an Indian as belonging to a neighbor named Riley St. John. The horse had been stolen the night before. St. John is remembered, among other things, as the man riding with George Reynolds when George was shot by an arrow in an Indian fight. St. John rode on to kill the Indian who wounded his friend.

The troublesome years that followed were fraught with danger. When the Civil War erupted, and federal troops were withdrawn from nearby Camp Cooper in what became Confederate Texas, the Reynolds family joined a number of other families at a civilian fort, named Fort Davis, on the Clear Fork of the Brazos River, in present-day western Stephens County. Along with his younger brothers and sisters, Ben attended school taught by Sam Newcomb at Fort Davis.

After the war ended, the family moved to the Stone Ranch, established by Capt. Newton C. Givens, of the Second U.S. Dragoons, in 1859. Several stone structures, including a two-room house, bunkhouse, smokehouse, and corral, had been built on Walnut Creek. Givens had spent little time there, and died not long afterward. At the time of their construction, these were the westernmost structures in this part of Texas, and sat squarely in the range of the great buffalo herds. Ben and his oldest brother George killed a very rare white buffalo on one of their hunting excursions, the main pastime of the Reynolds brothers. Some believe it to be the first white buffalo killed in Texas. The animal was a young bull, and its skin is in the Smithsonian Institute in Washington, D.C. In the fall of 1866, many buffalo cows were killed, and orphaned calves wandered the range. Ben, only fourteen years of age, gathered some of these orphans and ran them with his father's cattle herds, the first effort in Texas to domesticate the bison.

The Reynolds brothers were cattlemen and trail drivers, and

would eventually drive cattle all over the West. Ben was no exception, but he was frail. In 1868, on the advice of the post surgeon at Fort Griffin, Ben dropped out of school and became part of the crew of a trail herd his brother George was taking north over the Goodnight-Loving Trail. The surgeon felt the rigor of the trip would strengthen the lad. By fall, the herd was in Trinidad, Colorado, where the crew and herd wintered before venturing further into the mountains. In the spring, the men moved the herd to Laramie, Wyoming, with plans to go on to California. George sold the herd in Cheyenne. Ben's share of the sale was $500. Apparently, the activity proved beneficial to his health as well as his financial condition.

Ben then decided to return to Texas. George entrusted him with $2,000, with instructions to give it to Joe Matthews, a fellow rancher at Fort Griffin, to pay a debt. The Reynolds and Matthews two families would become closely related, through several marriages among the children on both sides of the families. Ben traveled by train from Cheyenne to Omaha, Nebraska, and then on to Kansas City, Missouri. He toured the city sights before leaving for Paola, Kansas, the terminus of the railroad at the time. His next stop was Fort Gibson, on the Arkansas River. There, he bought two horses, and rode across Indian Territory and on to Fort Griffin.

This trail drive was only the first of many for Reynolds. In 1872, at age twenty, he was put in charge of one of two trail herds from the Reynolds ranch in Colorado. The other was under the control of Bud Matthews, only nineteen years of age at the time. Their destination was the Humboldt River country in Nevada, to a man named Hoyt, who took the first herd. The buyer of the second herd backed out, and the men traded the cattle for horses, and drove them back to Colorado. Then, the two young men went to San Francisco, and recounted seeing sacks of gold in the banks there.

Trail driving suited the young man, Ben Reynolds, as did ranching in Nevada and Utah, and especially in Colorado. He established a ranch near La Junta. In 1875 he left the La Junta ranch with 200 head of Durham cattle, an English breed that promised better beef from range grasses than the hearty longhorns did. He wintered the cattle at Mobeete, in the Texas Panhandle, and in the spring took the cattle on to the family ranch near Fort Griffin. Unfortunately, more than half the animals died from Texas Tick Fever, a malady that did not harm the longhorns, but from which the Durhams had no immunity. His effort was, however, thought to be the first to bring Durhams to this part of the state. This British breed was important to the cattle business of the time. Charles Goodnight brought a number of Durham bulls to the Palo Duro Canyon ranch which he founded in 1876. The Durhams proved less hardy than the Herefords, and eventually lost out as the breed of choice of West Texas cattlemen for decades to come.

In 1876 Ben began construction of what became known as the Reynolds House, in Reynolds Bend on the Clear Fork of the Brazos, a site not far from the Stone Ranch, where the family had lived earlier. In her now-classic volume *Interwoven*, his sister Sallie Reynolds Matthews describes the house:

> The house was small without a suspicion of architectural design, built in an "L" plan with living room, combined kitchen and dining room, and a small bedroom on the lower floor. There were three bedrooms up-stairs, the stairway going up in the kitchen, and there were three fireplaces and one closet.

One of Reynolds's most dangerous roles was his part in the arrest of John Larn, who was married at the time to Mary Jane Matthews, a sister of Reynold's longtime friend, J.A. Matthews. The story of Larn has been told and retold, but the one-time lawman turned cattle rustler and his friend John Selman were becoming a threat to the Clear Fork community. Early on the morning of June 23, 1878, Sheriff W.R Cruger, Deputy Dave Barker, Ben, and other carefully selected men from the community arrested Larn at the milking pen on his ranch, near the site of abandoned Camp Cooper and took him, not to Fort Griffin, where Larn had friends, but to Albany. That night, several masked men entered the jail and shot

Larn to death. Great mystery still surrounds the story of this violent incident of Clear Fork life.

Reynolds settled down and began to devote time to expanding development in the region. In 1879 he married Florence Matthews, a niece of the neighboring ranching family. He became a commissioner, county judge, and county attorney in Throckmorton County, where for many years he operated an abstract office and practiced law. In 1888 he and neighbors Mart Dixon, Mart Gentry, and John Matthews built a schoolhouse in Reynolds Bend.

Benjamin Franklin Reynolds was indeed a pioneer cattleman, innovator, and productive citizen. The latter years of his life may lack the glamour and attention paid his more famous brothers, but he was definitely an important part of life in the American West. His nephew, Watkins Reynolds Matthews, later a legendary cowman along the Clear Fork, restored three of the structures mentioned here—Stone Ranch, the Reynolds house, and the schoolhouse—and they stand today as evidence of the old days along the Clear Fork.

TWENTY-SIX

THE SAGA OF THE STONE RANCH

The several structures that make up the Stone Ranch, a cluster of ranch buildings located between Albany and Throckmorton, stand today as elegantly as they did when constructed in the 1850s, The story of this complex of buildings is a fascinating one. The site is a mesquite grassland that lies along Walnut Creek, about twelve miles west of present Highway 283, one half mile south of the Clear Fork of the Brazos River, and five miles west of the location of abandoned Camp Cooper, where Col. Robert E. Lee spent some of his time in Texas as part of the Second U.S. Cavalry. Buzzard Peak is nearby, as are ruins of the small bake oven ordered built, either by Col. Lee or by his successor, for the short-lived relocation of nearby Camp Cooper. The name of the ranch, of course, derives from the native stone from which the buildings, sheep shed and pen, and the large corral were constructed.

Various families temporarily occupied the site in the early days. In 1865 a ranching outfit known by the names of Knox and Gardner lived there briefly. In 1866 the Barber Watkins Reynolds family and ranch crew moved there. The house was then the outermost one on the Texas frontier, with none between it and the New Mexico settlements. The largest structure is composed of two large rooms, about sixteen by twenty feet, with a fireplace in each end of the house. Double oak doors open to the north and south. A spacious entry hall once served as a spare bedroom when needed. One room has a floor of planks, the other of stone, into which were cut cattle brands of the region. A small two-room house to the north served as a residence for the young men and boys. About two hundred yards northeast of the two houses stands the sheep shed; the smokehouse stands almost due west of the main structure. Records show that this structure, important for preserving and storing meats, once held a huge store of salted buffalo tongues, a delicacy during the period. The grave of a child is located on top of a nearby hill.

Other families living there over the years included the M. V. Hoovers, who occupied the house from about 1872-1875; then the Millets, a ranching outfit known for its rough antics, moved in next. About the time this crew left in the winter of 1879, fire swept through the buildings, and with time, the stones tumbled down. The Millets founded the Hashknife Ranch, which still operates extensive holdings some miles north of Lambshead.

This remarkable complex of buildings was restored by Watkins Reynolds Matthews, an outstanding rancher and historical preservationist, who for many years has run Lambshead Ranch, where the structures stand. Watt had long hoped to restore the structures, but was unable to find a stonemason who could handle the work. He finally located, in Kerrville, a man who could do the rock work; and on May 12, 1983, Watt began supervising the task of cleaning up the site and sorting the stones. Extra stone was taken from the tumbled-down walls of the nearby corral, which as reconstructed, is smaller than the original version. The first rock was not laid until June, 1983, but Thanksgiving dinner was served in the main house that fall. To guide the project, Matthews followed the scant description recorded by his mother in her book, *Interwoven*, and old photographs made before the roof timbers collapsed. From this data, he decided the height of the walls and the pitch of the roof. The stone floor in the east room is the original one. Even the large oak doors were reconstructed. The original keystone, with the date 1856 cut into it, was placed years ago in the chimney of the cook house at the Lambshead Ranch headquarters but was returned to the house to complete the restoration. In addition, Matthews reactivated the well by having it cleaned out and replacing the stone top. He also decorated the interior with artifacts of the period.

Lawrence Clayton at the Stone Ranch

This collection of buildings in what is still an isolated area came to be built originally, legend says, by a Captain Newton C. Givens, who served with the Second U.S. Dragoons stationed at Camp Cooper. The military post, located not too far away, was under construction at the same time. Givens will be remembered as the commander of a small garrison of troops who set fire to the buildings at Fort Phantom Hill in 1854, when that post, despised because of the scarcity of wood and water and the harsh climatic conditions, was ordered closed by the army. In the absence of documented fact, the process of legend has taken over and allowed the creation of a romanticized version of what took place. The story is that Givens may have constructed the place as a lodge for hunters, since he was an ardent hunter himself, but he may also have intended to raise cattle in order to sell beef to the army, a situation he supposedly found illegal only after the buildings were completed. A study of documents relating the life of Givens, however, reveals that though the officer was involved, the extent to which he was involved brings into question whether his actual contribution may well have been far different from that with which legend has credited him.

A sketch of Givens' life reveals some interesting information. He served at various stations in the Southwest and in 1854, he was assigned with Company I, Second U.S. Dragoons at Fort Belknap, Texas, near present-day Graham. In 1855, Given's career took a decided turn for the worse.

On May 4, he was arrested and ordered to face a court-martial in Austin, Texas. The charge involved "conduct prejudiced to good order and discipline" and "conduct unbecoming an officer and a gentlemen." The evidence against him consisted of a letter, of which Givens was thought to be the author, published in the *Texas Gazette*, a newspaper in Austin. The text was highly critical of Givens's commanding officer, Major Enoch Steen, Commander at Fort Belknap, where Givens was then assigned. Their conflict stemmed from an incident in which Givens led a contingent of twenty soldiers to discover the identity of a party of raiding Indians.

B.J. Fisher summarizes a report to the Adjutant General in Washington dated November 17, 1854, which recounts that Lt. Givens

> was in pursuit of a group of Southern Comanche who had run off a number of cattle and oxen. He reported that he proceeded with 20 men to the Clear Fork of the Brazos. He found the river very high and was unable to cross it. A Mr. Burnett came down the river and told Givens that he had tracked the Indians to a place where they had crossed the river a few miles down. A Mr. Garner, who assisted in trailing the lost animals, swam the river and served as a guide for Givens. The soldiers came upon two oxen killed and portions of their flesh taken off, apparently for provisions. The carcass of another oxen was found thrown in the river but none of the flesh had been removed from this one.

Givens continued to follow the trail of the Indians. When he discovered that the guilty Indians were a surprisingly large party of Southern Comanches, he returned to Fort Belknap to seek more soldiers to "chastise" the Indians.

Major Steen refused to authorize the expedition, and Givens became angry at Steen's lack of action. This situation is reflected in the letter, which was signed "By one who knows," and seems to reflect the information known to Givens and emotion characteristic of the young lieutenant.

The Stone Ranch

Givens was in Austin in July of 1855 for his trial. According to Holden, Givens had gained the title to the Stone Ranch property on July 20 of that year. On July 23, 1855, only three days later, during testimony at the trial proceedings, Givens made several derogatory comments about Brevet Major General Persifor F. Smith, Commander of the Department of Texas. Although eventually found innocent of the first set of charges, Givens was subjected to a second court-martial, ordered by General Smith. While Givens awaited the result of his first trial, his unit was transferred from Fort Belknap to Fort Riley, Kansas. Givens remained at Fort Belknap, but was ordered for his second court-martial to Carlisle Barracks, Pennsylvania. He was there by Christmas of 1855, because he wrote, on December 26 of that year, a letter to Colonel C.A. May asking to be transferred to warmer climate for his health and noting that since his "act or neglect . . . [occurred] while serving in Texas," he expected to be tried there. No change was ordered, and his court-martial convened in Pennsylvania on January 15, 1856. Givens was found guilty, suspended from the army for nine months, and reprimanded. It is not apparent whether he served the full suspension, for he resumed duty with his company on May 15, 1856. It is possible, but unlikely, that during the time of waiting for the result of his first trial, he may have spent some time building the Stone Ranch complex. He had, as well, a period of suspension after January 15, 1856, and may have worked on the project then. If so, he traveled to the ranch in the dead of winter, probably primarily on horseback, since no other means were available, and worked in the worst part of the Texas winter. One cannot be certain that he was allowed the leisure for this work, however, because Heitman states Givens was "in arrest, suspended, and sick" from 1855-1857. Whatever he did during this time cost him heavily in his health. By January 7, 1857, Givens reported for duty in Austin, complaining of being ill. Concern for his health had become a dominant factor in his life.

By November 24, 1857, he was in Galveston, too ill from tuberculosis and intestinal problems to travel. A Dr. Heard, who treated him as best he could, wrote the following: "Captain N.C. Givens, Second Regiment of the Dragoons, called on me for medical aid on the 14th of November . . . I found him labouring under a diarreal affection associated with a high state of the gastro intestinal mucous membrane. His liver is involved functionally to a considerable extent. I have given him such medical treatment as in my opinion he required. In view of the fact that his lungs are tuberculous, I have advised him to remain here until he feels his health more improved before he makes the further attempt to join his post." Givens was on sick leave of absence after June 15, 1858, until his death in San Antonio on March 9, 1859. His effects were turned over to his mother.

Holden indicates, but does not footnote a specific source, that the cause of death was an accidental gunshot wound, suffered while hunting with Captain Kirby Smith, who had been stationed earlier at Camp Cooper. Heitman, a reliable military source, indicates that Givens died that day, but gives no reason. It is Heitman's pattern to give cause of death, if unusual, so the gunshot wound story may not be true. No mention of cause appears in a letter from Major General D.E. Twiggs, then Commander of the Department of Texas, to Colonel S. Cooper, of the Adjutant Generals Office in Washington, D.C. One would assume that if he were too ill to serve, he would not have been hunting, and probably died of complications of tuberculosis.

The idea that Givens built the ranch structures while stationed at Camp Cooper is erroneous. Givens was never assigned to duty at

Camp Cooper. Don Biggers, an early source on stories from the area, seems to be the origin of this false assumption, and later writers on this subject simply picked up his error. Camp Cooper was home to the Second U.S. Cavalry, an elite group created by Jefferson Davis in 1855 and staffed by many future Southern general officers. Givens' assignment was Fort Belknap, where the Second U.S. Dragoons were stationed, approximately fifty miles to the northeast between present-day Graham and Newcastle. These two units have often been confused because of the similarity in their names. The manufactured materials in the Stone Ranch buildings—oak planks and split shingles—are thought to have been diverted from the supplies sent to help construct Camp Cooper, but may not have been from that source. At least two reasons exist for this conclusion. First, according to Mr. Fisher, little in the way of materials was sent to the construction efforts of these frontier posts by the army. The structures at Camp Cooper were mostly tents, anyway. Whoever built the house probably had to haul in supplies by wagon. Further support for this generalization, about Givens' not using military supplies, comes from the fact, that at the time of this construction, Givens was not on active duty in the area near the ranch, because of the terms of one of his two courts-martial. Legend and fact meld together in this story, and Givens' true role in the construction of the Stone Ranch may never be known for certain.

Uncertainty over the person or persons responsible for construction does not detract from the significant accomplishment of erecting the structures, or of restoring them. They serve as a monument to man's perseverance and vision in the 1850s, and as an inspiration to those who see and enjoy the significant effort to preserve the past for the present.

TWENTY-SEVEN

Watkins Reynolds Matthews: Rancher and Historical Preservationist

Rare indeed is the individual who has both the vision and the means to preserve those things from the past which are important to himself and to others. One of these unusual individuals is Watkins Reynolds Matthews—rancher, cowman, historical preservationist, and philanthropist. Watt, as he is known to his many friends, has deep roots along the Clear Fork of the Brazos River north of present-day Albany, for his family on both his father's and mother's sides were ranchers who helped settle the area. His father, John Alexander Matthews, married Sallie Reynolds, the daughter of Barber Watkins and Anna Maria Campbell Reynolds, in 1876. They had nine children, six girls and three boys. Born in 1899, Watt was the ninth and last child.

Among Watt's most significant activities and contributions during his long life are his efforts at historical preservation. The main projects have involved five structures on his ranch: the Reynolds house, the Bartholomew house, the John House dugout, the schoolhouse built on the ranch in 1888, and his recent, most impressive accomplishment, the Stone Ranch.

Construction began on the Barber Watkins Reynolds house on January 1, 1876, in Reynolds Bend on the Clear Fork. The area around the house is rustic but modernized in many ways. It serves as the setting for the annual Fort Griffin Fandangle "Sampler," performed in the spring. Its location, a pecan-bottom river bend near a tall bluff, is one of the most serene in the region.

Lawrence Clayton and Watt Matthews

The Bartholomew house was built by Nathan L. "Barney" Bartholomew, former Throckmorton County judge and organizer of the First National Bank in Albany, in the summer of 1876. It is located on the Clear Fork not a great distance from the Reynolds house. Lumber used for its construction was transported by wagon about 150 miles from Eagle Ford, west of Dallas, the terminus of the railroad at that time. This home stands today as ready for use as it was in the frontier era when it was constructed.

The dugout is a more recent structure. Built by John House in the 1890s, it is set into a low hill overlooking the Clear Fork of the Brazos River bottom. The walls are built of native stone, which makes it somewhat unusual among dugouts. This structure was restored to a habitable condition in the 1970s. Mr. Matthews recalls that the dugout, as originally constructed, was occupied as late as 1912 or 1913, then fell into disrepair.

The schoolhouse in Reynolds Bend was built in 1888 by families living in the area. Those involved in its construction include Benjamin Franklin Reynolds, Mart Dixon, Mart Gentry, and John Matthews. Of the schoolhouse, Watt says it is as near a facsimile as he could arrange. The construction method, popular during this period, involves one-by-twelve-inch pine planks raised vertically with the joints stripped with one-by-fours. The schoolhouse stands on the same foundation, and is as nearly as possible the same size, as the original.

The Stone Ranch is Watt's most spectacular accomplishment. The ranch was founded by Captain Newton C. Givens in 1855 along Walnut Creek in southwestern Throckmorton County. The name of the ranch derives from a house built of native stone, completed probably in 1856 by workers gathered by Givens, who at the time was commander of a company of the 2nd U.S. Dragoons stationed at Fort Belknap. Commander Givens was an ardent hunter, and possibly established the ranch as a hunting lodge, but his aim probably included raising cattle in order to sell beef to the army. He died in San Antonio in 1859.

Other families temporarily occupied the structure, and in 1866 the Barber Watkins Reynolds family and ranch crew moved there. The house has two large rooms about sixteen by twenty feet each, with a fireplace in each end of the house, with an entry hall that served as a spare bedroom when needed. Also on the property was a sheep shed, a smokehouse, and a small two-room house—the residence for the young men and boys.

Fire swept through the buildings in the winter of 1879, when a ranching family named Millet occupied the premises, and with time the stone tumbled down. The property was transferred from the Givens estate to John H. Hancock of Austin, and in 1880 was sold to the Reynolds and Matthews. Judge John A. Matthews gained control of the property in 1885, and it remains part of Lambshead Ranch, so named because of an early English settler, Thomas Lambshead, of Devon, England. It is still controlled by the Matthews family, and

Watt himself is manager. The stone house and outbuildings stand today as proudly as they did in 1856, when Captain Givens erected this most unusual group of stone structures.

Matthews has devoted himself to the maintenance of a lifestyle reminiscent of pioneer days. The recently expanded cookhouse on Lambshead Ranch serves two meals a day to cowboys who work there, and others who come by. He also has constructed at the headquarters a picket-style house, made of vertically set cross-ties, but he still lives in the bunkhouse, his home for many years. In addition, Watt has been careful to disguise modern-day corrals and cattle guards by having cedar posts wired to them, and otherwise maintaining the appearance of an older time on Lambshead Ranch.

Animal life on the ranch also is reminiscent of pioneer days. Matthews has kept a herd of more than a dozen buffalo since about 1950. When the herd grows too large, surplus animals are slaughtered and used for meat to feed the crew. Buffalo hides are tanned and kept for future use. He also maintains a herd of longhorn cattle, bought from the herd at Fort Griffin in 1972. Deer, turkey, and domesticated hogs that have gone wild abound on the ranch. Matthews has long been a game conservationist, and many deer and turkeys have been transplanted from his ranch to other areas.

Watt's efforts have not gone unnoticed, for he has received several prizes and awards for preserving and conserving Lambshead's history and resources. His special-merit award from the National Cowboy Hall of Fame and a Texas preservation award from then Governor Preston Smith are among those honors garnered. His highest honors are two: The Golden Spur Award, given to him in 1981 by the Ranch Heritage Center at Texas Tech University; and the Ruth Lester Award, the state's honor for historical preservation, given to him in 1984 by the Texas Historical Commission. In 1984 he also received the Josiah Wheat Award, given by the Texas Historical Foundation, for his outstanding achievements in historical preservation.

When asked about these awards, Watt replies modestly that his hobby is "preserving the landmarks and traditions of the pioneers."

He insists that "as long as you are doing what you like to do, you don't deserve a lot of credit for doing it." Obviously Watt has enjoyed preserving the landmarks on the ranch he has managed since the 1940s, and contrary to what he says, he does deserve an enormous amount of credit for his efforts.

TWENTY-EIGHT
The Ice Man Comes to Ft. Griffin: An Oral History from the 1930s

In her address at the banquet at last year's meeting of the West Texas Historical Association, Dr. Lou Rodenberger, a writer and folklorist, highlighted the significance of oral history, a subject that tends to have much in common with folklore, because of the oral nature of both undertakings. I have been interested in the subject for some time, principally because of discussions with Dr. Rodenberger and others over the past decade or so and because on my wife's side of the family, oral history and legend have proved to be a particularly rewarding storehouse of information for me. One of my best informants has been my wife's father, J.C. Irwin, Jr., a descendant of the Irwin family who was among the first white settlers to come to this area along the Clear Fork of the Brazos River. His grandfather, John G. Irwin, was a first sergeant of dragoons at Camp Cooper and later, as a civilian, sold beef to the troops stationed there under a contract signed by Col. Robert E. Lee, then Commander of the Department of Texas. That story intrigued me from the beginning, and I found many more to keep me interested.

My father-in-law told me about a man named Raymond G. Little, an early-day ice delivery man in the Fort Griffin area, where Mr. Irwin has lived most of his life here, and he could recall the man's leaving ice at the Irwin ranch house. J.C. had thoroughly enjoyed a series of recent visits with him in Woodson, a small town in Throckmorton County, where the two often met while having lunch at the local café. Since it struck me as strange that the remote Fort Griffin area would have an ice delivery system in the 1930s, I was eager to interview Mr. Little, which I accomplished initially on February 23, and again on March 12, 1985.

Raymond Little, a man of medium height and slender build, presently resides in a comfortable, spacious home at the intersection of FM 209 and FM 578 in downtown Woodson. Although life in this community has a very slow pace these days, it was, in years past, a bustling area with considerable oil activity, in addition to the farming and ranching that still make up the mainstay of the region's economy. Mr. Little was born two miles southwest of Woodson, on a piece of property the family was then renting, but which he later purchased and still owns. The son of John R. and Pearl Little, he was the oldest of four children: Alton, now deceased; Ivan; and JoAnn. Mr. Little has been married twice, but both wives are now deceased. His first wife, Rosetta Good, bore him one child, Carolyn (Tate), now of Wichita Falls. His second wife, Mozelle McBride, who taught science in the Woodson schools for some years, bore two children: Thomas Randall, now residing in Arlington; and Susan Jane, of Oklahoma City.

John Little, Raymond's father, came to the Fort Griffin area in September of 1900 and, as chance would have it, spent his first night in the home of my father-in-law's parents, the John Chadbourne Irwins. The Littles were involved in agricultural pursuits in the Woodson area, and in the spring of 1930, Mr. Little helped Raymond assume an ice delivery route established earlier by Raymond's uncle. Raymond took the route in mid-June, and this step became the turning point in his life, because he gave up his plans to return to John Tarleton College in Stephenville to complete his education.

The ice was manufactured in Woodson at a plant, erected by a man named McGraw, on the Humble Lake built at Woodson in the late 1920s to support the oil refinery. In 1930 the plant was run by J.R. McGraw, son of the original owner. J.H. Good, later to be Mr. Little's father-in-law, bought the plant in 1931 or 1932. Most of the ice was sold in Throckmorton, hauled from Woodson in a four-wheeled trailer specifically outfitted to hold a number of the uncut 300-pound blocks in its wooden bed. Mr. Little bought a 1929 Ford Roadster pickup, and built a bed suitable for hauling ice. The apparatus was a staked bed with sides made of one-by-twelve planking. The arrangement accommodated the one hundred pound blocks of ice with scant inches left above the precious cargo. The top of the bed was covered by a tarpaulin, which insulated the load and allowed easy access from above. In this vehicle, Raymond was able to haul eight to nine hundred pounds of ice at one time. One of his routes went southwest from Woodson to Fort Griffin to the Lambshead Ranch of the Matthews family, and back to Air Plane Station, a point seven miles south of Throckmorton, now a park on Highway 283. He drove this stretch of ranch land every other day. On alternate days, the route took him northeast to Masters, Murray, and Hufstedler. It was a seven-day-a-week job. Roads were a problem in bad weather, and he can recall that some portions of the Albany-Throckmorton stretch of Highway 285 were being paved during his years as a deliveryman.

Raymond Little, The Ice Man

On his Fort Griffin route, most of his thirty to forty customers bought twenty-five or fifty pound blocks, although a few bought as much as a hundred pounds. The Matthews Ranch would normally buy a hundred pounds each time. In extremely hot weather, Mr. Little would have to make two trips because, as he explained, by the time he got to the end of his route, the blocks that had weighed twenty-five pounds when he left that morning were somewhat diminished in size. "Those at the end of the route suffered a little, I'll have to admit," said Mr. Little.

Payment for the ice was not always in legal tender. Customers who bought larger orders often paid with money, but many of his smaller accounts paid in goods of one kind or another. As he noted, "There just wasn't much money in those days." Many of his customers paid him in eggs, and he regularly carried egg cases in his truck, to haul the eggs safely to town. Market value of eggs at that time fluctuated around ten cents a dozen. Twenty-five pounds of ice cost the customer eighteen cents, so Mr. Little collected the equivalent of the current market value in eggs.

Many of the people, he recounted, did not have iceboxes, or if they did, they did not put their ice in it to keep comestibles cool. Most families kept their milk and other perishables fresh in cooler boxes in a window of the house; ice was too precious for the relief it brought, to be used for chilling food. Customers wrapped the ice in a blanket or quilt to insulate it. The main use for the ice, he said, was for cool drinks, especially tea. Usually, the ice would last his customers only the day on which he delivered it, so they would go one day without ice before he made his return trip. There were, of course, no electric refrigerators at this time, because electricity did not come to the region until 1947. A few families had Electrolux refrigerators that ran on kerosene.

Although Mr. Little began his delivery service in 1930, he did not deliver ice in '31 or '32. He resumed his route in 1933, and followed it without interruption until 1939. "Without interruption" does not indicate, however, that this job ran year round. He normally began his deliveries around the first of June, and ended his service after the end of September, when the weather began to cool down and the demand for ice dropped off. The last year that he ran the route, he drove a 1938 V-8 Ford pickup, a much improved method of transportation from the earlier Model A truck he had used.

Mr. Little's customers typically had a standard order, with which he was familiar. If someone were at the house when he delivered and wanted to change the order, they were free to do that. The cards used to indicate the size of the block of ice desired (so familiar, particularly in cities) were not used on Mr. Little's route at all.

The job was not an easy one. Since the ice was manufactured in Woodson, Mr. Little would go to the icehouse the evening before and, using a large handsaw, he would score the large blocks so that smaller blocks could be separated easily with an ice pick. Early the next morning, he would load the truck and start out on his route, which was some fifty to sixty miles in length. He would return home during the afternoon, at which time he frequently helped with the farming chores, before returning to the ice house late in the afternoon, to saw ice for the next day's run. He said, "As a young man, I thought I could work two jobs, but this convinced me I couldn't. I had to stay with just one."

In response to my question concerning the amount of profit he made, his response was clear: "I never made any real money at this job. The ice cost me forty cents a hundred, and my profit was only thirty cents a hundred. The margin was pretty slim when you consider my expense. There was so little money in those days that most of us were just looking for something to do to get by. I had a job, but it just paid my expenses. That wasn't any worse than most other people were doing at the time, so I kept after it for a while. It was really a grind, but it kept me off the W.P.A. crews. There was no money in my pockets when I quit. I just didn't eat much during those years, and I sure didn't spend much." He went on to comment on the value of his stint: "The ice business was good experience for me. For as long as I could remember, I wanted to be in a business of some kind. That ice business convinced me that I was not cut out to be a business man, and so I guess it was very beneficial for me. After that, I stuck with farming and ranching. I'm not sorry that I was in the ice business, but I am glad that I didn't stay with it all these years."

Mr. Little had many recollections about his business experience. He said, "Some people left without paying me, but I was never really hurt by that. I'd like to think I may have helped them, if they just couldn't pay me. I don't 'grudge anyone for anything that happened during those years." On an even happier note, he still sees people he served with the welcomed relief from summer's heat. They often say to their children, "There goes our ice man," and they recall the pleasure of a cold glass of tea on a hot summer day.

Mr. Little's story seems fairly typical of the 1930s period. I can remember hearing other stories of the depression years and shortly thereafter, when people did whatever was possible and necessary in order to survive. One reason, perhaps, that I was drawn to this story is my grandfather, now deceased, delivered ice in a mule-drawn wagon for the Southern Ice Co. in Dallas in his younger days, before moving to Live Oak County to pursue farming and ranching. I also recall that Conrad Dunagan, when he was president of the West Texas Historical Association, called for the study of business ventures in West Texas. This story as led me to consider doing an indepth study of ice production and delivery, in a region in which that commodity would have been even more precious for the comfort it brought during the hot summer months, than it was necessary for the preservation of fresh fruits and vegetables during shipping to distant markets, as ice was used in other areas. Nor was it used for the preservation of foods. This practice came when refrigeration became common in this region in the late '40s, after electricity was brought in. But that larger study would have to be researched from formal records, and it is oral history that interests me here.

TWENTY-NINE

The Fort Griffin Fandangle: History, Legend, and Lore in Dramatic Form

Settlement of the Fort Griffin area is a typical but fascinating one. Because of the remoteness of the region, however, a broad sketch of the activities of this period seems necessary to provide a framework for the information that makes up this book. I have chosen to offer this sketch in the form of a discussion of a most unusual dramatic production, the *Fort Griffin Fandangle*, which uses the history of the region as the vehicle for presenting its singing and dancing. The *Fandangle* is informal, entertaining, yet reliable in its presentation of the general events of the history, legend, and lore of the area.

HISTORY DRAMATIZED

Imagine yourself sitting in an outdoor amphitheater near Albany in late June. It is sundown, and the audience is talking excitedly. The harsh notes of a steam calliope boom a rousing song in the background. As darkness approaches, the spotlights click on and the eerie sound of an organ starts a chill up the backs of the viewers, and the words coming through the speakers highlight the tone of the evening by using Berta Hart Nance's poem, "Cattle," the last couplet of which states the general impact of this region:

Other states were made or born,
Texas grew from hide and horn.

Then follow the words "Ladies and Gentlemen, the *Fort Griffin Fandangle* of [year]." As the speaker ceases talking, riders bearing flags race across the grassy stage, and the spine-tingling figure-eight maneuver begins at breakneck speed as the music rises in tempo and volume. Dust swirls, but the speed never slackens. These are not town boys riding borrowed horses. These are men who this very day chased cows out of the brush along the Clear Fork of the Brazos River, or doctored a sick calf after roping it in the pasture. This is the real West, tamed just enough to bring it to town on toughened cowponies that like the thrill of the chase, and seem to enjoy seeing how close they can come to the other horses that should get out of their way. Only one horse has been killed in this chase in recent years, but one occasionally causes a spill. This is the *Fort Griffin Fandangle*, and its purpose is to recreate a sense of the spirit of the frontier. It is perhaps best characterized in this rousing horseback ride.

The development of the show is chronological, beginning before the habitation of the region by Indians. The opening scene depicts flora of the region—cacti, mesquite, bear grass, and others—by having a child carry a painted prop depicting each plant. The same holds true for the fauna—skunk, paisano or roadrunner, coon, deer, and yes, the mighty bison called the buffalo, Lord of the Plains. The intricate dance steps of these actors are an integral part of the show, and laughter ripples through the crowd as the child, wearing the costume of the rabbit, hops across the grassy stage.

In order to take the audience back in time, the story is dramatized through the memory of the Old Timer, a character played by an old-time cowman, recognized by area residents as one of the earliest still living. Joe B. Matthews played the role for years, and now

Watt Matthews, *Fandangle* president and veteran rancher, rides his "herd-wise pony" to the ranchhouse by the "creek" to tell the tales of the Old Timer.

The first settlement in the area was habitation by the Indians. These burst on the stage, riding bareback on spirited ponies, reflecting the Kiowa and Comanche bands which once roamed the area, mounted on fleet ponies that made them lord over all. One of the most remarkable openings ever used for the show was the appearance of a white horse ridden at breakneck speed by a cast member wearing an Indian costume. They first appeared on the rim of a hill about three quarters of a mile from the audience. The spotlight followed horse and rider, mane and feathered headdress flowing in the breeze. The viewer could surely feel the chill of vulnerability the settlers must have felt, seeing the mounted, able Comanche warrior.

Dependent upon the buffalo, which furnished flesh, bone, and skins, Indians lived close to the land, and found this area completely supportive of their way of life. They lived literally off the buffalo, which gave them food, clothing, and hide covering for their tepees. When eaten raw, the meat provided an almost complete diet, supplemented by nuts, berries, and various plant roots. Although not easy, life was fully accommodating to the Indians' nomadic style. The scene depicting this era features a tepee, erected by the cast before the audience's eyes, and later, a "dead buffalo" is carried in on a pole between two warriors. The Indians converge on the carcass, and when they withdraw a few minutes later, the stark bare bones are left lying on the ground. This scene celebrates the height of the Plains Indians' culture, when they had the buffalo, the horse, and no Anglo intervention.

The "calm" of Indian life, interrupted only by tribal warfare, was shattered by Anglos migrating from the East, although the first travelers appeared harmless enough, for they were only trappers and early cowmen. Mr. C.A. Boles portrays Jesse Stem, the first settler in the area, as he leads his burro across the stage. However, these early settlers simply foreshadowed the masses that would come later, to overwhelm the Indians and almost completely eliminate the buffalo.

A song, "Let's Settle in This Country," emphasizes the determination of the settlers to establish homes here. Another song, "Dugout," recalls the kind of habitation common in this early day, although a piece introduced in 1984, "The Stone Ranch," highlights this historic structure erected by Captain Givens in 1856. The Indians saw their way of life threatened and fought back, and the infamous Indian Wars resulted. Although these conflicts are often romanticized in fiction and film, they are made very real here in such raids as the one at Elm Creek, and the kidnapping of Minnie Durgan, and the kidnapping of John Calvin Ledbetter at the Ledbetter Salt Works south of present-day Albany. This action sets the stage for the appearance of one of the South's most beloved men, Col. Robert E. Lee, who commanded a contingent of soldiers at Camp Cooper from 1856 to 1857. He termed this post his "Texas home." Camp Cooper was located a few miles from the Clear Fork Comanche Reserve, upriver from Fort Griffin, the fort founded after the Civil War.

Fort Griffin, the military post which gave its name to the area, was located on a hill overlooking the

Clear Fork. Beneath it, on the flat in the river bottom, grew up the town of Fort Griffin, and it is this town that is the heart of the *Fandangle.* In song and dance, life at the fort and town are dramatized. Gamblers, buffalo hunters, camp followers, ruffians, and other types are included. Such names as Lottie Deno, Johnny Golden, John Wesley Hardin, John Selman, John Larn, Doc Holiday, Wyatt Earp, Big-Nose Kate, and others appear as the saloon scenes dominate the set. Central to all the action is the Beehive Saloon, where these famous words appeared printed on the front in large letters:

The photos on these two pages are from the annual pageant, the Fort Griffin Fandangle

Within this hive we are all alive,
Good whiskey makes us funny,
And if you are dry
Step in and try
The flavor of our honey.

In the midst of can-can dances, fist fights, and gunfights, the raw life of the town of Fort Griffin is dramatized. "Oh, That Town of Ft. Griffin" characterizes the place:

Oh, the town of Ft. Griffin
So rough and fancy free
The wildest town on the prairie—
The town that fits me to a T.

Cattle drives occurred during the 1870s, crossing the open plains east of present-day Dallas, and forging further westward each season. The Western Cattle Trail traced its way from South Texas up the Leon River, on past Fort Griffin, and across the Red River to Dodge City, Kansas, and the Santa Fe railroad there.

One scene in this segment always inspiring awe, especially in newcomers, is the arrival onstage of a herd of twenty to thirty full-grown longhorn steers, borrowed from the state herd at Fort Griffin State Park. As the animals come down the incline onto the stage, inexperienced members of the audience gasp in fright, but mounted cowboys hold the herd in check, while one member of the cast, for a long time now Clifford Teinert, sings "The Cowboy's Prayer."

From the side, these creatures are awesome, standing six feet or more in height at the shoulder, with horns reaching out about six feet, occasionally as much as nine feet. But, as J. Frank Dobie says, from the rear the creature shows "cat hams, narrow hips, and a ridgepole kind of backbone." These rangy beasts, direct descendants of those making up the herds that gave rise to the cattle kingdom, usually exhibit an exuberance for life sparked by the cooling evening temperatures, by now down to about 85 degrees.

When ready to move the herd out to a corral hidden in the mesquite brush over the ridge, the cowboys start riding in on the herd. Spotlights aim high to give a false light enabling the cowboys to see how to move the cattle. One rider turns and rides up the incline, and the herd leaves as if on signal. The animals snort and kick up their heels in the exit of one of the most exciting scenes in this or any other drama.

The cowboy life that grew up around these original herds of Spanish cattle is emphasized by a camp scene, in which the cowhands play a trick on the trail cook, busy preparing his meal off the tailgate of his chuck box, mounted on a covered wagon. A fire burns beneath a pot, and the traditional enameled coffee pot heats nearby. A Dutch oven sits ready. A song, "Come and Get It" rings in the night: "Come and get it, hear him shout, / Come before I throw it out." Then a calf is released onto the stage, hotly pursued by a cowboy swinging his lariat. The calf is roped, thrown, and branded right on the stage. The puff of yellowish smoke, as the hot iron scorches hide and hair, is obviously not a stage prop.

On the less serious side is an always well-received scene, depicting a confrontation between a drunk cowboy, returning to the ranch from a binge in town, and a huge, thirsty rattlesnake with a yearning for alcohol, and a knack for playing solitaire. Through the use of a cleverly constructed stage prop, the cowboy and the snake share a drink or two with their card game before the cowboy decides that the association is an unnatural one. He tries, unsuccessfully, to elude the snake, which follows him constantly from then on. This scene highlights two prominent occupants of the area—cowboys and rattlesnakes—and is a fine example of the humor present in the show.

The heyday of the wild, open range period having been depicted, civilization begins to close in. Into this turmoil of activity rattles the Butterfield stagecoach, linking this outpost with the rest of the world as it runs from St. Louis to San Francisco. As settlement progresses, families are established, schools and churches spring up, permanent houses rise, and fences are built. Songs and dances illustrate each phase of growth. Then the death knell sounds, as the night is shattered by the screaming whistle of the machine that doomed Fort Griffin, the Texas Central Railroad train, which followed tracks laid into Albany, leaving Griffin to dwindle away, as trade left and moved to the other city. The unique ranch culture was left to its own development.

An interesting note on this railroad occurred when the football field served as the theatre. The train ran on a schedule which always interrupted the show while passing by on the tracks behind the stadium. To offset this distraction, the directors arranged for the train to become part of the show. Actors boarded the train, which timed its arrival for an appropriate time in the play. This is just another example of how a local situation was modified to fit into *Fandangle*.

The finale of the show is always the same. The entire cast stands on the grassy stage and sings "Prairie Land," everybody's favorite piece, written by *Fandangle* creator Bob Nail. It captures the essence of the frontier spirit of those who came to the region and stayed:

Each man holds within his heart
The dream of a land all his own.
No other land will do,
No other land is home
Here beneath the Western sun—
I know at last my quest is done.

ALBANY'S RESPONSE TO THE OCCASION

No one doubts that the *Fandangle* has put Albany on the map for many people, and in response, the town shows its gratitude by staging a parade each year on the second Thursday of the performances. Storekeepers along the main street of Albany line windows with memorabilia from frontier days: books, tools, items of clothing, and the like. The parade itself is usually led by the Hardin-Simmons University Six White Horses, each rider carrying one of the six flags that have flown over the State of Texas. Following the White Horses are local cowboys, carrying flags of the United States, Texas, and the *Fandangle*, as well as another set of the six flags. Covered wagons rumble along the asphalt street and the Butterfield Stage rattles by, drawn by six feisty mules, fighting to tear loose and run out their energy. More cowboys appear, their hats pulled down and their horses prancing, frightened by the crowd, the strange sound their hoofs make on the asphalt, and the uncertain footing of their iron-shod hoofs. Morris Ledbetter drives his old 1947 red fire truck, children hanging off the sides, siren blaring. Bands play, and children wave from wagons and trucks. A replica of the Texas Central Railroad engine and its cars "steams" down the street, smoke billowing from its stack, its tractor chassis disguised by the skillful hands of its builder, Mr. Crutchfield. This is typically a grand parade, and spirits are high.

The parade follows the main street, which is also Highway 283. Beginning north of town past the old depot, now a museum where *Fandangle* scripts and other items are stored, the parade winds through the downtown area to circle the square with the unique stone courthouse, begun in 1883, the work of architect J.E. Flanders of Dallas. The crowd gathers on the grounds around the courthouse by the gazebo, to eat a catered barbecue dinner. The menu is typical: sliced barbecued beef brisket, pinto beans, coleslaw, sliced peaches, bread, and tea or coffee. Those early and lucky enough to find a place, sit at tables and chairs along the street to eat their meal. Others hunker down on the ground, or around the gazebo. Conversation is the main order of the day. People who see each other daily, or only once a year at the *Fandangle*, or perhaps not in ten years or more, share news, pictures of grandchildren, and old memories of past performances witnessed or participated in.

As the sun slants towards the west, the town empties of people. Cars stream along the street leading to the parking lot of the prairie theatre, on land once trodden hard by the hoofs of trail herds headed up the Western Cattle Trail. Patrons navigate around chartered buses and motor homes parked near the top of the hill. Shuttle trailers drawn by tractors scurry past, carrying those who are unable or prefer not to walk up the gravel road toward the amphitheatre. Friends greet each other with hugs and handshakes. The air, still usually in the 90 degree range, is nonetheless filled with expectation, and the audience settles in for the frontier reenactment.

THE HISTORY OF THE SHOW

How this show came to be created and produced initially, and how it has continued to thrive over the years, is a remarkable story. In 1937, then superintendent of schools, C.B. Downing, called to his office Miss Alice Reynolds, daughter of a locally prominent family. A graduate of Baylor University with a degree in music, and having done graduate work in music at Sul Ross State Teachers College, Miss Reynolds was a little puzzled by the invitation. And justifiably so, for the request was indeed a strange one: could she create and produce an outdoor drama, with high school students as the cast members? She immediately admitted that she could not, but she recommended instead someone who could, if persuaded. She went to visit a good friend, Robert Edward Nail, Jr., offshoot of another locally prominent family, who had just moved back to his hometown to see after his mother. He jumped at the chance. Shortly, Alice and Bobby, as they were affectionately known by scores of Fandanglers, were off and running, and so was born the genesis of the *Fort Griffin Fandangle*, a play originally entitled "Dr. Shackelford's Paradise," performed as the senior class play in the spring of 1938.

The creator came with rich credentials. Salutatorian of his high school class, Nail had attended Lawrenceville Preparatory School in New Jersey and Princeton University, where he studied drama and was named to Phi Beta Kappa. While at Princeton, he wrote "The Time of Their Lives," regarded by many as the "best play ever written by an undergraduate student at Princeton." Nail worked at theatres in New York, Fort Worth, Abilene, and Dallas before returning in 1937 to Albany, where he taught English and drama temporarily at his old high school.

He authored various one-act plays that proved popular, especially in the state's University Interscholastic League competition. In 1966, he was awarded an honorary Doctor of Humane Arts degree by Hardin-Simmons University in Abilene. He received numerous other awards, and was responsible for arranging the college education of numerous Albany youths, and starting several others on careers in technical theatre.

The performance of "Dr. Shackelford's Paradise" was so successful that, by popular demand, the show was reworked to include townspeople in the cast, and became known as the *Fort Griffin Fandangle*, a name that alliterates nicely on the tongue and is euphonious. Actually, the last word is a provincial use of the Spanish term *fandango*, a fast dance. Nail agreed to continue the show, but he laid down three rules from the beginning: first, anybody could be in it as long as the person had ties in Shackelford County; second, there would be no publicity, and the show would have to grow by word of mouth; and third, there would be no profanity.

A musical comedy from its inception, early versions of the show contained only traditional songs and dances, folk material at its best. Familiar tunes included "Whoopie Ti Yi Yo, Get Along Little

Dogies," which served as the basis for the "Huppi Hi" dance routine; "Those Texian Boys;" "Lottie Tu Dum;" "Shenandoah;" "Bring Me a Little Water, Sylvie;" and "Eatin' Goober Peas." The show's theme song is a version of the tune to "Bury Me Not on the Lone Prairie," the theme of the early John Ford film *Stagecoach*, which took John Wayne to stardom. As the show was presented by popular demand year after year, participants began to write new songs. Now, most of the material belongs uniquely to the *Fandangle*, although traditional songs are still included.

Annual performances of the show have not been without interruption. When Nail entered military service in 1942, the first hiatus occurred. During his military career, he was assigned to special duty writing plays and radio show scripts for the army. He won the Legion of Merit for his abilities as an author and scriptwriter. Following the war, he also wrote the Nativity, an annual Christmas pageant, put on by the citizens of Albany. Occasionally, other years were skipped for various reasons. No show was performed in 1969, the year following Nail's death on November 11, 1968. The shocked town mourned him, as did anyone else who knew of him and his work. The Board of Directors rallied, however, and under the direction of Watt Matthews, President and a Princeton graduate himself, the show was revived and has not missed a year of production since.

Nail saw the show as a uniquely Albany activity, and resisted efforts to "export" it to larger audiences. One conciliation was the formation of "Samplers," short previews of the show that were transportable to other settings, either indoors or out, to promote the summer performance. Samplers were produced in the spring, and really served as the core around which the larger show, usually three hours or more in length and involving several hundred people, was built. These Samplers have been given in many locations, but the most significant ones were at the Lyndon Baines Johnson Ranch in 1967 and 1976, and in England in 1980. The *Fandangle* cast presented its show in Palo Duro Canyon, and paved the way, under Nail's leadership, for the massive professional production entitled "Texas," written by Paul Green, and now staged in the canyon each summer. Although Nail was the catalyst who created the *Fandangle*, and held it together for many years, he did not work alone. Albany has more than its share of talented people who have contributed over the years.

Next to Nail, Alice Reynolds definitely made the greatest long-term contribution. In addition to playing for the shows over the forty-three years in which she was active, she wrote many of the songs added in later years. Some she authored alone and others with James Ball, Nail, and some with both men. She designed many of the stage props, as well, some of which are ingeniously constructed for transport onto the stage. She made drawings for and supervised the making of many of the elaborate costumes, though others certainly designed costumes as well. One of her major contributions was designing the replica of the Texas Central Railroad train, which Mr. G.P. Crutchfield built on a discarded tractor chassis. She also stretched and laid out the emblems and banners for the production, symbols which have come to represent the show itself. Miss Reynolds played each performance without sheet music of any kind, using only a cue sheet. Once, when she forgot the music and key of a particular song during a performance, the singer, Harold Law, started by himself, perfectly on key, and gave her the needed stimulus. In early performances, she played only a piano with a microphone set beside it; later she used an organ. Although the longtime accompanist for the show, she has not played for all of them. Lloyd Letz played for some of the shows in the late 1930s and the 1940s. Alice was an enormously accomplished person. She studied painting in New York and New Orleans, and lived for a time in Taos, New Mexico. She painted a mural on the wall of the Post Office in Robstown, Texas, which was kept when the Post Office was recently restored. She died on May 20, 1984.

Others also loom large in *Fandangle* history: Marge Bray, an exceedingly alented dancer and choreographer, who was in the first performance, is now the director of the show; Bill Overton is a college trained drama director from Abilene; James Ball has directed the show and has written many of the songs; Louann George is now the music director, since Alice Reynolds retired in 1981. Her experience includes having been Miss Reynolds's assistant for some years. The list goes on and on.

The current prairie theatre was not the site of the early shows, which were held on the Albany High School football field from 1938 until 1965. Then the one-acre outdoor theatre was built on a thirty-acre site northwest of Albany, on land leased from the J.A. Matthews family for a dollar a year. Built by the people of Albany under Nail's supervision, it is a unique and very efficient theatre, arranged to permit the diverse activities and sets used in the show. Not every stage will accommodate running horses, a herd of longhorn steers, the Butterfield Stagecoach, and a replica of the Texas Central Railway train. The battery of spotlights and the flexibility and quality of the sound system far outstrip what one would expect from the resources of a town of fewer than 2,000 people. When one considers the support generated among Albany's oil-related business community, the reason for this quality becomes more obvious.

The content of the show each year depends upon a general direction chosen by the directors, and upon the talent available. Nail would often pick out someone present at early rehearsals, and assign them a role. One of Nail's strengths was his ability to spot talent, and showcase it in some part of the show. Now Marge Bray is in charge of casting, but she has the advantage of having inherited much proven talent with years of experience. The presentation of the historical material in the *Fandangle* is a simple but effective one. An event or period is mentioned, often with factually correct dates and persons, and then a song or dramatic skit presents the human side of the event. This technique is especially noticeable in the Camp Cooper and Fort Griffin segments. A major historic event, the drought, is dramatized by the song "Windmill," the title and words evoking recollections of that emblem of the developing West. This important source of water supply enabled ranchers to run cattle in fenced pastures away from natural water sources, such as creeks and rivers. Earthen tanks catching rain runoff are less often romanticized, because they lack the appeal of the windmill, although they became prominent later in the development of the West. Favorite songs and scenes are repeated annually but new songs and scenes are also regularly added. The theme is always the same—depicting the raucous, challenging settlement of the area. The details are simply variations on this theme. Even the show's program makes a unique contribution, for in addition to listing the members of the cast and the scenes involved, it is filled with information from old local newspapers—the *Frontier Echo*, the *Ft. Griffin Echo*, the *Albany Echo*, the *Albany Star*, and the *Albany News*; all early newspapers, and except for the *Star*, linked through their historical development.

The production schedule usually begins in November and December, when the directors start talking about what to include. Then in January and February, casting and rehearsals begin, and a Sampler is put together. This shortened version is important for several reasons, but primarily the Sampler becomes the core around which the larger show is built. Additional songs and rolling stock are added to flesh out the story. The Sampler is always presented to members of the Fort Griffin Fandangle Association at Reynold's Bend on the Clear Fork in May. Expansion of the show follows soon after, picking up speed as school ends and more actors from the schools become available. Nail always timed the show by figuring three minutes for each song, and then timing the narration to be included.

The old clock in the courthouse tower marks the conclusion of each *Fandangle* performance, just as it has done the lives of Albany citizens over the years. Nail felt the "weathered face" of the clock was a reminder of the town's past. The crowd departs, people already promising to return next year to this most unusual homecoming. Comments often dwell on whose former costume was in what scene and was worn by whom. The *Fandangle* is so thoroughly woven into the fabric of life in Albany, that to think of the city without the *Fandangle* is impossible.

The myths of the frontier are the gist of this production, and they are presented in a nostalgic, romanticized fashion that eases the original traumatic impact felt by the many institutions and individuals depicted in the story. It is "history not as told in books, but as remembered by the Old-Timer." We remember the good times and learn in later years to laugh at the bad. That is human nature, and the positive example shown by the Griffinites in this production makes the *Fandangle* what it is, a celebration of life in the Fort Griffin area of Texas.

THIRTY

A Brief Guide To Some Historic Sites Important To The Clear Fork Of The Brazos River Culture

The following material was gathered with the help of Morris Ledbetter, descendant of one of the earliest settlers in the region now known as Shackelford and Throckmorton Counties of northwest Texas. Morris was one of the best raconteurs of the history and lore of the region. An excellent historian, archeologist, and anthropologist, Morris always looked for opportunities to tell about the area he loved, whether it was before the Texas State Historical Association, or sitting in his favorite rocking chair at Blandon-Caldwell Trading Company in downtown Albany.

As a birthday present to his cousin, Sonja Irwin Clayton, he offered to take her and her husband, Lawrence, to all the historically significant sites in the region, if they would document the sites. Although he died in 1999 before the project was completed, the following represents part of the material gleaned on two day-long trips with Morris in 1998.

Each entry contains the name, location, and description, of the site. This essay is not intended as a tour guide for travelers. Most of the sites are on private property, and not open to the public. This is, to steal a phrase from modern life, a "virtual" tour, designed to familiarize interested persons with where these sites are and why they are significant.

Lawrence Clayton at the Site of the Commanche Indian Reserve

THE SITES

Site: Bush Knob Cemetery

Location: A small cemetery on FM 923 between Throckmorton and Woodson.

Description: Of principal interest here is the murder by John Larn and some associates of the Hays outfit, seven apparently innocent cattlemen, and seizure of the herd of cattle belonging to the murdered men. The victims were buried where they fell, their graves marked with pieces of uncut stone. The site was later used as a cemetery by local residents.

Site: Camp Cooper

Location: The Putnam Ranch on the Clear Fork, upriver from Fort Griffin.

Description: Founded on June 3, 1856, this pre-Civil War military post served primarily as home to members of the U.S. Second Cavalry, whose duties included patrolling the frontier and seeing after Comanche Indians on the nearby Reserve. Perhaps the best-known period of the fort's existence is the time Robert E. Lee commanded the post before assuming command of the Department of Texas. The post closed in 1861 when state forces demanded and accepted the surrender of the post by federal troops. What could well have been the first battle in the upcoming Civil War might well have been fought here had the federals resisted. Several structures stood at the site, but citizens have dismantled them and carried the stones away for other use. All that remains today is an historical marker.

Site: Civilian Cemetery near Fort Griffin

Location: East of Hwy 283, one-tenth of a mile south of Fort Griffin State Park

Description: This cemetery is visible from the highway. The site is thought to have been used by civilians at the town of Fort Griffin, particularly by Scottish stonecutters, because of the presence of cut native stone, rather than naturally formed stone in the headstones and grave covers.

Site: Col. Ranald MacKenzie's Campground

Location: West of Fort Griffin

Description: The staging area, on which MacKenzie organized his forces to launch the famous raid on the Palo Duro sanctuary of the Plains Indians, was a broad plain northwest of the Fort, now on private property. In 1874 the force routed the Indians with little loss of life among the native Americans. The buffalo soldiers, however, destroyed the horse herd and winter supplies, leaving the Indians destitute, forcing them onto the reservation in Oklahoma, and ending their way of life in the region. The trail from Fort Griffin to the High Plains came to be called the MacKenzie Trail. The crossing he used on the Clear Fork came to be identified by his name as well.

Site: Comanche Indian Reserve

Location: On the Clear Fork and FM 2584

Description: An area of several thousand acres set aside as a reservation for Comanche Indians, in hopes of civilizing them into becoming sedentary farmers. Friction between whites and Indians was frequent and potentially volatile. The effort failed, and the

Indians were moved to Oklahoma (Indian Territory) not long before the outbreak of the Civil War. John G. Irwin moved his family into the Indian agent's house, and the Irwin family took over the blacksmith shop. Later Ennis Irwin, a grandson, opened a blacksmith shop at Fort Griffin.

Site: Fort Davis

Location: On the Clear Fork in western Stephens County, east of Hwy 183, fifteen miles from Camp Cooper.

Description: This civilian stronghold on the Clear Fork served several families as a gathering point in order to protect themselves from Indian raids during the latter stages of the Civil War. It was one of several such regional civilian "forts," though it was never fortified nor manned by soldiers. Sam Newcomb taught school here and kept a diary of considerable importance to the history of the region during the time of the fort's existence. The Comanches noted that the soldiers had been withdrawn for the Civil War battlefields and saw a chance to inflict damage on the white settlers, perhaps driving them out. The dwellings built in the form of a large square were picket houses made of the trunks of small trees from the area set upright in the ground, and are now long since rotted away. The only surviving structure is the stone house that anchored one corner. It has been outfitted as a hunters lodge by present owners.

This civilian fort should not be confused with the military post in the Davis Mountains of far West Texas.

Site: Fort Griffin (Military Post and Town)

Location: On Hwy 283, about twenty-three miles North of Albany.

Description: The military post founded in 1867 on a hill overlooking the Clear Fork, and the town by the same name established on the flat between the fort and the river both proved important to frontier life. The mission of the post was protection of settlers from raids by mounted Comanche raiders. The soldiers were black, or Buffalo Soldiers, so called by the Indians because of the soldiers' curly hair.

The town was a magnet for all sorts of people, especially cowboys and cattlemen, as well as notorious outlaws, buffalo hunters, gamblers, prostitutes, and gun fighters. It was a major outfitting point and market for hunters, who destroyed the massive buffalo herds on the Southern Plains. The Western Cattle Trail ran through the area.

A fascinating locale during the frontier period, Fort Griffin represented much that is popularly considered typical of the Old West.

Site: Fort Griffin Bridge

Location: North of the fort and town, at the Old Crossing on the river.

Description: This elegant structure, closed to traffic in 1998 because it was considered unsafe by transportation authorities, carried vehicle traffic on the old Albany to Throckmorton Road. The gravel road south of the bridge was Griffin Avenue, the main street of the town of Fort Griffin. This road now feeds into a road that connects to Hwy 283 to the east, and other county roads to the west, but the original road continued up the hill to the fort. The bridge is in the *National Register* as a historic structure.

Hwy 283, which parallels the old road, also had a bridge with a metal superstructure, but this bridge was later replaced by a more modern one.

Site: Fort Griffin Cemetery

Location: Northwest of the fort.

Description: The burial ground for civilians in the area after the fort and town were founded. Many of the markers are sandstone and bear no inscriptions.

Site: Greer House

Location: About twenty miles southeast of Albany, between Hwys 6 and 183.

Description: James Greer, one of the earliest settlers in the area along Hubbard Creek, came in 1859. The house was an important landmark on the old military road, connecting posts to the north with the Headquarters of the Department of Texas at Fort Sam Houston in San Antonio.

Site: Jackson House

Location: At the entrance to Fort Griffin State Park.

Description: This impressive two-story structure was built by T.E. Jackson, an early settler who was also a dealer in buffalo hides, as a residence. Neighbors often visited the house to attend dances held on the second floor. Limestone to make the mortar used in the construction of the house was burned in a makeshift kiln a few miles north of the house. It currently serves as the headquarters of the Fort Griffin State Park.

Site: John Larn House and Grave

Location: A ranch near the Camp Cooper site.

Description: John Larn is one of the most controversial but fascinating figures in the lore of this region. The one-time lawman, his neighbors believed, was rustling and slaughtering their cattle to furnish beef on his contract with Fort Griffin. John Chadbourne Irwin, an early settler, recounted to his family two serious confrontations with Larn, both involving death threats to Irwin. One involved several cowhides carrying a variety of his neighbors' brands, weighted down with rocks in the river below Larn's slaughterhouse. Larn was captured by a posse of vigilantes led by Sheriff Bill Cruger, and jailed in Albany. That night several men entered the jail and shot Larn, who was in irons, chained to a large log. He is buried near the house in which he and his family lived. The cupola on top of the house is thought to have been used as a lookout point by Larn and his friends. The house is on private property and is not open to the public.

Site: Ledbetter Picket House

Location: Downtown Albany.

Description: This unique structure, currently located in downtown Albany, was constructed by the W.H. Ledbetter family on the banks of the Clear Fork just east of Hwy 283, about a mile below the town of Fort Griffin. Not a typical picket structure, this house has the pickets mounted on sills which form the foundation, rather than having the bottom ends buried in the dirt. The space between the small logs was chinked with mud. It has two rooms and a dog trot. At one time it was covered with buffalo hides to make it warmer in the winter.

Site: The Ledbetter Salt Works

Location: South of Albany, east of Hwy 283.

Description: A strong, saline spring south of Albany proved to be one of the major resources in the area, for Indians and early settlers. In the day before refrigeration, salt was an essential part of food preservation as well as a dietary supplement for people and livestock. Cal Greer discovered the spring in 1861, and in 182 W.H. Ledbetter found the spring and set up the necessary equipment to boil water from the salt, producing a product of very high quality. Settlers came in wagons to haul the precious commodity back to distant points. Indeed, some of the salt went to aid the Confederate cause in the South, during the Civil War. In March of 1868, settlers battled Comanche Indians at the site. While living there, the Ledbetter family had a son, John, kidnapped by Comanches.

Later, the family moved to the Fort Griffin area and erected a picket, cabin now in a park setting in downtown Albany, where some of the pots from the Salt Works also are located.

Site: Lynch House and Cemetery

Location: Near FM 601, about nine miles southeast of Albany.

Description: This house, built in 1876 on Hubbard Creek, served as the headquarters of the J.C. Lynch Ranch. Lynch was one of the area's most prominent citizens. He founded a school for area children, and it was from this school that Johnny Ledbetter was taken by Indians. Lynch served as county judge. The house burned and has not been restored. It stands on private property and is not accessible to the public.

The cemetery near the road holds the remains of the Lynch family and relatives, as well as other frontier settlers.

Site: Negro Cemetery at Fort Griffin

Location: Northwest of the fort.

Description: In a pasture northwest of Fort Griffin is an unfenced cemetery, where civilian Negroes were buried. No soldiers are buried here. The most noticeable gravestone is that of Mariah Williams, a black woman who lived in the region for decades. The cemetery is located on private property, and is not accessible to the public.

SOURCES

The following sources provide beneficial reading on the sites described above.

Biggers, Don. *Shackelford County Sketches.* 1908; rpt. Joan Farmer, ed. Albany, Texas: Clear Fork Press, 1974.

Cashion, Ty. *A Texas Frontier: The Clear Fork Country and Fort Griffin, 1849-1887.* Norman: University of Oklahoma Press, 1996.

Clayton, Lawrence and Joan Farmer. *Tracks Along the Clear Fork: Stories from Shackelford and Throckmorton Counties.* Abilene, TX: McWhiney Foundation Press, 2000.

Holden, Francis Mayhugh. *Lambshead Before Interwoven: A Texas Range Chronicle, 1848-1887.* College Station: Texas A&M University Press, 1982.

Matthews, Sallie Reynolds. *Interwoven: A Pioneer Chronicle.* 4th ed. College Station: Texas A&M University Press, 1982.

Robinson, Charles, III. *Frontier World of Fort Griffin: The Life and Death of a Western Town.* Spokane: The Arthur Clark Co., 1992.

Rister, Carl Coke. *Fort Griffin on the Texas Frontier.* Norman: University of Oklahoma Press, 1956.

Rye, Edgar. *The Quirt and the Spur: Vanishing Shadows of the Texas Frontier.* 1909; rpt. Austin: Steck-Vaughn, 1967.

THIRTY-ONE

My Last Christmas????

At this time of year, our minds automatically turn to the first Christmas. This year, however, my mind is turned to the reality that this is one of my last Christmases, perhaps the last. In October of 1999, I was diagnosed with Lou Gehrig's Disease, or ALS. My quality of life has deteriorated since that time to a very frustrating level of physical ineptness, especially with my hands. I will not try to list the multitude of small manipulations of everyday life that I can no longer do.

I feel fortunate that my disease does not require radical surgery or therapy, convalescence, trips to Houston for treatment, or other interruptive procedures. Several friends my age have cancer and heart problems, catastrophic disorders. My disease, in contrast, is a calm, gradual, disgusting, maddening encroachment on the quality of life for me and my family and friends. It is a surreal nightmare from which the only awakening is death.

What is one to do in this situation? I grappled with the ultimate reality and decided to do nothing different from what I have always done—enjoy my family, my work and my life—but to a greater degree of comfort in that knowledge. Like the mythic Sisyphus in

Camus's discussion of absurdity, I find some comfort in knowing the rules, what to expect, and what not to expect, from life.

Lawrence Ray Clayton

I have chosen as my model for living the rest of my life an example told to me by Keith Wells, a close friend and one of the few bonafide heroes I know. As a marine attacking the Japanese fortress of Iwo Jima in World War II, Lt. Wells knew that chances were good he and many of his men would be killed in the coming battle. Wells made his decision not to despair but instead to do what he had been trained to do up to the time he could no longer do that. He remained true to the code of a warrior. I have made the same decision. I am, in a sense, dead already. I will work and write as long as I am able and then accept the inevitability of death, a reality that has been here since I drew my first breath more than sixty years ago. I long assumed I would die in battle, as so many young men did in the wars that bracketed rather than interrupted my life. I remember several friends and a multitude of acquaintances who did not live this long.

I do not know when the end will come or what physical failings will accompany my last gasps on this earth. I just know for certain that the end will come. But I have known that all my life. Dying is part of living. Christ proved that centuries ago with the death of his physical body. With that knowledge, I can face this Christmas the same way I have all of those other wonderful Christmases—with love, hope and joy.

And I am beginning to be curious about what waits for me on the other side.

BIOGRAPHICAL SKETCH OF AUTHOR

Lawrence Ray Clayton was born on April 21, 1938, in San Antonio, Texas, to Donald H. and Loberta Isabella (Sawyer) Clayton. Shortly after his birth, the family moved to Del Rio, where they lived for nine years before returning to San Antonio. After one year, the family moved to East Texas, living near Jacksonville and then in Tyler and Rusk. Following graduation from Rusk High School, he attended Ranger Junior College where he married Sonja Irwin of Albany. He graduated *Scholaris* from Ranger Junior College with an Associate of Arts degree. He earned Bachelor of Science and Master of Education degrees at Stephen F. Austin State College and taught English in Rusk High School for five years, a tenure that was interrupted by a tour of duty with the 49th Armored Division at Fort Polk, Louisiana, during the Berlin Crisis in 1961-62. In 1965, he moved his wife and young daughter DeLys to Farmers Branch where he and Sonja taught for the Carrolton-Farmers Branch Independent School District. While teaching at R.L. Turner High School, he began work on a Master of Arts degree in English and history at North Texas State University and, in 1968, took a position as Instructor of English at Hardin-Simmons University. The M.A. was conferred in 1969. Following a leave of absence from 1971-1973 to do doctoral work at Texas Tech University, he became Chairman of the Department of English in 1974, just before the Ph. D. in English was conferred. A second child, Lea, was born in 1975. Dr. Clayton was appointed Dean of the College of Arts and Science at Hardin-Simmons University in 1980.

His research interests and publications were in the areas of American literature—especially of the American West—, English composition, and folklore. He was also President of the Texas Folklore Society. Lawrence Clayton died on December 31, 2000.

APPENDIX

Books by Lawrence Clayton

Benjamin Capps and the South Plains: A Literary Relationship. Denton: University of North Texas Press, 1990. (No. 2, Texas Writer's Series).

A Centennial History of Hardin-Simmons University. By A. Yvonne Stackhouse. Ed. by Lawrence Clayton. Abilene: HSU Press, 1991.

Chimney Creek Ranch. Privately Printed, 1993; reprinted in shortened form as a Special Publication, Friends of the Texas A&M University Library, 1994.

A Christmas Pudding. Edited by Lawrence Clayton. Abilene: Chestnut Street Press, 1989, 1995, 1996, 1997, 1998, 1999.

A Christmas Pudding. Abilene Writers on Abilene. Abilene: Santa's Helpers Press, 1994.

Clear Fork Cowboys: Contemporary Cowboys along the Clear Fork of the Brazos River. Photographs by Sonja Irwin Clayton. Abilene: The Cowboy Press, 1985.

The College Man and Our Rural Civilization. By Rupert N. Richardson. Introduction by Joe B. Frantz. Ed. Lawrence Clayton and Alice B. Specht. Abilene: Rupert N. Richardson Research Center and Richardson Library, 1989.

Cowboys: Ranch Life Along the Clear Fork of the Brazos River. Austin: Eakin Press, 1997.

The Dodge Jones Foundation: A History. Privately issued by the Foundation, Abilene, Texas, 1992.

Elmer Kelton. Boise: Boise State University Press, 1986. (No. 73 in the Western Writers Series).

Give Me Fifty Marines Not Afraid To Die. By John Keith Wells. Editorial Assistance and Afterword by Lawrence Clayton. Abilene: Privately printed, 1994.

Historic Ranches of Texas. Art by J.U. Salvant. Austin: University of Texas Press, 1993.

A History of Texas Music: Beginnings to 1950. With Joe Specht. College Station: Texas A&M University Press, 2002.

Horses, Their Role on the J.R. Green Ranch. (with Bob Green). With photographs by Sonja Clayton. Abilene: Hardin-Simmons University Press, 1998.

Horsing Around: Contemporary Cowboy Humor. Co-edited and Introduction. Detroit: Wayne State University Press, 1991; rpt. Lubbock: Texas Tech University Press, 1998.

Horsing Around, Vol. II. with Kenneth Davis and Mary Evelyn Collins. Lubbock: Texas Tech University Press, to be published.

I'm Still a Cowboy at Heart. Abilene: Cowboy Press, 2000.

In Memoriam: A Final Tribute to Watkins Reynolds Matthews by Some of His Friends. Ed. by Lawrence Clayton. With photographs by Sonja Clayton. Abilene: Cowboy Press of Abilene, 1997.

Litt Perkins' Book. Limited issue, privately printed. Abilene, 1979.

*Living and Writing in West Texas: Two Speeches by Elmer Kelton.*Intro. by Al Lowman. Ed. by Lawrence Clayton, Randy Armstong, and William Curtis. Abilene: Hardin-Simmons University Press (4-0-Imprint), 1988.

Longhorn Legacy: Graves Peeler and the Texas Cattle Trade. Abilene: Cowboy Press, 1994. Excerpted in *Texas Longhorn Trails*, 11, No. 6-8 (1999).

The March to Monterrey: The Journal of Lt. Rankin Dilworth (with Joseph E. Chance) El Paso: Texas Western Press, 1995.

Three Contemporary Ranch Women of Shackelford County: Mildred Palmer Diller, Doris Miller, Sue Diller Balliew. (With Darlene Bellinghausen and Lou Rodenberger. Photographs by Sonja Clayton. Abilene: Cowboy Press of Abilene, 1999.

Ranch Rodeos in West Texas. With photographs by Sonja Irwin Clayton, Lea Clayton, and Lawrence Clayton. Abilene: Hardin-Simmons University Press (Four-0-Imprint), 1988.

Remembering Dean Peacock. With photographs by Sonja Irwin Clayton. Abilene: Cowboy Press, 1998.

Texas Ranch Heritage. Photos by Wyman Meinzer. Austin: UT Press, to be published.

There's Always Another Chance and Other Stories. By Elmer Kelton. Edited and with Introduction by Lawrence Clayton. San Angelo: Fort Concho Museum Press, 1986.

31 by Lawrence Clayton. (Ed. Lou Rodenberger) Abilene: McWhiney Foundation Press, 2002.

Tracks Along the Clear Fork: Stories from Shackelford and Throckmorton Counties. (With Joan Farmer) Abilene: McWhiney Foundation Press, 2000.

Vaqueros, Cowboys and Buckaroos. (With Jerry Underwood & Jim Hoy), Austin: UT Press, to be published.

Watkins Reynolds Matthews: A Biography. Drawings by Paul Cameron Smith. Abilene: Hardin-Simmons University Press, (4-0-Imprint), 1989; 2nd ed. as *Watkins Reynolds Matthews: Biography of a Texas Rancher.* Photographs by Sonja Irwin Clayton. Austin: Eakin, 1994.

The Wonderful Country. By Tom Lea. Ed. By Randy Armstrong, William Curtis, and Lawrence Clayton. Abilene: Hardin-Simmons University Press (4-0-Imprint), 1995.

PHOTO CREDITS

The photo of Lawrence Clayton at Hardin-Simmons University Western Heritage Day, courtesy of Hardin-Simmons University. Lawrence Clayton and Watt Matthews, courtesy of Steve Butman. All other photos are courtesy of Sonja Clayton.

INDEX